THE SILENCE OF HEAVEN

AMOS OZ

Translated from

the Hebrew by

Barbara Harshav

The Silence of Heaven

AGNON'S FEAR OF GOD

Princeton University Press

Princeton, New Jersey

Copyright © 2000 by Amos Oz
Published by Princeton University Press, 41 William Street,
Princeton, New Jersey 08540
In the United Kingdom: Princeton University Press,
Chichester, West Sussex

ISBN 0-691-03692-6

This book has been composed in Adobe Electra by Princeton Editorial Associates, Inc.,
Roosevelt, New Jersey, and Scottsdale, Arizona

The paper used in this publication meets the minimum requirements of ANSI / NISO
Z39.48-1992 (R 1997) (*Permanence of Paper*)

http://pup.princeton.edu

Printed in the United States of America

10 9 8 7 6 5 4 3 2 1

CONTENTS

In quoting from literary works, I have referred whenever possible to published English translations and have cited corresponding page numbers. Occasionally, however, the published translation did not fit the point of Amos Oz's analysis and I had to provide my own translations.

Barbara Harshav

Shmuel Yosef Agnon, the dean of modern Hebrew prose and a recipient of the 1966 Nobel Prize for literature, is not well known in the English-speaking world. *Only Yesterday,* Agnon's greatest novel, is now being published for the first time, by Princeton University Press, in Barbara Harshav's translation. It is a special thrill for me to have my book on Agnon published in English at about the same time. I regard Agnon as one of my literary mentors; his sage, subtle, ironic voice helped me, back in my formative years, find my own voice—partly by struggling to free myself from Agnon's linguistic spell.

The Silence of Heaven focuses on Agnon's theological soul searching. Judging by his novels and stories, Agnon believed in God, yet felt that God was no one's friend. Agnon was an observant Jew—a synagogue-goer—but his heart was tormented by theological doubts. He often wrote about an omnipotent yet merciless God. This theme is never stated directly by the narrator in Agnon's stories and novels; rather, it is expressed by minor, esoteric, eccentric, unreliable characters. Yet the tragedy of Isaac Kumer in *Only Yesterday* and the misery of many other "believers" in Agnon's novels convey the subtle subversion of Agnon himself, a man who must have felt that the silence of Heaven is loaded with horrors.

Amos Oz

ARAD, ISRAEL, AUGUST 1, 1999

This book comprises three readings of three works by S. Y. Agnon, written not by a scholar, but by a reader of Agnon who loves what he has read.

Agnon's heroes and their creator usually treat questions of reward and punishment, the ways of the world, and the reasons for actions as religious issues—providing that the term "religious" is broad enough to encompass doubt, heresy, and bitter irony about Heaven. The Hebrew critic Shlomo Tsemakh has stated, "A person doesn't curse God if God is not in his heart." Agnon's heroes and the narrator who accompanies them sometimes approximate that religious position.

Nevertheless, in Agnon it is not always "Vanity of vanities; all is vanity" (Eccles. 1:2), nor is the end necessarily "everything is heard, revere the Lord." A broad spectrum of theological, metaphysical, and ethical possibilities is laid out in Agnon's stories. Whenever I reread them, I see how close Agnon's positions toward Heaven, Eros, Judaism and Zionism, clamorous rhetoric, or humility and silence are to the positions of several other great writers of the new Hebrew literature, especially Haim Nachman Bialik and Yosef-Hayyim Brenner, and at times also to those of Uri Tsvi Greenberg: between faith and the shock of doubt, between yearning and revulsion, between love and hate, and between intimacy and disgust. But the blazing rage in Bialik, Brenner, and Greenberg is not in Agnon—instead there is a mockery bitter as scorpions. Yet with all his mockery, Agnon is sometimes full of compassion for man and his situation within "the work that is wrought under the sun" (Eccles. 2:17).

The book begins with "The Heart, the Dead Space, and the Way Back"—my talk at an Agnon commemoration at the Hebrew University in Jerusalem in 1975, previously published in my book *Under This Blazing Light* (1978). "The Mockery of Fate and the Madness of the Righteous Woman" was published in the Rosh Hashanah edition of *Ha-Arets,* September 22, 1991. "Stolen Waters and Bread Eaten in Secret" was published in a different version in *Ha-Arets,* April 19, 1989. The fourth and by far the largest part of the book, "Guilt and Orphanhood and Fate: A Reading of *Only Yesterday,*" is published here for the first time.

Each chapter should be read along with the story it discusses.

Many years of reading Agnon with high school students at Kibbutz Hulda and Givat Brenner, at Ben-Gurion University of the Negev, at the Hebrew University in Jerusalem, and in several institutions abroad, as well as with many literary evening circles, have contributed to this book. If a whiff of an oral presentation lingers in it, I won't be sorry. I learned a great deal of this material from my students, and if I thanked every one of them by name, I could fill a book. Thanks to them and to my first teachers, Aharon Apelfeld, Dov Sadan, Shimon Halkin, and Gershon Shaked, who taught me how to approach Agnon's stories. Special thanks to my friends Haim Be'er and Rafael Weizer, who opened my eyes to large and small things, showed me what I didn't see, and saved me from many bad mistakes. Thanks also to Tirza Vardi of the Department of Hebrew Language and Literature at Ben-Gurion University for checking and correcting the citations and references and providing good footnotes, and to Tsruya Shalev and Orna Levi, who brought this book closer to my vision of it.

Amos Oz

CHAPTER **1**

The Heart, the Dead Space, and the Way Back

*Because of that historical catastrophe when
Titus the Roman Emperor destroyed Jerusalem
and Israel was exiled from its land, I was born
in one of the cities of Exile. But all the time I
imagined myself as having been born in
Jerusalem.*

S. Y. Agnon

Those words, as all readers of Agnon know, are true. But, strangely enough, their opposite is also true. Had Agnon chosen to say "Because of that historical catastrophe when East European Jewry fell apart, I became a Hebrew writer in Jerusalem. But I always saw myself as one who was born in one of the cities of Galicia and destined to be a rabbi there"—those words would also be true and right on target.

Perhaps it is in this paradox, the tormented tension between one tenet and its opposite, that we must recognize the trauma that made Agnon what he is. For every true writer becomes a writer because of a profound trauma experienced in youth or childhood. And if we hedge our statement with a myriad of reservations, with all kinds of "although" and "nevertheless," perhaps we might venture to say that the flight of the narrator's imagination is as high as the depth of his wound, or, in other words, the force of his scream is as intense as his pain. Indeed, the title of one of Agnon's short stories is "The Reward Matches the Pain." (Yes, I hear you, there are people who suffer a trauma and don't become writers, but rather saints or murderers or whatever, but I did say "with a myriad of reservations.") If, for instance, we take a Hebrew writer today, we shall find that he is tormented with the question of whether it is good or bad to expel the population of an Arab village, and his hero suffers emotional distress because it is good according to one system of values and bad according to another, and he accepts both systems and both have shaped his beliefs. Or another writer is torn between admiration for brute force, on the one hand, and respect for the spirit in general and the ethical spirit in particular, on the other. Yet, beyond all differences in talent, perhaps we may say that the trauma, the rift, in Agnon's soul was deeper and more painful than those; hence the creative tension, the vigor of the sources of energy, the depth of the torments are of a different order altogether. For Agnon's pain and the distress of his generation were malignant: incurable, insoluble, inextricable. There is One Who hears our prayer or there is not. There is Justice and there is a Judge or there is not. All the acts of our forefathers are meaningful or they are not. And while we're at it—is there meaning to our own acts or isn't there? And is there any meaning in any act at all? What is sin and what is guilt and what is righteousness? In all these, Agnon is neither guide nor model, but he and his heroes run around from one extreme to another in dread and despair. Such dread and such despair are the source of great works of literature in other nations as well, in other languages and in other times. And with all the restraint that imbues Agnon's writing, writing that comes "after the writer has immersed himself in ice water" ("The Tale of the Scribe"), with all the moderation and dissimulation and muting and circumlocution and irony and sometimes even sophistry—with all that, the sensitive reader will hear a muffled scream . . . an open wound. For there is a genuine creator here.

|

Agnon's fictional world is made of sin and punishment, temptation and responsibility, the normal and the abnormal, the system and outside the system, guilt and judgment.

Man is a guilty creature. All the characters in Agnon's fiction are guilty souls. But Agnon is neither preacher nor theologian—he is not Rabbi Grunam May-Salvation-Arise of *Only Yesterday:* There is guilt, but we cannot know where the accusing finger arises, who is the judge, and who administers the punishment. And perhaps, most horrible of all—the ultimate dread oozes from between Agnon's lines—perhaps there is no Emperor in the city and there is nothing, for in that case all existence is an ugly joke and a senseless abomination.

Everyone is guilty in Agnon's fiction: Isaac Kumer in *Only Yesterday,* who deserted his hometown and abandoned his father and brothers and sisters and violated "Thou shalt not covet" and other prohibitions; and the guest in *A Guest for the Night,* who stayed the night and desired greatness—to be nothing less than a miracle-working saint who can restore his hometown from its destruction. Menashe-Haim in "The Crooked Shall Be Made Straight," and Manfred Herbst in *Shira,* and Hirshl Hurvitz in *A Simple Story,* and even the wretched Farenheim in "Farenheim," who "embezzled from the firm"—they're all guilty.

Indeed, a reader of Agnon's *The Bridal Canopy* might think there is refuge from sin and guilt under the wings of faith, or, as Agnon says, "within the system." But Agnon himself, jester and tormented man that he was, wrote *The Bridal Canopy* so that we readers will never know if Reb Yudel and his miraculous adventures really did exist or were only a parable; and if they were a parable, was its point aimed at the system and its crooked ways or against us and such "light human beings" as we are? My teacher, Dov Sadan, caught this double meaning long ago.

Moreover, within the system we can expect to find not only peace of mind and proper order, reward and punishment, integrity,

Torah and its rewards; within the system—according to Agnon's fiction—also lurk the internal contradiction, the absurd, the iniquity the mind can't bear, the repression of desire, the repression of emotion, the disgustingly smug petit bourgeois obesity, and the sacrifice of Eros, that life force, as a victim on the altar of harsh religious principles and laws. Ask the righteous woman Tehilah, who suddenly became a desperate chatterbox at the end of her days and even "raised herself in a kind of dance," and she will tell you what's going on "inside the system." Ask the "Exiled One," ask Menashe-Haim, ask the guest who came for a night and wanted to restore the system to its former glory. I am indicating all these possibilities and people here to refute those who want to find in Agnon's works a mine of simplistic "Jewish consciousness."

In the depths of his fiction, did Agnon hope "to restore the old system" after his heroes discovered that, outside the system, what lies in store for them are evil lust, lies, hollow phraseology, and, above all—madness and death? An innocent reader may be misled into thinking that Agnon is seeking a way back. Another innocent reader may mistakenly think that Agnon is not seeking a way back. It is the ancient dilemma: "From You to You I shall flee." Does not Arzef, the taxidermist in *Only Yesterday,* kill animals, take away their souls, and grant them a kind of eternity in exchange? And the animals, the story relates, love Arzef and come and plead with him to kill them so they will live in another dimension.

And one reader, a character in *Shira,* says to the writer Hemdat, who appears in *Shira* and other stories: "Our contemporaries expect to find new tidings in creative works." As for Hemdat, he replies, as is his wont, with a blend of innocence and cunning: "I didn't come to give an answer to the question 'Where are you going?' but sometimes I do respond to the question 'Where did you come from?'"[1]

Thus a great Hebrew writer apparently told us where we came from. But is that what he really told us? Daniel Bach in *A Guest for the Night* says: "I'm a light human being, and I don't believe the Almighty wants the good for His creatures." And if these horrible words aren't enough, Daniel Bach adds: "I'm only a human being, flesh and blood, and when my flesh rots and my blood stinks, my lips cannot utter the praise of the Almighty." Elimelech Kaiser in the same novel adds: "If you think the Supreme Being won't accept our prayers like that, He'll ask Esau to pray to Him."[2] This heresy sounds infinitely bolder and more bitter than the heresy of those who simply say that there is no God in Heaven and everything comes from primeval matter and ancient microscopic creatures.

Thus from Agnon's stories of the past a repressed truth emerges: What was broken, was broken irremediably. The walls of religious law and tradition were broken neither by the perpetrators of pogroms nor wicked gentiles nor Hitler nor the assimilationists nor the men of the Enlightenment nor the Zionists; the Temple collapsed from within, under the burden of its own contradictions, under the weight of its laws and judgments and prohibitions. Even a simple gentile woman, Krulka, Mrs. Sommer's cleaning woman in *A Guest for the Night,* is sorry for that guest, who stayed "far from his wife and children and [could] not distinguish between a thing that can be repaired and a thing beyond repair."[3]

Therefore, there is no way back. Akavia Mazal may drool as nostalgically as he likes over the tombstones in the old graveyard. The gate is locked and the demons mock him. And, in quite a different case, Dr. Schimmelmann in *Only Yesterday* may correct the Bible to his heart's content according to modern taste, and with the foam of his words he may turn the Prophets into journalists—even so the demons mock him too, and Agnon mocks with them. There is no way back. Hence many slops of mockery are poured out in Agnon's fiction onto all "who take refuge in the shadow of wisdom," all who return to the ruins like archaeologists who collect shards (in the words of Haim Nachman Bialik's poem "Facing the Bookcase": "Mines in the graves of a nation and in the ruins of the spirit"). The archaeologist's return to the ruins is not the return of a lost son to his father's quarry. Woe to Weltfremd and to his erudition. And all of Manfred Herbst's rummaging in the remnants of Byzantium that crumbled to dust makes no sense. Not to mention Gamzu in "Edo and Enam," whose erudition cost him his life. If the way "back to Gumlidata" doesn't lead to the madhouse, at best it leads to the leprosarium. And, as I said, the demons mock, and the innocent-cunning Hemdat often mocks with them.

Demons, I said. But I didn't mean Baruch Kurzweil's daemons—those belong to another song altogether.[4] As for me, I find in Agnon's fiction a wild and dark vein of pagan provocation. There is the hand of fate. There are bloodthirsty gods, forces of destiny, fatum. And there are all kinds of demons—as in *Jaffa Belle of the Seas*, described in

"A Vow of Faith," and of course in "Edo and Enam" and in "Forever." After Daniel Bach realized that the Holy-One-Blessed-Be-He had removed His Shekhinah, in other tales other forces seemed to appear and fill the vacuum with some dark, idolatrous flapping of wings. Here are the demons who play with destinies, like the dog Balak with Isaac Kumer and the nurse Shira with Manfred Herbst—the finger of fate.

I am certainly not pigeonholing Agnon here into a faith or ideology or "worldview," for he was far from all that. The Agnon who wrote in one place in *Shira,* "The gods who mock one another led Manfred," is the same Agnon who wrote in the same novel, "A man and a woman . . . who were touched by the hand of God which the faithless call Destiny." By simple analogy, you can stand at this point and proclaim that Agnon's own words show that he is faithless. But Agnon defies simple analogies—except, perhaps, when he himself parts the curtain for a brief moment and peeps from behind the screen of intelligence and "wisdom" and says—in the story "Tehilah"—"I stood at times among the worshippers, at times among those who question."[5] There is no way back.

But what about the way forward? What does Agnon say about the return to Zion and about building the Land of Israel? In fact, he says the same thing Yosef-Hayyim Brenner says, though in a manner diametrically opposed: while Brenner smashes puffed-up falsehoods with hammer blows, Agnon appears holding a sharp pin.

In Agnon's fiction, as in Brenner's, the new society in the Land of Israel has a few Pioneers endowed with the modesty of hidden saints, the enthusiasm of Hasids, and the dedication of "devoted scholars." Yet there are also others, who made their way to the Land of Israel afflicted with the diseases of Exile we know from Agnon's "With Our Young and Our Old" or from Brenner's "Around the Points," those who spout hollow rhetoric, who are devoured by doubts and torments, who pursue small positions of power and honor in a nutshell, pursued themselves by hysterical frenzy—the frantic con artists and the eccentrics seeking Repair. And on the other hand again, in Agnon's tales of Jaffa and the settlements, as in Brenner's, the Old Yishuv appears as a ritual bath of stagnant water. And like Brenner's and Bialik's, Agnon's heart went out to "the eternally modest people who keep silent." As for the others, Brenner assaults them furiously in his fiction with Dostoevskian fists, while Agnon slices them with a Thomas Mann–like razor of irony. In the Petah Tikvah of *Only Yesterday,* Rabbi Menahem, the "Standing Menahemke," lives quietly, unlike frantic pushers like Grisha and Gorishkin. In *Only Yesterday,* in the Old Yishuv in Meah Shearim, Reb Grunam the mad preacher runs rampant, unlike the blind seer Reb Haim-Rafael, who is humbler than grass. Brenner himself appears in *Only Yesterday* when a lie is smashed to smithereens— an incident that may indeed have taken place at the Bezalel Art School during the time of its founder Boris Schatz. A Hanukah party was held "with licentiousness and gluttony"; a statue of Matityahu the Hasmonean holding a sword was put up, and the guests danced around it as on Christmas night. Agnon writes that if the spirit of life had been breathed into the statue, it would have come down off its pedestal and stabbed them all with the sword in its hand. For Matityahu the Hasmonean was an iconoclast and a zealot for his religion. Indeed, all the time the Greeks enslaved his nation, he didn't budge; only when they moved to forbid the practice of religious commandments did he rebel against them. (And with that, some comfortable Zionist stereotypes cracked: the Hasmoneans as the "Shomer" of ancient times, and Matityahu's revolt as a "national liberation movement.") When the Brenner of Agnon's tale hears this, he bursts out laughing with "a vulgar laughter," and Hemdat also smiles thinly.

|

Let us digress briefly from the discussion of Agnon's work for a personal story. In 1961, a young student assigned a paper on the Eretz Israel fiction of Brenner and Agnon learned of the paternal affection that Brenner—a respected and admired writer—showed for Agnon, a young beginner. That friendship, which originated in Jaffa during the Second Aliya, amazed the student, who found it hard to understand why on earth a bitter, sensitive, slovenly, and quarrelsome man like Brenner, a Russian and perhaps a bit Dostoyevskian, had become fond of the young Agnon-Hemdat, a delicate, shy young fellow, a poetic dandy, a kind of fragrant citron indulging himself in his wrapping. So that student, in his youthful naïveté, went to see Agnon and asked him: Venerable Mr. Agnon, what bound you and Brenner together in Jaffa? Weren't the two of you different souls? Agnon looked obliquely at the questioner, smiled at the young fellow, smiled again to himself, and then said: "Between me and Yosef-Hayyim, there was a closeness rooted in a mutual love." The student was excited. He thought he had stumbled onto the trail of some piquant love affair, and if he would just go on pulling at Agnon's sleeve, the writer would tell him marvels to make his head spin. And so, in his youth, the lad pleaded with Agnon to reveal to him what that mutual love had been. Once again Agnon smiled (the smile, as the lad later learned, of a butterfly hunter at the sight of a splendid specimen), almost winked, and said something like: "Well, I'll tell you a deep dark secret: In those days, when we lived in Jaffa, Yosef-Hayyim and I were both deeply in love with Shmuel Yosef Agnon."[6]

I will not analyze the irony in that little Agnon anecdote. But I will tell you that it was not mutual love but—first of all—reciprocal hatred that bound the two of them. And if what Agnon told that young student was cruel to Brenner as well as to himself, it was cruel in Agnon's particular way and by his particular system: subtle, sober, and slicing. Brenner, in his cruelty to himself and to others, was cruel tooth and nail. Both Brenner and Agnon pinned on the Zionist dream the ultimate hope, the hope after all hope is gone, but they weren't taken in by it, and they clearly discerned all those seeds of calamity that befell us from inside ourselves many years later. Agnon's fiction is filled with relativism and skepticism about politics and the "tools of the state" (the same tools that later excited the poet Natan Alterman and many other distinguished people). That skepticism is also evident in *The Book of the State* and in *Shira*—especially in some of the things Manfred Herbst tells his daughters.

Is there consolation, a way out, a path that may emerge from or be implied by Agnon's fiction? Sometimes you are tempted to generalize and say, "Blessed are the undefiled in the way" (Ps. 119:1). Yes and no. There is the extreme innocent, Reb Yudel Hasid, whose innocence perhaps stands him in good stead and perhaps doesn't, and he is liminally saved yet not saved at the end of *The Bridal Canopy*. Yet, on the other hand, there is an equally extreme innocent, the son of the son of the daughter of Reb Yudel's daughter, Isaac Kumer in *Only Yesterday,* who has no miracle and no trace of a miracle, and who succumbs to madness and death. There is an innocent named Taglicht, Light of Day, and there is a similar innocent named Gedalia Ziemlich, about whom *A Simple Story* relates that he "didn't despair [!] at calamity," that is, he expected it to come every day, and it certainly did come to him. There is Mr. Mintz, father of Tirza, on the one hand, and on the other hand there is the righteous woman Tehilah. These are the undefiled in the way. If any of them survives, it seems only by chance or almost by a miracle. The others go to the leprosarium or to the madhouse or to the "House of the Living," the graveyard.

And serenity? If there is serenity, it is granted in Agnon's fiction only to a handful of exceptional individuals, savagely strong people who succeed in bursting out of the general cycle of temptation-sin-guilt-punishment that comes from within or descends as a disaster from without. In *Only Yesterday,* Yohanan Leichtfuss—Sweet Foot—for example, establishes his power over women and dogs by force and lives outside the circle. Samson Bloykof, the painter, exercises iron control over his sick body and rebukes his languishing lung for not being ashamed before his empty belly, and his empty belly for not being silent before his defective heart, and all three of them for raising their voices when he—Samson—even though he is sick and hungry, doesn't say a single word. And above all, Arzef, who lives alone, "like the first Adam in the Garden of Eden," in the desolation of Eyn Rogel, where he plays the lord of life and the lord of death. These individuals, because they are like animals or gods, have peace. But their peace entails shedding the image of man, which is an image of temptation-sin-guilt-torment-remorse.

There is, of course, yet another kind of peace of mind in Agnon's fiction, as in Brenner's. That is the peace of humility, in the sense of the tragic law Shakespeare expressed through Othello: "'Tis the plague of great ones; Prerogativ'd are they less than the base" (3.3.273). This is the bovine peace of Tsirl Hurvitz in *A Simple Story,* "who gave up everything for eating and drinking," of Heinz Steiner, of some desiccated professors and smug social activists. But their serenity is bought at the cost of "giving up everything." Giving up emotional life. Giving up the power to love. Castration of the soul. As Hirshl in *A Simple Story* says of his uncle who went mad: "His heart was a dead space inside him."

It is a kind of choice, and ultimately it is forced on Hirshl himself (and, in another way, on Tirza Mazal née Mintz): to love, and "to pay for the conflagration with your fat and blood" (in Bialik's words), with madness, torments, death—or not to love, and to purchase tranquility at the price of "a dead heart." Hirshl may have found a crack to pass through between the horns of that dilemma, even though he also pays at first with torments and madness.

And now, a few sentences about Agnon's narrative art. In Agnon, there is "the forest" and there is "the town." The Agnon town has been thoroughly studied, perhaps even more than Adiel Amzeh studied the antiquities of Gomlidata in "Forevermore." Now let's go to the forest, that vegetative artery of savagery and dread, often veiled in seven idyllic and even pastoral veils. In Agnon, they do not come in a dramatic torrent but rather accumulate and unwind slowly, restrained as under a thick shell. The storyteller tells his tales, including even his seething tales, as Doctor Langsam in *A Simple Story* cures his patients: as if inadvertently. Slowly. Casually. As if by themselves. Without a "peak" and without a "climax." One possible title for this study of Agnon might be "The Narrative Art of Doctor Langsam."

|

I shall end where I began: with all-embracing generalizations. Keep in mind, readers and lovers of Agnon, that, when all is said and done, the language of Edo and the Enamite Hymns in "Edo and Enam" *are not* the exciting remnants of a mighty culture that declined and was lost; they are merely the songs and language that a father and daughter invented to amuse themselves.

And therefore, and especially for that reason, the entire life work of Doctor Ginath in that story comes to dust and ashes: "The wind . . . whirleth about continually, and the wind returneth again according to his circuits" (Eccles. 1:6). "Vanity of vanities; all is vanity" (Eccles. 1:2).

The secret "remedies" in the story are really nothing.

And all of Gamzu's rare books will never bring his wife back to him. She left and is no more. Never was she really his.

Gunther and his girlfriend have no house and wander the streets of Jerusalem like two stray dogs.

And who has it good in the world? Of whom can we say "Blessed are they for the Land is given unto them?" Mr. Greifenbach and Mrs. Gerda. All kinds of smug intellectuals. They and their apprentices, and social activists, and Makhersons and Makherovitches and Makheranskis, and all the other "enlightened rich who were clearing their homes of sacred literature," in the words of "Edo and Enam."[7]

"On the ruins of their hearts the mezuza was declared unfit," in the words of Bialik. Their "heart is a dead space inside them," in the words of Hirshl Hurvitz.

"The wind . . . whirleth about continually, and the wind returneth again according to his circuits." "Vanity of vanities; all is vanity." Or again, in the words of that good-hearted wretch Hirshl of *A Simple*

Story, who thinks to himself: "How badly made is man, he sleeps to wake up, he wakes up to sleep, and between sleeping and waking—sorrows and torments and injuries and offenses."

I apologize if I have cast a shadow on Agnon. I shall end with the words of Adiel Amzeh: "For twenty years a man must be hidden in wisdom's shadow in order to utter such a simple piece of wisdom."[8]

I apologize if I have not introduced anything new; I was not invited here to be innovative. I came to talk about torments, about love, and about pain in Agnon, that Ecclesiastes who disguised himself in all sorts of beautiful disguises. And it is with great love that I talked of him as I did, and not otherwise.

CHAPTER 2

The Mockery of Fate and the Madness of the Righteous Woman

Covering and Revealing in the Story "Tehilah"

In "Polarity in Agnon's Fiction," Baruch Kurzweil summarizes "Tehilah" as "an ancient picture that conveys wholeness and harmony of the soul." For Kurzweil, Agnon's polarity is that the hand that sketched the ancient picture of wholeness and harmony is the same hand that depicted in *The Book of Deeds* and "Edo and Enam" a "demonic and split" picture. And ever since Kurzweil published this analysis, generations of literature students have memorized "Tehilah" on the altar of their matriculation examinations as if the story and its heroine are simply a honeycomb of "wholeness that is the asset of the past." Even Leah Goldberg, a precise and careful reader, found that "the joy of a pure and innocent heart . . . hovers over that story, over the life of poverty and grief and even over the sin."

Shalom Kremer, who thinks that "one big and pleasant spirit moves in" "Tehilah" and in Agnon's entire fictional world, agrees with Leah Goldberg and Kurzweil and insists that "this is a populist-national decision of a Jewish artist to see things as our forefathers saw them since the time of the Talmud," et cetera. Eli Schweid goes even further in his harmonious view, classifying "Tehilah" as "a holy story" in the traditional Jewish sense of the term. "The work itself," writes Schweid, "is a process of self-education and subduing the heart to faith."

Thus, in the wake of Goldberg, Kurzweil, Kremer, Schweid, and other critics, an icon of the righteous woman Tehilah has been hung on the Eastern Wall of that literature designed to convey the charms of the Jewish faith to the souls of matriculating students, somewhere between Haim Nachman Bialik's poem "My Mother of Blessed Memory" and Y. L. Peretz's story "Three Gifts."

This chapter reexamines the question of how whole is the spiritual wholeness of the righteous woman and how harmonious is the harmony the seekers of harmony impose on this work. We shall also try to determine whether the story "Tehilah" really is a "polar opposite" of the world of *The Book of Deeds* and the nightmares of "Edo and Enam," or if perhaps many elements of the horror, injustice, and madness we know from *The Book of Deeds* are also hiding between the folds of the character of the righteous woman Tehilah: not "an ancient picture that conveys wholeness and harmony of the soul," but a story of covering and revealing. The covering is a splendid Torah Curtain embroidered with the words "All that the Merciful One did He did for good"; and the revealing—what sprouts through the rips in the Torah

Curtain, what is increasingly exposed toward the end of the story—is the revealing of an abusive and mocking god, a jealous god furious and vengeful, visiting "the iniquity of the fathers upon the children unto the third and fourth generation," and without forgiveness.

What made Agnon link in this short story one of the classic peaks of the sweetness of faith and acceptance of judgment with one of the sharpest expressions of bitter heresy, heresy in the spirit of Daniel Bach of *A Guest for the Night,* who says of himself, "I'm a light sort of person and I don't believe that the Holy-One-Blessed-Be-He wants the good for His creatures"?[1] What made Agnon create in this story a hybrid of theodicy and Candide?

One possible answer lies in Dov Sadan's comments on *The Bridal Canopy.* According to Sadan, the three heretical generations that are removed from the scope of "the bridal canopy" so as not "to damage the wholeness . . . have plotted to enter that innocent world, dressed in its garb and crowned with its diadem and using all its characteristics, in order to subvert the enemy capital [that is, the fortress of Halakhic and harmonious Judaism!—A.O.] from inside its citadel. . . . He who sailed with a heart full of hymns to the past, overcame . . . that past. . . . The secret subversion from within—even if at its root is religious awe and at its base is cunning—is stronger than any ideological war from outside." Sadan also says of Reb Yudel Hasid in *The Bridal Canopy:* "You can't tell whether the author wanted to shape a character of innocence in its full expression, while he really supplied it . . . with materials of keen criticism . . . or whether he wanted to spread before you a scroll of criticism, while really singing in your ears a great hymn to Innocence. . . . Here you don't know and you wouldn't know even if the author made a public declaration on it."

2 |

If we find that critics and readers have generally accepted "Tehilah" as a kind of canonic icon,[2] perhaps we should begin our protest by stating that this story is not an icon at all, nor does the term "character story" apply to it, because neither the story nor its central character is static. There is a plot, there is development, there is a series of fatal encounters, there are scandalous revelations, there is great upheaval, and finally there is also a conscious choice of death. Tehilah the righteous woman, who enters the story as the embodiment of humility and Hasidism and piety, the personification of graciousness and mercy, almost like a popular Russian Orthodox saint, leaves the story and this world half mad, and divests herself of life in a gesture of disgust and horror. Not even a trace of "wholeness and harmony of soul" remains in Tehilah as she leaves.

3 |

Among other things, "Tehilah" is concerned with the explicit and implicit contrast between the past and the present. The story unfolds before the reader with a series of encounters, parallelisms, and comparisons between "representatives" of the past and "spokesmen" of the present. It is no accident that the spokeswoman of the past is an impressive *character,* while the present is represented in this confrontation primarily by various inanimate, easily moved *objects,* such as a fountain pen, a portable heater, and a walking stick.

The righteous Tehilah, spokeswoman of yesterday's world, does not completely reject the "innovations" but regards them with a blend of timid curiosity and censored attraction: "They slander your generation in saying that all its innovations are only for evil," says Tehilah at the sight of the fountain pen in the hand of the narrator. Yet she wants her letter to be written with a quill (p. 45).[3]

The narrator himself (who is, to some extent, a representative of the present, with his fountain pen and the portable kerosene stove he brings) is skeptical and ironic about the present and its inventions: "We made our way amongst the stones and through the alleys, avoiding the camels and the asses, the drawers of water and the idlers and the gossip-mongers," the narrator says at the beginning of the story (p. 24). Immediately after, at the home of the Jerusalem sage, he finds the sage so steeped in his innovations that he does not notice who is standing before him; he goes on piling up his innovations so that the narrator cannot interrupt him with the question of who Tehilah is. That mockery of innovations and innovators recurs often in the story: all inventions and innovations are merely spots of shadow the artist places on the canvas to emphasize the sublime halo of light surrounding the heroine, and, if not for the fact that women do not resemble angels, the narrator would compare her to an angel of God. But the narrator, who paints the world of yesterday out of monumental excitement, will gradually and incidentally expose in it a side of dark dread, which is also monumental.

Several critics and readers, influenced by what they see on the surface, have accepted the description literally, as if "Tehilah," were only about the "progressive decline of the generations," or about the idea that "the ancients are human beings, while we are donkeys." They interpreted the story as if it told us that the past is Paradise and the present is regrets for Paradise Lost, that it is "a subduing of the heart to faith" or a "hymn to love, humanity, and faith." We have already suggested that the idyllic-harmonistic fallacy about the story and about the righteous woman is inherent in the mistaken definition of the story as "a picture." "Tehilah" is far from a picture and much closer to a story with a quite dramatic plot with a proper exposition, complication, climax, and resolution—a story in which extreme changes take place, at least in its main characters, between the beginning and the end. For example, Tehilah enters the story as a woman who resists old age despite her 104 years ("if not for the old lady's clothes on her, not a trace of old age was seen in her"), but by the end of the story we find that "a change had come over her. Although she had always walked without support, I noticed that she now leaned on a stick" (pp. 39–40). This Tehilah, who meets the reader when "kindness and pity were the light of her eyes, and every wrinkle in her face told of blessing and peace" (p. 23), leaves the story—and this world—when "all her serenity had gone and her face took on sorrow and anger." At the beginning of the story, Tehilah hoards her words like gold coins because she wishes for life and knows that talking too much squanders your allotment of words and shortens your days; at the end, she testifies about herself: "I have become a chatterer" (p. 44), abandons all the years she has left to live in this world "to you and to all those who delight in life" (p. 63), and even longs explicitly for death. This is not a portrait or a brilliant icon of a paragon, but a dynamic character and vicissitudes of plot that shift from one extreme to another.

Or more precisely: shift from one ostensible extreme to another.

4 |

Perhaps the decisive question for a new understanding of "Tehilah" is: What has changed?

What causes the change in the righteous woman? Is it not the memory of Shraga's offense and her own catastrophes, which Tehilah has borne silently in her heart for ninety years without uttering a peep? What, therefore, has suddenly changed in her? What prevents her from going on in her graceful and glowing justification of the Judgment until the age of 120? (In that case, the story would deserve to be called a "portrait," and Kurzweil and Schweid and others would have been right.) The answer seems inherent in the story, and there is no need to seek an answer outside it: Tehilah's encounter with the narrator is what opens the sealed cellar and releases the ghosts; and even wounds that had fallen silent a generation ago, two generations ago, three generations ago, gape open and start screaming.

The encounter with the narrator is a fatal one for Tehilah, and, at least once, the narrator himself raises the possibility that it is he who inadvertently shortened the righteous woman's days (p. 49). Of course, we can insist on an "external" explanation: Tehilah represents the world of the past, a world undermined, unfortunately, by the invasion of the modern world, Heaven forfend, and thus Agnon is forced, as it were, "to kill off" the righteous woman at the conclusion of the story. But this is to reduce the work to a didactic allegory.

5 |

Eli Schweid and others talk of a "literary synthesis" between a realistic character story on the one hand, and allegorical and legendary elements on the other. If this were a character story, a legend, or an allegory, the narrator could be eliminated or reduced to an amazed observer with no active role in the plot. But behold: it is precisely in this story that Agnon makes a detailed autobiographical appearance, rare even for this writer who often endows his narrators with features from his own life and experience. If we identify the narrator of "Tehilah" with the personality of his author, we could collate his profession (writer), his departure from the Land of Israel before World War I (1912), his residence (the new city of Jerusalem, in the neighborhood of Nahalat Shiv'a, where Agnon lived after his second immigration to the Land of Israel in 1924), and even the "proper scroll" the author wrote in his youth, which won universal praise. Incidentally, in a talk titled "In Honor of Myself" delivered in 1958, Agnon told his audience about Tehilah as if she were a real person and not simply a parable. It is not only the autobiographical details that identify the narrator in "Tehilah" with the author of "Tehilah," but also—even more important—the spiritual position of the narrator within his story, a position typical of Agnon: he admires the righteous woman and clings to her world, but he himself is not part of that world, and does not stray from the beaten path to join it. He lives in the new city, carries his fountain pen around with him, leads travelers on tours of Jerusalem,[4] and yet—his heart goes out to what Tehilah represents. He is a person who stands here and longs to stand over there, but in fact, he does not take a single real step from here to there, and in the confrontation between the two worlds, both ultimately emerge before him with equal validity, and toward both, directly or indirectly, he expresses mixed feelings in a blast of irony, either overt or covert.

Jews stand at the Wailing Wall, the narrator tells us, some praying and some bewildered, and he says of himself: "I was standing at the Wall, sometimes among the worshippers, and sometimes among the skeptics." This may be the most revealing statement of all the autobiographical details Agnon has strewn in "Tehilah," a statement that applies not only to the narrator's place in this story, but perhaps also to the place of other narrators in Agnon's other works who tell of their creator. In Barukh Kurzweil's favorite words, this may be a "key to understanding the Agnon phenomenon."

It is this narrator, who straddles two domains, who causes the turning point that took place within Tehilah: what was not shaken by her encounters with "the world of innovations," with the new Yishuv, with the Jerusalem of "autobuses" (her word), is undermined at long last when she comes upon a man standing "beyond the fence" but very close to her world and admiring her world, at least ostensibly—a practicing Jew, a religious scholar, and yet planted in the new world. Furthermore, that man is a modern writer who not only can put words on parchment in fine calligraphy, like a traditional scribe, but can also understand and express the vicissitudes of the heart and embrace people's secrets and hurt feelings. Certainly those qualities of his draw Tehilah to choose him as a listener for her tragic confession, someone who might make literary use of it. And the evidence is this: except for one word, she does not dictate the formulation of her story but allows him "literary freedom."[5]

The encounter with the narrator determines the righteous woman's fate: "I do not know if there was any real need to return so soon," says the narrator (p. 49). "Perhaps if I had waited longer, perhaps it would have lengthened her life." There is an abyss between the double "perhaps" in this paragraph and Tehilah's phrase (p. 32) "that all a person's deeds are appointed, from the hour of his birth to the hour of his death."[6]

In Tehilah's deterministic world, everything is fixed ("even how many times a man will recite Psalms"), and there is no room for "perhaps." The "perhaps" the narrator inserts into Tehilah's world acts as a kind of delayed explosive or a venom that spreads slowly, for when Tehilah reexamines her life in light of what she has absorbed from the narrator, perhaps she asks herself if perhaps things couldn't also have happened differently from the way they did. And the narrator himself? He who wants to draw inspiration from the certainty of the righteous woman, from the full faith of her statement "All that the Merciful One did He did for good," ends up infecting her with his own doubts (or legitimizing doubts that had been dormant in her from time immemorial). At any rate, the dimension of his "perhaps . . . and perhaps" also becomes hers. He who stated at the beginning of the story, in Tehilah's own vein, that "it is appointed for every man to meet whom he shall meet, and the time for this, and the fitting occasion" (p. 23), ends up ascribing Tehilah's premature demise to the fact that he did not postpone his meeting with her. He who wanted to warm himself in Tehilah's light ends up inadvertently cooling and extinguishing that light, simply by coming close.

6 |

Several encounters—more precisely, seven encounters—between the narrator and the righteous woman indicate the axis of the plot. The first five are "chance" encounters, and the reader is emphatically invited to see a guiding hand in them (in the vein of "it is appointed for every man to meet whom he shall meet, and the time for this, and the fitting occasion"). These are chance encounters in the sense of summonses, linked with the concept of appointing, that is, destiny, fate—as "for this was not the last occasion that *was appointed for me* to see her" (p. 29; my emphasis—A.O.). But afterward, there is a sixth encounter, initiated by Tehilah: she asks the learned man who spawns innovations to tell the narrator she would like to see him. The narrator hears this and goes to her. The next day, the narrator comes to Tehilah on his own. And of this seventh, critical encounter, the narrator says: "Perhaps if I had waited longer, perhaps it would have lengthened her life" (p. 49).

Alongside this series of seven encounters whose causes change between the first and the last, the story also presents a system of internal parallelisms: every primary character has a parallel secondary character, either a caricature or a negative.[7] The sick and complaining old woman, who from her age could have been Tehilah's granddaughter, is a kind of "shadow" of Tehilah. And the innovating learned man is the absurd reflection of the narrator, for in his somewhat autistic way, he also stands between old and new. The narrator treats his inventions with a blend of pleasure (p. 40, for example) and subtle mockery (pp. 24 and 40). The sage wallows in his innovations and does not notice the mountains of Jerusalem, which never have innovations (p. 40) or Jerusalem itself, which is constantly being renewed, a kind of innovation he doesn't grasp (p. 40). The characters of the grumbling old woman and the innovating sage are similar to Bialik's descriptions of the stupefied old men in "My Return"—"old, antiquated, nothing new"—but instead of fleeing from their desolation, he clings to them and promises: "Together we'll rot until we stink." And when the innovating sage explains to the narrator the source of his wife's name (a name that now seems invented today), he emphasizes the idea that "there is nothing new under the sun" (p. 41). On the other hand, the narrator's position toward "the new world" is just like his position toward "the old world": complex and ambivalent.

The parallel characters are characters who bring about encounters: the narrator first comes upon Tehilah, and it is she who shows him the way to the learned man's house. A few days later, on his way to the complaining old woman—"if she was unfamiliar with stoves of this kind, it would be as well to show her the method of lighting it" (p. 26)—the narrator again comes upon Tehilah. Tehilah praises the narrator for the stove he bought, and thus she does the work of her "mirror image," for the other woman is bitter and incapable of saying a good word. And it is the learned man, again as a connecting character, who finally sends the narrator to Tehilah's house, at her request, and thus seals her fate.

Another system of parallels can be found in the blows that landed on Tehilah and her offspring for the sin of her father: just as Tehilah's father sinned by canceling the match between Tehilah and her husband-to-be, thus offending the bridegroom (and "such an offense of the bridegroom is like bloodshed"), so, a generation later, the match is canceled between the father of the grumbling old woman and Tehilah's daughter, who converted to Christianity on the eve of her wedding. And we have already mentioned the large and small parallels in the story between the embodiments of the past and the representatives of the present: a fountain pen, a kerosene stove, a walking stick, portable objects, inanimate objects that are not static.

7 |

"Everything is in the hands of Heaven"; "The Lord Blessed-Be-He, everything is equal in His eyes"; "The Holy-One-Blessed-Be-He gives to all His creatures according to their need"—this is the harmonious world of Tehilah, and thus, by deduction, is the world of full Jewish faith: "There is a leader in the capital" and "All that the Merciful One did, He did for good." But in this story, God appears not as a merciful father who allots to His creatures all their deeds for their good, but as a jealous God, vengeful and furious, visiting the iniquity of the fathers upon the children "unto the third and fourth generation."

A great many legends and midrashim deal with the punishment in store for someone who cancels a match and thus commits the sin of offense "like bloodshed," as in the legend "The Weasel and the Well" and its many modern adaptations.[8] But it is Tehilah who is punished—she and her children—not for the sin she committed, but for the sin committed against her. And the narrator who yearns so much to cling to her world is reluctantly forced to recognize that the world of faith also has its dark and dreadful side. Divine Providence, as it were, whose every action is supposed to be done with wisdom, is revealed to him—and is revealed also to Tehilah after ninety years of justifying the Judgment—as a kind of cruel fate that mercilessly strikes future generations, as if "Every man shall die for his own sin" (2 Chron. 25:4) had never been. It is not enough for the punishing God that He trample the innocent; He must also joke about it: Tehilah's father canceled the match because the bridegroom became a Hasid. Instead, the father married his daughter off, against her will, to "a proper Misnaged." Yet Tehilah's husband wound up becoming a Hasid, and it is Shraga, her former betrothed, who "sours" and becomes a Misnaged: mockery of destiny. Or, in the words of my teacher Dov Sadan in his article on *A Simple Story:* the horror of fate.

None of this places "Tehilah" at the opposite pole from *The Book of Deeds* and "Edo and Enam" (as Kurzweil and others have argued), but, rather, close to the world of those and similar works. This proximity is reinforced by a close analysis of the description of Tehilah's end: all the signs of distortion, cracking, and madness are manifest in the righteous woman when she suddenly decides on her own to leave the world. Tehilah's world was whole and at peace as long as she accepted the old without reservation and did not approach the new. But her encounter with the narrator makes her look back at her life and reevaluate her fate, without the defensive spectacles of "All that the Merciful One did, He did for good." This reexamination leads Tehilah to crack and fall apart: the first signs of old age appear (the need for a cane) in a woman who seemed to be blessed with eternal youth (p. 41), then grumbling and bitterness are revealed in a woman who seemed to be all grace and charm and mercy (p. 43), and finally "the learning of that old man was forgotten," and Tehilah, who had always been stingy with words in order to prolong the days of her life, says: "I have become a chatterer" (p. 44). Even later, her words betray half-repressed thoughts of heresy: "She sighed and said: if I knew that tomorrow our Redeemer would come, gladly would I drag out another day in this world. But . . . what is my life? And what is my joy" (p. 46). And further on, angrily and ironically, she is fed up with her life and wants to be rid of it: "Yet I cannot help but ask myself how much longer these bones must carry their burden. So many younger women have been privileged to set up their rest in the cemetery on the Mount of Olives, while I remain to walk on my feet till I think I shall wear them away" (p. 46). And finally there is a description of the collapse of harmony and the shattering of the justification of the judgment: Tehilah asks the narrator to write a letter of apology for her to the dead Shraga. (What, in fact, was her sin against him?) She whispers the name Shraga again "as if she were dozing off." Her face, which had always expressed "blessing and peace," now puts on "grief and anger."

As Tehilah unfurls the torments of Job of her life in the narrator's ear, it becomes clear to the reader, and certainly also to the narrator, and perhaps even to Tehilah herself, that there is no atonement for the punishments decreed for her and her children. The description of Tehilah's son, who was horrified and died because the image of a madman wrapped in a shroud appeared to him in the prayer house on the same date her wedding was canceled (p. 56), is a description that suggests the experience of *The Book of Deeds* and perhaps even the plot of the wanton and devastating fate visiting the iniquity of the fathers upon the children "unto the third and fourth generation" in Micah Berdichevski's story "The Orphan and Two Distant Relatives."[9] And the very collapse of the righteous woman's principle of justifying the Judgment is described in tones that verge on madness: "'I suppose you are thinking that this old woman's wits are beginning to fail her.' She rose, and picking up the clay jar, raised it high above her head, intoning in a kind of ritual chant: 'I shall take this letter—and set it in this jar.'" (pp. 59–60). In an ancient custom no longer practiced by the Jews, she intends to take the jar with her prematurely to her grave so that it will reach her dead bridegroom. And after she "intones a kind of ritual chant," she smiles "a little smile of triumph, as of a precocious child who has got the better of an argument with her elders" (p. 60), and once again she seems to doze off. When the narrator reads her the letter to the dead man that he has composed in her name, Tehilah doesn't listen to him but "[seems] to have lost interest in the whole matter." This is a precise, almost clinical description, including chants and smiles and dozing off, of a person who has gone mad.

Even when she gets up and goes "to confirm the bill of sale" between her and the True Benevolent Society (that is, the Burial Society) and informs the amazed clerks, "I have already ordered the corpse-watchers and the layers-out and it would be ill-mannered to make sport of these good women" (pp. 62–63)—even this ostensibly cold-blooded act also bears a trace of madness. It may be interesting to compare Tehilah's parting from this world with the parting supposedly prepared in cold blood by Leah Mintz, the mother of Tirza in Agnon's story "In the Prime of Life," who orders her friend Mintshe Gotlieb: "Go to your house . . . and prepare everything for the Sabbath and tomorrow afternoon come down to accompany me to my grave."[10] In both cases there is a shadow of suicide in a woman who is still standing and is lucid, and who sets her funeral for the next day. Finally, Tehilah declares that she gives up the years she has left to live and grants them "to you and to all who delight in life" (that is, she herself no longer delights in life), and she sends the narrator about his business.

Eli Schweid finds that "Tehilah on the verge of her death goes beyond complete innocence," yet the story portrays not complete innocence but a woman driven almost mad by the bursting of her repressed torments, a woman whose life no longer has meaning. Indeed, Eli Schweid, unlike Kurzweil, distinguishes carefully between the innocence of the *heroine* and the dialectical position of the *text* toward the heroine's innocence. Nevertheless, even for Schweid, the final conclusion that rises from the work is, as we said, "subduing the heart for faith." Far from him, yet close to him, is Adi Tsemakh, who gives up the harmonistic view of this story and argues that Tehilah is punished because she has not stopped thinking of Shraga throughout the years of her marriage, and in fact throughout her life—and thus she committed the sin of adultery and went on in her rebelliousness despite the punishments imposed on her from Above. For Adi Tsemakh, "Tehilah willingly accepts the horrible results." Tsemakh also indicates the connection between "Tehilah" and the legend of "The Weasel and the Well." Parts of his brilliant article come close to hairsplitting, however. The theological position Tsemakh attributes to Agnon according to "Tehilah" is close to what I have described here, although in the end Tsemakh returns through a new path to "the harmonistic position" and categorizes the story as "a hymn to love, humanity, and faith."

8 |

In the first part of the story, we do not know the Job-like nature of Tehilah's catastrophes, and we do not find it out all at once, but gradually, drop by drop, progressing in horror.[11] We (and the narrator) first learn that Tehilah became impoverished (p. 42), her daughter converted to Christianity on her way to her wedding (p. 58), and her sons and her husband died (pp. 56–57). We learn last of the first blow that befell her: the betrayal ninety-three years before (p. 53) and the imposed match. The cancellation of the match she desired and the imposed match instead are two acts of erotic iniquity perpetrated on Tehilah, the root of all her torments. Like "In the Prime of Life," *A Simple Story, Only Yesterday, Shira,* Berdichevski's "Kalonymos and Naomi," Bialik's "Behind the Fence," and many other stories of the generation called the Generation of Revival in our literature—so "Tehilah" is also basically a story about an act of an erotic iniquity, an injustice forced on the individual by the laws of religion and society, that permeates and poisons its victim's life. In this story, the force of the iniquity is revealed to the victim only after three generations have passed, when her principle of justifying the Judgment has cracked, and she responds to the revelation like a person waking from a slumber when all his wounds begin to scream.

In Federico Fellini's film *Roma,* there is an unforgettable scene: archaeological digs under the city bring a burst of daylight to ancient Roman murals hidden in darkness for thousands of years. At that first contact with light, the murals start to fade and to be wiped out from one moment to the next right before our amazed eyes. In "Tehilah," it is the encounter with the narrator that is the destructive light that inadvertently devastates Tehilah's "wholesome and harmonious" world, in whose depths she had entrenched herself for ninety years against understanding the iniquity that was done to her, iniquity both by human hands and by divine hands.

9 |

Like many of Agnon's stories, this one is wide open to midrashic and allegoric or Kabbalistic and symbolic interpretations. Eli Schweid, for example, sees "Tehilah" as a complex combination of a realistic-psychological story and an ancient myth in the style of religious literature, and he notes that the story opens with Tehilah carrying a can of water and ends with the water in which Tehilah is purified. Schweid emphasizes that the water is a symbol of grace in the Kabbalah. And surely some critics are tempted to erect midrashic interpretations on the play of words of "Tehilah" (praise, glory)—"Tefila" (prayer) at the end of the story, and others will infer from this that Tehilah is the Community of Israel. According to this reading, Shraga must fill the role of the Holy-One-Blessed-Be-He in person, and the cancellation of the marriage is comparable to our many transgressions, and so on. But this way, too, even the diligent interpreter is not likely to salvage "the wholeness and spiritual harmony" that Kurzweil ascribed to this story, for Shraga the Hasid turned sour and became a Misnaged and wound up dying before Tehilah could ask his forgiveness for the sin she did not commit against him. Thus the allegorical interpretation loses its force, especially since the repair—if there is a repair in this story—is an even more dubious repair than the repair of the iniquity visited upon Job. This is neither an allegory nor an icon, but a tale of past and present, of faith and doubt, and especially of one person who wonders at the nature of two poles, when he stands "sometimes . . . among those praying and sometimes among those wondering." Therefore, it is difficult to accept Schweid's conclusion that "the essence of the idea embodied in the story—is the idea of Providence that everything is guided by it with supreme wisdom." It is easier to agree with Schweid when he states in the same article that "the evaluation of the past and the present in this story is dialectical."

10 |

Ostensibly, "Tehilah" concerns the clash between the innocent and harmonious past on the one hand and a future that is all dubious innovation on the other: a stove that isn't a stove, an autobus that isn't a cart, a pen that isn't a pen, innovations that offer nothing new, tourists who don't immigrate to the Land of Israel, Jews who aren't Jewish enough, Jerusalem outside the Walls that isn't Jerusalem enough, and so on. Ostensibly, what is juxtaposed here is the world of faith and the world of maybe, and the narrator—who may be seen as the real hero of the story—wants to be helped by Tehilah, the righteous woman, to get out of the absurdity of "the world of maybe" and rise to the sublimity of the "world of certainty": to repair the world, in the Kabbalistic sense of the term. Just as Tehilah, on leaving this world, tries with her letter to Shraga to realize a "repair" in the Kabbalistic sense of the term.

But ultimately it is not Tehilah who exalts the narrator to the sublimity of innocent faith, but the contrary: the narrator—inadvertently—drags Tehilah to the abyss of "the torments of post factum," of absurdity and dread. She who enters the story as a kind of Reb Yudel in a dress leaves the story and this world as a kind of Job in a dress. And as we said, "Tehilah" is not close to the stories of awe, the tales of the righteous, and ethical sermons; rather it is close to *The Book of Tales* and "Edo and Enam," or close to the stories of Kafka, with their victims who don't understand and the hidden forces that abuse her in what looks like mocking arbitrariness.

This is a story about two sides of the coin of faith: on the one hand, "wholeness and spiritual harmony," confidence in Divine Providence, charm and grace and mercy and benevolence—and on the other, the price of "a hollow heart," the price of erotic iniquity and erotic sacrifice. For Tehilah is destined for Shraga according to the match and according to desire, and she is taken away from him with a broken heart. As the desperate Hirshl whispers into the ear of his wife, Mina, in *A Simple Story:* "Our lives aren't our own, Mina, and others do what they please with them."[12] And there is not much difference between the fate of Tehilah and the fate of Leah Mintz, except that the former lived to an extreme old age and the latter died in the prime of life, perhaps because she loved Akavia Mazal and was engaged to him, but powerful forces took her away from Mazal and gave her to Mintz. (Incidentally, her daughter Tirza says of her "As a righteous woman she died," thus shrinking the difference between Leah and Tehilah, of whom similar things were said.)

Hirshl Hurvitz's maternal forefathers, the Klingers, carry a repressed and censored incident, a "skeleton in the closet": a very ancient curse hovers over that family from one generation to the next— that every single generation has its lunatic. Or perhaps it is not a very effective curse but rather a tradition of erotic iniquity that is operating, for in every single generation, one of the family is forced into a match he doesn't want and the match he does want is canceled, and the victim goes a bit mad: "His heart was a dead space inside him." Tehilah is like that too: after ninety years, it becomes palpably clear to her that in her childhood, erotic iniquity befell her, and more and more iniquities branched out from it. And when she does understand that, with all her 104 years, she "intones a kind of ritual chant," picks up a jar, raises it high, and puts a wish in it. Her heart is a dead space inside her, and she passes out of the world slamming the door like a precocious girl who has gotten the better of an argument with her elders, or like someone who is about to go mad.

11 |

In sum, to find in "Tehilah" an apotheosis of the world of faith is to violate the story and perhaps also the world of faith. Yet is it possible that everyone who interprets that story as a story of canonic Judaism (and some of its interpretations have themselves been granted canonic status) — is it possible that the devotees read only the first half of the story? For by the end of the story, the religious predestination — reward and punishment — is cracked and, as we said, between the cracks the "horror of fate" peeps out. The modern, skeptical existence, easygoing and unbelieving, bursts the walls of the righteous woman's righteousness, stirs doubt in her, and opens her wounds, and she leaves the world slamming the door. Contrary to the widespread psychological cliché that the past incessantly shapes the present and the future in the soul, with Tehilah, in her extreme old age, the present (the character of the narrator who becomes friendly with her) reshapes the past and exposes in it the face of a monster hidden under the cover of idyllic faith.

Indeed, the story "Tehilah" is not as close to Bialik's "My Mother of Blessed Memory," in which the mother "was a perfect saint," as it is to the tales of erotic iniquity that penetrate and pass from one generation to another and undermine the world of tradition from inside. We have already mentioned "The Prime of Life," and *A Simple Story, Only Yesterday,* and "The Crooked Became Straight," "Kalonymos and Naomi," and "Behind the Fence."

The root of this story is not in the Book of Esther or Psalms or the Book of Ruth, but perhaps it is in Bialik's "The Scroll of Fire."

1990–1991

CHAPTER 3

Stolen Waters and Bread Eaten in Secret

Reading *A Simple Story*

Understanding the Source of the Torments

> [Agnon's] typical situation is that he does not explain
> to himself where his desire is tending, and what are the
> actions done by him or to him, he confronts them with
> ambivalence. . . . The conflict between the soul that
> does not relinquish and his actions that are nothing but
> relinquishing.
>
> Dov Sadan

Which of Agnon's heroes is described in these lines? Manfred Herbst
of *Shira* or Isaac Kumer of *Only Yesterday*? The hero-narrator of
"Thus Far" or the wounded souls of *The Book of Tales*? Hemdat or
Jacob Rechnitz? That short paragraph, in which the critic Dov Sadan
characterizes Hirshl Hurvitz of *A Simple Story,* could well describe
most of the young heroes of Agnon's fiction. What Sadan says about
Hirshl could be said about Isaac Kumer in *Only Yesterday.* Both of
them are more or less cousins of the tormented "externs," the nonresident students in the early twentieth-century fiction of Mordechai
Ze'ev Feyerberg, Hersh David Nomberg, Micha Berdichevski, Uri
Niroah Gnessin, and Brenner.[1] But their heroes, Nahman and Fliegel-
man and Kalonymus and Hagzar and Ezekiel Hefets, all possess powers of thought, some more and some less, and a tendency to question,
qualities that prepare them to cope intellectually with their situation—
although that coping ends in failure. On the other hand, Agnon's
heroes, who are not "externs" and intellectuals, come to defeat and
renunciation without understanding what has struck them or what lies
at the root of their wretchedness; or perhaps they do understand but
are only unable to articulate it.

    In the following pages, we will examine the possibility that
Hirshl did understand, in his own way, what struck him—and perhaps
we will find that ultimately he is not really one of the defeated or the
relinquishing.

    Dov Sadan has also stated that understanding the source of
the torments in *A Simple Story* may be even more complicated than
understanding the source of the torments of the heroes of Feyerberg,
Brenner, and Berdichevski, because in *A Simple Story* two systems
of argumentation are operating that appear to contradict one another,

or to cast doubt on one another; or at least to put one another in a relative light.

2 |

It Is All the Fault of Society, or Perhaps It Is Mother, or Perhaps Grandfather, or Maybe Even the Draft Board

> The lady doth protest too much, methinks.
>
> Shakespeare

Hirshl's madness, like Isaac Kumer's ascent to the Land of Israel, is explained too much. Like the lady's excessive protest in *Hamlet*, the abundant overflow of convincing explanations in *A Simple Story* and *Only Yesterday* invites a certain doubt.

Dov Sadan seems to have been the first critic to understand the double meaning of Hirshl's madness: "Behind the psychological explanation," he wrote, "the face of another explanation peeps out at you, and if you remove its calming swoon—you will see the horror of Fate." Then came Malka Shaked, who recommended a "pluralistic view of the plot of *A Simple Story.*" She doubled the double meaning of Hirshl's madness, indicating no less than four systems of argumentation to explain why that young man went out of his mind—four systems of explanation that are all convincing, all detailed, and all capable of meeting the explanatory obligation in a family novel of the realistic-social-psychological tradition. Yet it is precisely when they are combined that the various arguments cast doubt and a light of relativity on one another. Thus the superfluous explanations burst the bounds of a traditional family novel and grant *A Simple Story* the nature of the kind of modern novel in which actions are presented in microscopic detail, while their reasons and meanings are left in the dark. When Baruch Kurzweil chose to connect *A Simple Story* to the tradition of "European literature from the time of Balzac and Stendahl to Tolstoy," he apparently did not discern the surplus of explanation that amounts to a lack of explanation.

Malka Shaked enumerates these systems of explanation: (1) The psychological explanation—Hirshl's erotic frustration leads to his "collapse" and "unconscious craziness." (2) "The horror of Fate"—Hirshl's madness stems from the realization of an ancient and traditional curse that hovers over the heads of the Klinger family because of the offense committed by one of Hirshl's forefathers against the rabbi of the city. (3) The social explanation—the source of Hirshl's madness is in a revolt, conscious, unconscious, or semiconscious, against the social framework and its castrating conventions. (4) The "utilitarian" explanation—Hirshl's madness saves him from the draft board, which supposedly cannot be bribed.

To these four systems of explanation, we must add the genetic—for the rabbi's curse on the Klinger family may also be seen as an inherited genetic defect conveying the tendency to mental illness from one generation to the next. Every single one of these explanations is enough to make a hero of Stendahl or Tolstoy or Thomas Mann go mad. Piled on top of one another, the explanations take *A Simple Story* out of the "explicit" tradition and bring it into the world of modern authors. In Kafka or Peter Weiss, the hero is liable to go out of his mind without the text bothering to offer the reader even a trace of an explanation.

The polyphonous abundance of explanations for Hirshl's madness in *A Simple Story* and for Isaac's immigration to the Land of Israel in *Only Yesterday*—psychological social, hereditary, erotic, pre-destination, and utilitarian explanations that are all designed to explain the deed itself—such an abundance does not explain the mystery but only deepens it.[2] Thus the story loses its simplicity and departs from social-psychological realism.

3 |
"There Is Method to This Madness"

> He's a God-given con-artist, but still entirely loony.

The Sergeant Major

Malka Shaked writes: "It is impossible to say that Hirshl is crazy and at the same time to claim that he is pretending to be crazy." But why is that impossible? Just as a sane person can sometimes successfully pretend to be crazy, and just as a madman sometimes succeeds in pretending to be rather sane (even leading masses of enthusiasts), so a person who "isn't right in the head" can pretend, cold-bloodedly and precisely, to be a run-of-the-mill lunatic or to assume by calculation the form of a drooling moron. Hamlet, prince of Denmark, may be the quintes-sential literary example of a madman pretending to be a madman, a mental case who plays the fool for others and yet warns his friend Horatio that he intends to play the fool. In this case, Hirshl is Hamlet, prince of Shibush. Like Hamlet, even though his soul is genuinely shattered, he is still able to appear a drooling moron—or the embodiment of submission and conservatism. And like Hamlet of Denmark, so Hamlet of Shibush warns his only friend (Mina) that he may soon appear to be a complete moron.

Keep in mind that, even during the grotesque feast in the Ziemlich house, after the announcement of the engagement and before the wedding, Hirshl cold-bloodedly weighs madness as a tactical option that in a twinkling can get him out of the erotic trap, which, he clearly discerns, "the whole world" is trying to spring on him. Hirshl weighs his options: "All I need to do, he thought, is say something beastly and I'll be rid of her for good" (p. 75). As the story continues, after his marriage, Hirshl again weighs precedents that occurred both in his family and outside it, precedents in which madness served "as a calculated escape hatch" from the rack of social constraints. Amazingly, Hirshl will weigh these "underground" considerations not in the depths of his heart but aloud, and to his wife, Mina, of all people, even though she would seem to be the trap he wants to escape from. This looks like an insoluble contradiction: a person intends to go out of his mind a bit to break the yoke of a forced marriage—and he lets the "enemy" in on his plan. But this is only an ostensible contradiction because, in truth, Hirshl's staged madness is not aimed at Mina and is not intended to get him out of her hold—but almost the opposite.

4 |
"The Good Breeding of Home"

> And the essential thing is not the last question
> Or the morals of the story, or a statement
> Of purpose. It is listening closely.
>
> Nathan Alterman, "Summer's Feast"

Did Hirshl Hurvitz and Isaac Kumer, two sons of shopkeepers "in our hometown," know each other? Logically, they had to know each other: both are from the same small town, and if they aren't the same age, they are more or less of the same time.[3] Of course, status differences separate them, and Kumer probably never did or could set foot in the

Hurvitz home. Tsirl Hurvitz, Hirshl's mother, certainly would not have looked with favor on any contact between her son and "inferiors." Kumer, the grandson of the granddaughter of Reb Yudel Hasid, is a wretched pauper, while Hirshl, the son of the daughter of Reb Simon Hirsh Klinger, is rich and getting richer, and his match doubles his fortune. When Simon Kumer, Isaac's father, preaches morality to his son, he points to Isaac's friends who "had already taken wives and opened shops for themselves, and they're distinguished in the eyes of folks. . . . They enter the bank and the clerk sits them down on a chair," and so on.[4] When Simon tells these things to his son, he may be thinking of Hirshl Hurvitz and praying that his son will be like him.

As for Hirshl, he may be thinking of Isaac Kumer and his family when he says to himself: "There were those who claimed that the whole problem with the world was its being divided into rich and poor. Indeed, that was a problem. Certainly, though, it was not the main one. The main problem was that everything was so painful" (p. 10).

Despite the differences in status, those two shop owners' sons in the town, both of them excellent and modest, both afraid of women, both connected with Zionism, may well have crossed paths. Perhaps they exchanged a few words on a winter night in the newspaper reading room at the Zionist club. Perhaps Hirshl agreed to buy stamps or Zionist Shekels of the Jewish National Fund from Isaac, who devoted himself to selling them. In all the vicissitudes of their fate, despite the differences of place and status and incident, either of them could have said that "the good breeding he had received at home was not easily overcome" (p. 29).[5]

A careful examination of the abundance of "explanations" for Hirshl's madness reveals the fascinating similarity between Hirshl and Isaac and the gamut of reasons for Isaac's immigration to the Land of Israel. What Malka Shaked wrote about the madness of the one can apply to the immigration of the other.[6] We may conclude that Hirshl in his madness and Isaac in his immigration to the Land of Israel take themselves "out of the routine" and "out of the system," in Agnon's words. And keep in mind that both of them take themselves out of the *same* routine and out of the *same* system—and both of them discover some time later that it is easier to get out of the system than to get the system out of your soul. Moreover, Hirshl, as far as we know, will not immigrate to the Land of Israel—but Isaac will go mad. For all the differences between Hirshl, who put his shoe on his head and cried "Ga-ga," and Isaac, who drooled into his beard and cried "Arf arf," we must remember that Hirshl's mad rooster is an erotic rooster, just as Isaac's mad dog is an erotic dog.

Here are the systems of explanation for the two works, superimposed on one another:

Hirshl's Madness (*A Simple Story*)	Isaac's Immigration to Israel (*Only Yesterday*)
Psychological explanation: attempt to get away from the tyranny of the mother.	Orphan with no mother. Seeking an ideal mother figure and imagining he has found her in "Our Mother Zion" (p. 39).
Erotic motive: power of the erotic transgression.	Lack of erotic opportunity in the towns of Diaspora—erotic "promise" in the Land of Israel.
Genetic reason: inherited-latent madness in the family.	Descendant of Reb Yudel Hasid, heir to his innocence and devotion.
Predestination reason: ancient curse.	The deeds of the forefathers are a sign for the sons of the great-grandsons.
Social reason: madness rescues Hirshl from social torment.	Immigration to the Land of Israel guarantees the wretched pauper that he will be a "property owner" and will improve his social position.
Family calculation: the in-laws believe that going mad is a ruse to thwart the draft board.	Isaac's father fears that his son "will ruin" the other children and prefers that he go to Israel—and return sober from his dream.
Immediate cause: the draft board is about to come and cannot be bribed.	The draft board is about to come, and there is nothing to bribe them with.

And so, in *A Simple Story* and in *Only Yesterday,* a great heap of explanations for issues is piled up where the realistic novel would have settled for one. And in both works, the abundance of explanations does not shed any light but rather dazzles the reader so much that the true internal cause remains a profound mystery.

5 |
Hirshl and Isaac—Two Orphans

> *You are too pure to be my friend*
> *You are too holy to sit with me;*
> *Please be my god and angel . . .*
> *And my tremor is in my teardrop.*

H. N. Bialik, "She Wrote Me a Little Letter"

Isaac Kumer's mother—as her memory is inscribed on his heart—would seem to be the complete opposite of Tsirl Hurvitz, Hirshl's mother. Tsirl is the daughter of rich shop owners, strong and domineering, like the greeting cards she sends every Rosh Hashanah to her poor relatives: "of stiff, heavy paper, blazoned with gold letters" (p. 5). And: "She would sit herself down at the table, her body overflowing her chair" (p. 26). Or: "Tsirl . . . had reached the age when what concerns a woman most is what she has to eat and drink" (p. 25). A. B. Yehoshua has discerned Hirshl's repressed hatred for his mother, a woman who is not feminine and a mother who is not maternal.

Unlike Tsirl, Isaac Kumer's mother, Judith, is pictured in the eyes of her orphaned son as an angel of God, "dressed in white clothes, and her voice . . . full of compassion."[7] Isaac recalls with a tremor of holiness "her white hand stretched out to him . . . and it was clear in his eyes that there [was] no woman in the world like his mother. And when his mother died, another woman who *would come* in her place would be modest and pious as his mother."[8] The words "would come" are italicized here because in Hirshl's world—as in the world of Hemdat in "Hill of Sand," as in the world of Isaac Kumer, and as in the worlds of Rechnitz, Manfred Herbst, and other Agnon heroes—the obligation of "coming" is imposed on the woman. She is the lady on a white horse, while the man need do nothing but wait until he is awakened and until he awakens, and until salvation comes along and saves him from his virginity. (This issue has been explored further by Moshe Shamir and Gershon Shaked.)

There seems to be no greater contrast than that between Isaac's pure, white, angelic mother, who died in her youth (and is reminiscent of Leah, Tirza's mother, in "In the Prime of Her Life"), and Hirshl's coarse, domineering, "red" mother.

But this contrast is merely an optical illusion. In point of fact, the role both mothers play in their sons' lives is almost equally destructive: Hirshl and Isaac are both bereft of a mother. Both of them have to let go of the image of the mother before they can realize their sexuality. And in both of them, the image of the mother distorts erotic autonomy and causes torments that lead to madness. A. B. Yehoshua expands on the issue of Tsirl's destructive role in her son's life and argues that the decision of Hirshl and Mina at the end of the story to entrust their eldest son to the care of Mina's parents is merely a symbolic expression of Hirshl returning "his self" to the parents' generation to reproach them for their failure in his education—as if to give them a "make-up exam."

Neither Isaac's mother as an angel of God nor Hirshl's mother as a coarse cow is portrayed as a human being. Both the latter in her bovine heaviness and the former in her angelic nature are castrating mothers. Both make their sons seek in their lovers not spouses and friends but, in Bialik's words, "a mother and a sister." Isaac wants in Sonya the angelic mother he had, and Hirshl, who wants in Bluma the mother he never had, ends up finding in his wife something of the flesh-and-blood quality of his mother and is glad about that.

In both cases, these two excellent and modest young men turn to the beloved in their youth in a manner Bialik describes: "You are too pure to be my friend / You are too holy to sit with me; / Please be my god and angel." And: "Take me under your wing and be a mother to me and a sister." True, it turns out that Sonya Zweiering in *Only Yesterday* has no interest in being a mother and a sister to Isaac, except perhaps for a few weeks, while Bluma Nacht in *A Simple Story* isn't capable of playing the role of mother and sister—and she may not be able to play any "feminine" role at all, as will be discussed later.

In the end, Hirshl breaks off with Bluma just as Isaac Kumer breaks off with Sonya, but even after their love has died and become a suppressed offense and a repressed passion, those two innocents go on paying lip service to their past love and stubbornly maintaining a pathetic ritual of disappointed love. Both torture themselves with guilt, one toward Sonya and the other toward Bluma, not for the sin they have committed but for the sin the beloved woman has committed toward them. And the heart grows more resentful.

Incidentally: do the comparison between Bluma Nacht and Sonya Zweiering, the similarity between Isaac and Hirshl, and the parallel between the two love affairs all perhaps hint that the character of Shifra, whom Isaac marries, and the character of Mina, whom Hershl marries, are also close? This deserves a discussion by itself, "only God knows when."

6 |
Kalonymos, Noah, and Hirsh

> And one night, Noah escaped with Marinka?
> You don't know the soul of a man from the forest suburbs.
> On the Sabbath of Hanukkah, Noah married
>   a proper virgin.
>
> H. N. Bialik, "Behind the Fence"

At the center of A *Simple Story* are Hirshl's love for a servant relative, his marriage to "a proper virgin," his madness, his healing, and his adjustment to the "mother's repast" that is forced on him. According to one of the systems of explanation operating in the story, Hirshl's madness expresses a planned revolt designed to burst the erotic fetters that bind him and to escape from slavery (with Mina) into freedom (in the arms of Bluma).

Hirshl appears to be a victim of manipulation, a bachelor who has been maneuvered by his mother and "society," with fraud and cunning, into marrying a woman who horrifies him intellectually (pp. 109 and 112–13) and revolts him physically (pp. 114, 124, and 125). Ultimately—according to most interpreters of A *Simple Story*—Hirshl restrains the desolation and adjusts to the revulsion and, with great difficulty, manages to make do with what is available. According to Gershon Shaked, Hirshl's recovery at the end of A *Simple Story* is an emotional castration, an extinction of the heart, a bourgeois thickening at the expense of the youthful fire that Tsirl and Toyber and Langsam and the whole host of them turned into ashes. Shaked believes that the narrator weeps for the dying out of the erotic fire in Hirshl, as is obvious in the texture of "blind motives" in the story, as well as in the elegiac tone that controls the final chapters. A. B. Yehoshua finds less gloom in the conclusion of *A Simple Story* than does Shaked, and he thinks that Hirshl's recovery comes from his partial consciousness of the fact that the previous generation sinned against him. Either way, most readers and critics seem to accept Gershon Shaked's notion that Hirshl is depicted at the end of *A Simple Story* as a man who has lost the romantic spark bought with torment and has become a settled shop owner who displays exactly what Sonya sees and loathes in Isaac Kumer: "a petit bourgeois on a holiday."[9] Habit seemed to blunt Hirshl's disgust for Mina's body, and his erotic interest shriveled with the passing years, until—following the custom of Jewish males—he "lived in peace with Mina and did not turn his eyes to other women."

It is fascinating to compare what looks like "an extinguished conclusion" in *A Simple Story* with the extinguished conclusion in Berdichevski's story of "Kalonymos and Naomi." Like Agnon's Hirshl and Bluma, Kalonymos and Naomi are young lovers "intended" for one another by bonds that originate in the previous generation. Bluma is "like a twin" to Hirshl because her mother was intended for his father. Naomi is Kalonymos's stepsister because of the second marriage of his father to her mother. As in *A Simple Story* and "In the Prime of Her Life," an erotic "disruption" takes place in the previous generation, and the love of the young couple is supposed to repair it. As in *A Simple Story* and to some extent also in "In the Prime of Her Life," in "Kalonymos and Naomi" the lovers first encounter a fortified wall of social convention and the refusal of the Orthodox "guards of the walls" to allow the lovers to repair what their forefathers ruined. Here and there, the lovers rebel and try "to break the rules." Bluma Nacht goes to work in the home of excommunicated pariahs who live in the Christian quarter, outside the Jewish community. Tirza is afflicted with a serious illness, and—just as it is illness that kept Akavia from her mother—it is illness that grants him to Tirza herself. Agnon's Hirshl steps "out of the order"—the social system—and goes a little crazy. With the help of the forbidden philosophy, Kalonymos rises above the "order," while Naomi becomes a cow and crawls on all fours under the order.

In all three works, breaking out of the order seems to end with the capitulation of the rebels. Tirza Mazal, née Mintz, achieved her goal but found herself stuck where her mother had stood—and flickered out—married to an extinguished, grayish man. Hirshl and Kalonymos return ashamed to the slot destined for them from the start—one becomes a schoolteacher, and the other becomes a shopkeeper.

Yet there is a big difference between the two outcomes. Kalonymos and Naomi seem to succeed in breaking the forced match and realizing their desire to live with one another, while Hirshl fails in that. But the success of Kalonymos and Naomi has the taste of total defeat, just like the success of Tirza Mintz-Mazal: they are condemned to live "extinguished" lives. And some crushed victory, even if it is an entirely secret victory, may be inherent in Hirshl's defeat. More about that later.

In both *A Simple Story* and "Kalonymos and Naomi," the social system—"the order"—is determined to extinguish the erotic fire and to turn it to ashes, lest it spread and endanger the entire "order." But in Berdichevski's story, the fire turns so thoroughly to ashes that there is no longer any danger that it will be rekindled, that Naomi and Kalonymos will be allowed to marry one another like two "defectives." In *A Simple Story*, the social system—Tsirl and her whole host—thinks the fire has turned to ashes, but the careful reader will discern at the conclusion of the work that Hirshl and Mina manage to preserve a few hissing embers, and to warm one another in secret.

Perhaps if Hirshl's madness had been so complete that they were forced to end his marriage to Mina, and if his madness had gone on until the system finally married him off to Bluma, as damaged goods with inferior goods, perhaps then the conclusion of *A Simple Story* might be as extinguished and awful as the conclusion of "Kalonymos and Naomi." Then Bluma's implied frigidity would certainly have brought down on Hirshl "the dreariness of life" that concludes Berdichevski's story.

This dreariness is much like that which concludes "In the Prime of Her Life." Tirza wanted to love her mother's lover to avoid her mother's fate—"a life of ashes" with her father. In the end she married a man whom time made into the twin of her father, and thus—great tragic irony—her life became a copy of her mother's extinguished life. Tirza's victory is just the same as the defeated life of her mother. It is no accident that the last scene of "In the Prime of Her Life" is almost a reflection of the first scenes. Tirza Mazal, née Mintz, also went to the fire and found ashes.

Note, too, that in "Kalonymos and Naomi," as in *A Simple Story*, the roots of erotic distortion seem to derive from some genetically predestined curse passed from one generation to the next: "I shall begin with the father of her mother, with Natan Halevi." There too, couplings that are useful and reasonable in social terms but cruel in erotic terms produce madness: first in Samuel, then in Naomi.

But, as we said, A *Simple Story* is different from "Kalonymos and Naomi," different from Bialik's "Behind the Fence" and from Agnon's "In the Prime of Her Life"—because A *Simple Story* does not end with the defeat of Eros but with its secret victory over those who would destroy it.

A *Simple Story* provides a solid basis for the view that Hirshl's disgust for Mina's personality and body is merely one side of the coin, while the yearning for Bluma that drives Hirshl out of his mind has at least one clear component of a staged performance, for which Hirshl holds a secret "dress rehearsal"—before Mina, of all people. The extinguished reconciliation, the falling into domesticity, the castration of impulse are merely a "cover story" Hirshl concocts to hide from the world his erotic joy, his and Mina's, a joy suggested at the beginning of their marriage that grows deeper and more exciting and has to be hidden from the evil eye of a society that sees in it the danger of an erotic wildfire.

Thus, A *Simple Story* can be seen as a fascinating continuation, an innovative variation, a dialectical development of the subject Berdichevski raised in "Kalonymos and Naomi." The Romeo and Juliet of the town of Shleyva (tranquil), Kalonymos and Naomi joined in a tacit conspiracy against the tyranny of their families in order to break the advantageous match forced on Kalonymos and to realize their love. But, like Heraclitus's fire, "their victory is their defeat": when they at last receive permission to unite in marriage, their sexual impulse has been castrated and their love has turned to ashes. The victory of the lovers destroyed love. Kalonymos, like Hirshl's crazy uncle, is described at the end as a man "whose heart was a dead space inside him."[10]

After Hirshl has rebelled, he apparently succumbs, gives up his Juliet, and obediently makes do with what his mother has put on his plate (ostensibly like Noah in Bialik's "Behind the Fence"). But in point of fact Hirshl privately discovers Bluma's latent frigidity (p. 224). In his heart, the beloved Rachel turns into the hated Leah—"His heart bore a grudge" against Bluma (pp. 26–27)[11]—while Leah (Mina) turns into Rachel. Hershl and Mina light a secret and joyous erotic bonfire— far from the madding crowd, far from the evil eye, very far from the "gloom of life" that characterizes the extinguished souls at the conclusion of Berdichevski's story and from the obedience of the domesticated Noah at the end of Bialik's.

7 |

The Fire and the Ashes

I swear not to bite my bread
Until my teeth are set on edge by your sour grapes.

Nathan Alterman, "Song to the Woman of My Youth"

We must reexamine Hirshl's relation with Bluma and its opposite, his relation with Mina, as well as the first, profound pattern that stamped both those relations—the complex network of Hirshl's relations with Tsirl, his mother. For at least on one issue all the critics of this work agree: *A Simple Story* is far from simple. (Gershon Shaked was correct, nevertheless, when he indicated that the fabula of this story could also serve as an emotional potboiler and is certainly suitable for one of the dime novels that Haim Nacht used to read to his daughter, and that Hirshl and Bluma might have read at night by candlelight.)

A. B. Yehoshua has noted the chill and barrenness that characterize Tsirl Klinger-Hurvitz, who is remote from the stereotype of a Jewish mother and is incapable of functioning as a wife, a mother, or a housekeeper. Bluma and her cookies, Bluma and her cooking, Bluma and her ways that radiate softness and sorrow bring Hirshl his first experience of love. And indeed the orphaned boy—orphaned because his mother is not a mother—is not exactly seeking erotic charm in Bluma. On the contrary, throughout the story there is hardly a sign that Bluma interests Hirshl erotically. It is Mina who stirs his sexual impulse, even though her table is full of "abominations"—and perhaps even because of her "abominations" (p. 80). Hirshl imagines he has found in Bluma not the promise of erotic satiation, but rather a maternal bosom. And incidentally, Bluma indirectly represents a kind of sister to Hirshl and even his twin, according to the Platonic myth (p. 27). But just as Bluma is not sexually ebullient, she is also unable to grant Hirshl the "wing of a mother and a sister" that he begs for. Bluma is like Tsirl: "[a] princess with the skin of a fish."

From this point, the tragedy follows the logic of a comedy of errors. Tsirl, summoned to frustrate her son's love for Bluma, a poor relation who is like a servant, hurries to insinuate Mina Ziemlich, a wealthy girl with a fat dowry, into his lap. In Tsirl's plan, Mina Ziemlich—Ziemlich means "approximately," "more or less," "quite"— is to put out the erotic fire Tsirl thinks Bluma has ignited in Hirshl's body. Indeed, Hirshl, who sees himself in love with Bluma and in fact is only in love with his emotional love for Bluma, first exhibits a certain disgust for Mina, whom he imagines as "like having to wear a coat all the time that never keeps you warm" (p. 123). She often inspires such physical revulsion in him with her coddling and her cosmetics (that is, with her overt femininity) that he "[turns] his nose away from her."

But that is not the whole truth. The truth is that, because Hirshl does not seek a surrogate mother in Mina or try to see her as a sister or attempt to nestle like a baby under her wing or elevate her as if she were "too pure to be his friend" or form an emotional ritual around her as he did with Bluma, he ends up discovering in her what he didn't find and didn't seek in Bluma: a flesh-and-blood woman. While the infantile and sentimental Hirshl responds with disgust and fear to the discovery of Mina's femininity, the young man Hirshl finds that Mina can really starve his sexual impulse (starve—and also satisfy, according to several subtle hints scattered here and there in "hidden places" in the story, which will be discussed later). Thus, gradually, with hesitation and denials and repressions and an internal struggle between the sensitive orphaned child and the young man in Hirshl, the fellow discovers that Mina, even though she can't be "a mother and a sister" to him, can be to him what his body wants and his heart does not reveal to him: not a surrogate mother, but an opposite mother.

One by one, invisibly, the basic alliances at the beginning of the story are undermined and disrupted, and instead a surprising alliance is secretly made. At the beginning of the story, it is a secret "genetic" alliance that Hirshl and Bluma make against Tsirl's tyranny, against social conventions, against the erotic iniquity that prevented his father and her mother from marrying in the previous generation, and against Mina, whom Tsirl has chosen to be the long arm of the mother in the son's future bed. But gradually and secretly that alliance is violated and a new alliance is made. These changes of coalition are the true internal plot of A Simple Story. From the very beginning of the marriage, Mina serves not as a castrating instrument operated by Tsirl by remote control, but as Hirshl's secret refuge from his mother's tyranny and from Bluma's cold shadow.

When, exactly, did Hirshl violate his alliance with Bluma against Tsirl and replace it with a secret alliance with Mina, against both Tsirl and Bluma? This is a gradual process, and it is impossible to point to any clear turning point. Even near the end of the story,

"Blumaesque recidivism" still twitches in Hirshl, as when he "throws" himself on his sick son and thinks that "if Bluma were taking care of him, he would be all right by now" (p. 221). Note that here, as everywhere in the story, Hirshl's vision of Bluma is sterilized of any sexual dimension and is merely one of the last spasms of "be a mother to me and a sister." And indeed, a few pages later, he finally dares to look at Bluma's barrenness and formulate to himself the previously turgid observation of the sexual and emotional coldness that emanate from her: "The reason she doesn't marry must be that it might give some man pleasure" (p. 224). Thus, after prolonged blindness, Hirshl succeeds in locating Bluma not as a soft and delicate opposite of his coarse mother, but as his mother's double, a citizen of the love desert of those who indulge in narrow-minded calculations. In his thoughts, Hirshl had previously called Bluma "the accountant," thus comparing her to his mother, Tsirl—even though for a long time he rejected and repressed the conclusion to be deduced from that.

As we have said, there is no discrete and specific turning point where Hirshl trades his childish attachment to Bluma for a manly attachment to Mina. Nevertheless, we can certainly follow the process of a gradual emotional and erotic opening up, as Hirshl grew closer to "his hated wife."

The expression "his hated wife" is in quotation marks because, with a ritual stubbornness, Hirshl continues to pay lip service to his love for Bluma, just as he persists in paying lip service to his hatred for Mina—long after his love for Bluma has evaporated and his attachment to Mina has deepened. Indeed, as the story progresses, the love Hirshl feels for Bluma turns to rage and resentment, while his initial disgust for Mina gives way to desire, affection, and intimacy.

It is the soft, submissive Hirshl who finds a flame where at first he imagined he saw only "abominations." Mina, to whom his mother exiled him as to an erotic wasteland far from Bluma, reveals herself to him as a promised land.

Incidentally, perhaps something similar happens between Manfred Herbst and his wife, Henriette, and his lover, Shira, in Agnon's *Shira*. To get to the root of this subtle and slippery subject in Agnon's work, it is rewarding to examine its most primeval, archetypal, and mythic form in the nocturnal race at the conclusion of "The Oath of Faith."

8 |

An Underground of Two

> *Therefore shall a man leave his father and his mother,*
> *and shall cleave unto his wife: and they shall be*
> *one flesh.*

Gen. 2:24

We must examine in detail the hints of a secret emotional and erotic alliance that Hirshl concluded with the woman who was planted between his sheets to represent the long and castrating arm of the mother and the society.

Malka Shaked indicates the many examples in A *Simple Story* that express Hirshl's hatred for Mina and the spiritual and physical revulsion she evokes in him, including fragments of Hirshl's internal monologue on pages 131 and 154. She also points out the allusions that appear, in combined discourse, on pages 155–56 and connect Mina to the story of Jacob and Rachel and Leah and to the story of Elkanah and Hannah. From this and other examples—such as the tale of the candle that was extinguished under the wedding canopy, and the tale of the leaders of the Indian sect—Malka Shaked concludes that "this madness is a result of . . . unrealized love on the one hand, and a miserable marriage on the other."

But this "miserable marriage" seems to be the least simple thing among all the not-simple things in A *Simple Story*. For example, on the very night of Hirshl's "ensnarement" at a ball at the Gilden-horn home, which Dov Sadan sees as a "coterie of clowns in a horror party," some solidarity of the persecuted is already taking shape in secret between Hirshl and Mina. In that horrible scene, Hirshl is depicted as a hunted animal in a trap, and Mina is the bait the hunters set in that trap. Hirshl, wretched and lost among the jesters who are making fun of him, feels "as if he were going to swoon or vomit" when he is surrounded by "black and red . . . and mocking faces." In his despair, he turns to Mina and finds in her a saving anchor from the grotesque isolation imposed on him by the other guests at the party: "A thousand things Hirshl told Mina . . . God in Heaven knows where Hirshl got so many measures of conversation. . . . And he said things Mina had never heard in her life. . . . He didn't feel that she was silent since his heart felt that she was listening." Gershon Shaked has commented on the connection between these two formulaic phrases, "a thousand things" and "God in Heaven," in *A Simple Story*. Of course, there is no description of "disgust and revulsion" here, but, on the contrary, a description of the beginning of a delicate intimacy between an introverted and quiet young man surrounded by mockers, who generally doesn't have anyone who wants to listen to him, and a girl who grants him attention and feeling. (The verb "to feel" dominates this paragraph!) Thus the beginning of a subtle closeness between Hirshl and Mina is forged, two souls spoiled by their parents but disdained and unimportant, two only children who have "all the good things" but have no one truly close to them. In this scene, Hirshl feels so close to Mina that, even at this early stage, he compares her tacitly to Bluma. And miraculously, with that very first comparison, Mina comes out on top: "yet Mina's eyes left a good memory for they were not suspicious like Bluma's eyes."

That same evening, it becomes clear that "unlike what Hirshl thought did Divine Providence think of him. Forty days before his creation, a divine voice emerged and said: The daughter of Gedalia for Hirshl. He stood up and took Mina's hand and held it. Her hand clung to his and a new light gleamed in her eyes, the light that was hidden away in her since the day the voice said: The daughter of Gedalia for Hirshl, and now it shone in her again."

Never had Bluma's hand clung to Hirshl's hand. Never had such a light shone in the eyes of Bluma Nacht.

That evening in the Gildenhorn home, the angel that comes forty days before the creation of a man is mentioned for the third time, when Gildenhorn congratulates Hirshl the way you congratulate a winner in a card game, with the words "Ich gratuliere," and the narrator quickly "corrects": "Yet the divine voice that said The daughter of Gedalia Ziemlich to Hirshl Hurvitz spoke from the throat of Gildenhorn" (p. 108). This emendation deserves our close attention: the story permits the suspicion that there is a secret agreement to use the ball at the Gildenhorn home to advance the goal of Yona Toyber the matchmaker, who promised Tsirl to make Hirshl and Mina fall into each other's arms so that even they would not understand that their embrace was the product of careful manipulation.

The plan is to make Hirshl the brunt of mockery and isolate him until his only refuge is in Mina's corner, for she is also isolated from all the other guests at the party. Unwittingly, the two will confer, and that will give the mockers the opportunity to declare that they are engaged, thus blocking any possible evasion—any attempt at denial will entail a public scandal, and we know that children from good homes would prefer "a thousand deaths to one disgrace." Thus "a fait accompli" is established. This satanic caprice is what lies behind the mocking words of Gildenhorn—the head of the coterie of clowns—who bursts out laughing when he says "Ich gratuliere," as if Hirshl had won at cards. The narrator turns the mockery into the finger of God, and the manipulation by Toyber and Tsirl into an instrument in the hand of Providence, by saying: "But the divine voice that said The daughter of Gedalia Ziemlich to Hirshl Hurvitz spoke from the throat of Gildenhorn."

The "divine voice" that "announces the daughter of so-and-so to so-and-so forty days before the creation of the embryo" originates in the Talmud Tractate Sotah, page 2, and in the Tractate Sanhedrin, page 22 (where there is an explanation of the difference between the first match and the second that may be relevant to our discussion). Those who agree with most of the interpreters of A Simple Story that Hirshl and Mina are not a match made in Heaven but a "miserable marriage," and those who argue that the right match, the match "made in Heaven," was the match between Hirshl and Bluma, who were meant for one another because Hirshl's father was meant for Bluma's mother—both will surely conclude that the "divine voice" plays a clearly ironic role in the scene in the Gildenhorn house. This opinion should be examined carefully, for it is easy to say here, Woe unto Heaven and woe unto its divine voice that blesses an artificial and clownish match, a wretched match of money with money, a match that was created merely to get Hirshl away from Bluma. But a careful reader must ask whether this divine voice in the Gildenhorn house is indeed an ironic divine voice. Agnon's works assume that the younger generation—Hirshl and Bluma, Tirza and Mintz—is condemned "before its birth" to repair the erotic distortions of the previous generation. Is the Platonic myth about "the twins who yearn to reunite" indeed the narrator's position?

For is it not possible that Agnonian irony may "strike twice"? Perhaps he who laughs last laughs best, and he who laughs last is not necessarily the reader who quickly concludes that a match according to a divine voice that emerges and announces is a distorted match. "He who sits in Heaven will laugh"—and the match of Mina and Hirshl is revealed in the end to be a match made in Heaven—just as it is revealed to the reader that Bluma, who was "like a twin" to Hirshl, was not created to be his wife.

Because Mina Ziemlich is not Hirshl's twin, and *because* she is not the reflection of his mother, she is truly the one intended for him. After many vicissitudes and torments, Hirshl himself understands this. And when he does understand it, toward the conclusion of the story, then he "will leave his father and his mother [and his "twin sister"] and cleave unto his wife: and they shall be one flesh."

And Mina?

"Impossible to say that Hirshl . . . is the bridegroom Mina had dreamed of and impossible to say he isn't. There's something in Hirshl Hurvitz that attracts the heart to him . . . and her heart was attracted to him." And when Hirshl takes her hand in the Gildenhorn house, "a new light gleamed in her eyes, the light that was hidden away." If, in that same chapter, the "divine voice" appears no less than three times along with "a hidden light," perhaps the reader had better not be too hasty to see Hirshl and Mina's match as a matter of irony and blindness.

The bait that Tsirl and Toyber and the whole Gildenhorn coterie of clowns tied to their fishing rod, and the innocent fish that was drawn to that bait in his great loneliness, created a mute bond between them: to make a virtue of necessity.

Hirshl will indeed go on tormenting himself over Bluma, not exactly because he misses Bluma, but because he misses his childish love for Bluma. It will not be easy for Hirshl to reconcile himself to his position as a desired man, and for a long time it will be hard for him to give up his position as a rejected child seeking the wing of a mother and a sister to curl up under. This is the wing his mother didn't spread over him, and the wing Bluma couldn't spread over him because she was neither a mother nor a sister, and especially because she didn't live her femininity, the painful lesson poor Getsel Stein was also to learn.

The torments that distance Hirshl from his wife, as many readers have discerned, are the same torments that finally return him to his wife and bring him close to her, something that few have noticed. Either way, at a very early stage of the plot of *A Simple Story*—at the end of chapter 7—it is clear that while Hirshl sees himself in love with Bluma, his heart is already "resenting" her.

At the betrothal feast of Hirshl and Mina, held in the Ziemlich home in the village of Maly Krovik, Hirshl initially sits sullen and displeased. He despises his mother, despises the lush feast, despises himself, entertains the idea of becoming a vegetarian, and even cold-bloodedly considers how he might get out of the match: he merely has to utter something disgraceful, and he is free of it forever. Clear and sober as a strategist preparing a battle, Hirshl calculates the advantages of causing a scandal that would get him "out of the order" and release him from the social-family rack. As in other places in the story, Hirshl considers some precedents he has heard of: tales of people who deliberately pretended to be mad because madness is a sure refuge that gets them out of (social and erotic) slavery to freedom. Why doesn't Hirshl blow up the feast in Maly Krovik and the match forced upon him by uttering "something disgraceful"?

On the contrary, instead of uttering something disgraceful, Hirshl suddenly becomes "like an inexhaustible fountain" and charms his bride so much that "she [lifts] her eyes to him." Here is the first flickering of a process that will intensify and ripen in Hirshl's heart: "Just then he didn't see Mina as the same Mina his parents wanted to marry him off to, but as a woman he gave his heart to and his mother came and separated them. He immediately held out his hand and took Mina's hand and clasped it like a man holding onto something when everything is against him."

Once again, the change of heart he experienced at the ball at the Gildenhorn house takes place—and this time more strongly. Hirshl holds Mina to remove from his face both the shadow of his mother and the shadow of his beloved. Perhaps more clearly than in any other line in the story, the decisive revelation is contained in the words "a woman he gave his heart to and his mother came and separated them." Those words clearly locate Mina in Bluma's place and Bluma in Mina's place. Here, Hirshl stopped seeing Mina as a tool in his mother's hands: he wants to see himself and Mina holding out against a mother who is trying to separate them.

Of course, after that scene, Hirshl will relapse several times. The oedipal-infantile option will often win out over the adult erotic option. The attraction to the "maternal apron strings" will sometimes still push aside the attraction to the "feminine apron strings." The attraction of the flesh to his own flesh and blood (Bluma) will not easily give way to mature eroticism turned outward, beyond the family circle. The suckling instinct "to give birth inside" will still cause Hirshl suffering and delusions before he surrenders to the adult instinct "to give birth outside." (The struggle between these two contradictory instincts is perhaps the central subject of Thomas Mann's novel *The Holy Sinner* and of A. B. Yehoshua's novel *Mr. Mani.*) Hirshl will be disgusted with Mina and will loathe her; often he will still yearn for the chilly virginity of Bluma, "his twin," that "princess with the skin of a fish." Hirshl's pungent expressions of loathing for his wife's flesh-and-blood femininity and his longing for Bluma's asexual angelic nature may of course be found in several places in *A Simple Story.* Hence, Bluma is depicted as a "fish," while Mina, at the banquet table in her parents' home full "of abominable dishes . . . with tempting smells" (inspiring thoughts of vegetarianism in Hirshl), is depicted as "meat" (flesh). Between "fish" and "meat," Hirshl's contradictory desires ramble through most of the pages of the story.

Despite all its vicissitudes, the alliance begun between Hirshl and Mina in the Gildenhorn coterie of clowns and concluded at the banquet in Maly Krovik is to last and overcome all the fatalistic forces that attract Hirshl, as they attracted Tirza Mintz, to repair a distortion that occurred before his birth, a repair that is just short of incest. The alliance will also overcome the predestined, or mantic, genetic force that condemns Hirshl to madness and destruction. It is to Mina that Hirshl "[gives] his heart," and it is Bluma "his heart resents." Mina's red color will gradually intensify and push aside Bluma's blue color, as Yair Mazor has shown. Even in the desolate days after the wedding, the text hints dimly, erotic fireworks fly between Hirshl and Mina.

During the great crisis, in the desperate dialogue between Mina ("You want me to die") and Hirshl ("Why should I want you to die?"), Hirshl suddenly tells Mina his most intimate secret—not the secret of his love for Bluma, but a much more awful secret: the story of his uncle, his mother's brother, who went out of his mind, the secret of that Klinger family curse of inherited madness. That is the secret locked up tight that no one in the story has ever talked about, not to anyone else in the family, and certainly not outside it, for "the seal of good breeding isn't soon wiped out" and "far better to die a thousand times than to be disgraced even once." And it is in a time of crisis that Hirshl reveals the dark secret to Mina, "who had never heard that story," just as she had never heard about Tsirl's grandfather who had put a chamber pot on his head instead of tefillin, or about the man who, "when he wanted to get rid of his wife, he went out of his way and put his tefillin on the cat." All those great secrets Hirshl tells Mina, and he also tells her that he doesn't think those men were lunatics, but heretics who broke out of the boundaries. One of them went "outside the order" because they were about to marry him off to "a woman he didn't love," and another because "he wanted to get rid of his wife," and both of them because "others have control of us, Mina," and because "his heart was a dead space inside him." Their madness, Hirshl whispers to Mina in the dark of their bedroom, was merely make-believe, a trick to protect sanity from the threat of social forces that drive you mad through erotic repression.

There seems to be a stunning contradiction here: if Mina is a hated wife Hirshl is plotting to get rid of by pretending to be crazy—which will involve divorce, which will bring erotic release (like Kalonymos in "Kalonymos and Naomi" when he turned to philosophy)—then Mina should be the last person he would involve in this plot. After all, the man who exposes himself here to his wife is not a poor wretch pouring out his heart to anyone who happens by, but a plotter recruiting an accomplice in rebellion. At any rate, he is definitely hinting broadly to Mina and warning her that he also plans to get up one day and put on a chamber pot instead of tefillin, or to put the tefillin on the cat, or to call out "Ga-ga." And when that day comes, Mina is not to take things literally: Hirshl's wink as he acts like an idiot and breaks out of the boundary is entrusted here to Mina in advance.

Hirshl knows that Mina now has the power to thwart his plan. In retrospect, we know that Mina did not reveal his secret to those "who sought his soul"; she pretended to be even more amazed than others and didn't hint even to her own mother that Hirshl had planned his madness in advance. Mina did not "betray" Hirshl as Bluma "betrayed" him (in his opinion) when she abandoned him to the matchmakers and left the Hurvitz house. All that—even though Mina seems to have good reasons to "betray" Hirshl: ultimately, a breaking out of the boundary that was ostensibly intended to get rid of her. And wonder of wonders, even though it is Bluma who seems to be beyond that boundary, and even though it is Mina who seems herself to be part of the rejected boundary, nevertheless, Mina will choose not to "denounce" Hirshl.

On the night Hirshl led Mina to the family "vaults," to the hidden repressed eroticism that drives people out of their minds, to places no stranger ever beheld, a wonderful underground bond was formed between them. And there is a distant echo here—perhaps a reverse echo—of the bond Kalonymos and Naomi formed in Berdichevski's story. But in "Kalonymos and Naomi," as we said, the rebels' victory is their defeat, while in *A Simple Story*, Hirshl's submission and domestication conceal the victory of the couple, Hirshl and Mina, who succeed in preserving the erotic ember from the freezing hand of "God in Heaven and Tsirl and Toyber on earth." If Hirshl's madness had caused them to separate him from Mina and place him in Bluma's bosom, *A Simple Story* might have concluded as did "Kalonymos and Naomi." Even closer: if Hirshl had succeeded in using his illness to force his will on his mother and "get" Bluma, *A Simple Story* would have turned into another version of "In the Prime of Her Life." Tirza went to seek an erotic kingdom (Akavia Mazal) inherited from her mother and found foolishness. If Hirshl's madness had succeeded in getting him the "erotic kingdom" of Bluma, the heritage of the previous generation (Mirel and Barukh Haim, whose match was called off), he too might have discovered foolishness where he had hoped to find a kingdom. It is important here that Bluma Nacht's emotional aridity is not only a result of her thwarted relations with Hirshl: even in her youth in her father's house, there is a strange description of Haim Nacht and his daughter Bluma reading a book together. As the father is "soaking the pages with his tears," "troubles and torments do not stir [the daughter's] heart," and she doesn't shed a single tear but states coldly that "if [somebody] had acted differently—he would have saved himself his trouble." At that, Haim Nacht sighs and says: "Daughter, daughter, how can my daughter talk like that." From her youth, then, Bluma is described as a cold calculating girl, incapable of emotion.

Hirshl wanders around at night like Reb Yosef Dela Reina of the town. He stands gazing at Bluma's (assumed) window—Hirshl, who once, in front of the Mazal house, "rested his head on the latch of the gate and began to cry" (p. 148); Hirshl, who persists in reciting to himself that "only Bluma [is] expert at making the bed." When all is said and done, it is Hirshl who creates good sexual bonds with his wife and bonds of conspiracy against his mother and against the forces of society. Such bonds did not and could not exist between him and Bluma. His heart still pays lip service to his immature feelings for Bluma, his feet still carry him to her house at night, but his mind and his loins are now directed not toward her but toward Mina. And deep in his heart, he knows already that it is not Bluma but Mina who is "expert at making the bed." And the reader now discerns that in fact the "divine voice" that emerged "forty days before his creation" did not say the Nacht girl for Hirshl, but the Ziemlich girl for Hirshl. Thus, relatively early in *A Simple Story,* the seed of Hirshl's future infidelity to his love is sown—his infidelity with his legal spouse.

Thus we can understand that Hirshl goes a bit mad, not to force his parents to release him from the punishment of Mina and allow him to escape to the closed night bloom (Bluma Nacht), but rather to be freed from his mother's embrace. His liberation from his mother's clasp is connected to his liberation from his devotion to Bluma, for the addiction to Bluma was—at least to some extent—the product of a perverse response to his mother's clasp. And when he is liberated at last from the mother's grasp and from his addiction to the sensations for Bluma, he can unite "without any separating partition" with the one "lying before him and breathing."

Hirshl, "the castrated male" who was driven out of his mind by "God in Heaven and Tsirl and Toyber on earth" and whose watch stopped, that crushed man whose "heart grew hot and pounded. . . . He also gasped for breath. . . . His voice trembled. . . . The blanket covering Mina fell back a bit. Hirshl's lips clung to Mina's. After awhile, she drew breath and said, You're here, Heinrich. Hirshl hugged her with all his might and gave no answer." At the end of the story, the erotic conspiracy between Hirshl and Mina is still hidden not only from Tsirl and Toyber, but also from the reader, who feels that the bedroom door has been shut in his face and he can learn of it only indirectly: "[Mina's] once pallid face became ruddy, her mouth . . . began to smile. Truth to tell, lines did appear on her cheeks near her ears, but Hirshl is fond of those lines and calls them kiss pockets because of matters intimate between a man and a woman."

What are those "matters intimate"? Behind that locked door, the reality of husband and wife hints that they are the complete opposite of the experience of the extinguished couple at the end of "Kalonymos and Naomi" and of the gloomy couple at the end of Agnon's own story "In the Prime of Her Life." There is enough evidence to assume that the "matters intimate between a man and a woman" are things Bluma's nature wouldn't allow. At last, the liberated Hirshl awakens to say words about Bluma that his heart has not revealed to him before, words he utters with a trace of the sarcasm he has after all inherited from his mother, Tsirl: "That maiden didn't love me and I doubt she loved anybody in the world. She doesn't get married because she begrudges a man any pleasure he might get from her." And so Hirshl now understands "that maiden's" erotic stinginess: not a romantic incarnation of the beautiful Mirl who was intended for his father in the previous generation, but an incarnation of his castrating mother, Tsirl. She is a shopkeeper of love whose purse is fastened forever, the opposite of the disappointed romantic lover depicted in "The Hill of Sand" as "a beggar of love with a torn rucksack."[12] Against Tsirl and Bluma, cold and stingy shopkeepers of love, stands Mina, who "flashed a blossom of light from her eyes . . . and a pleasant warmth from her body . . . to Hirshl's body." She is the warmth that Hirshl wanted and didn't find in his mother. She is the warmth that Bluma seemed to promise him and didn't grant, perhaps because she couldn't grant what she didn't have. It is the warmth they tried to cool once and for all by chaining Mina and Hirshl to one another, yet those two, sent to freeze together in the erotic snow, manage to outwit their captors, establish a small underground, and make the best of a bad bargain, or bring fire out of snow.

9 |
Not a Mother and Not a Sister

> For the cause of things and their end did disappear
> And the world happens in between.

Nathan Alterman, *A Feast of Summer*

Said Mina to Hirshl: "I used to think that love is wont to grow with every single one of us. Hirshl lowered his eyes and said, No, it comes if there is no one between it and us." Gershon Shaked cites these fascinating words at the very end of the story and claims they mean that Bluma Nacht no longer stands between Hirshl and Mina. A. B. Yehoshua, on the other hand, thinks that Mina and Hirshl's love flourishes at the end of the story, not because Bluma no longer comes between them, but because Tsirl "has dwindled" and no longer comes between them: "Tsirl had changed greatly, she is no longer passionate for fine foods and not eager to eat and drink." If we accept the advice of the narrator and "look into the matter," we shall find that Shaked's interpretation that Hirshl and Mina's love flourishes because Bluma is diminished does not contradict Yehoshua's interpretation that it flourishes because Tsirl is diminished. The shrinking of Bluma and Tsirl are the same. It is not Mina, Tsirl's choice, who is the heir of the frigid Tsirl, but Bluma, Hirshl's own infantile choice. Moreover, the whole issue of Bluma was merely moving a piece on the board laid out between mother and son in a game where the mother wanted to perpetuate her rule and the son wanted to rebel against it and find himself a surrogate mother. When the game ended, both Tsirl and Bluma "dwindled."

Slowly, in stages, on a very gradual slope, in a calm epic tone that tells the story naïvely, as it were, Hirshl learns to accept what his heart told him on the night of the party in the Gildenhorn coterie of clowns, when Mina was imposed on him: he learns that he has to realize the mature reconciliation between emotion and the sex drive. Some see the novels Dr. Langsam gave Hirshl during his madness as instruments of castration, and some see Dr. Langsam as the great castrator, who executes the deeds of Tsirl and Toyber with incomparable sophistication. But those novels Langsam gave Hirshl may be seen as a way of legitimizing ripe and mature eroticism, and as a warning against the childish, romantic, emotional eroticism that cost the doctor's wife her life. According to this notion, Langsam serves not as a deus ex machina of social conventions, but as a man who "hath seen affliction"—his wife's suicide—helping Hirshl change from a child to a man.

By the end of the story, Hirshl no longer wants "his twin" to be a mother to him, no longer wants his mother to be a wife to him, and no longer wants his wife to take him under her wing and be a mother and a sister to him. On the contrary, Hirshl "makes order" in his spiritual house. In his reexamination of *A Simple Story,* Gershon Shaked maintains that at the end of the story, the tormented lover became middle class and sold the noble pain and the "wondrous princess" for a mess of lentils of shopkeeper comfort and the lush "feast of the mother," to the grief of the narrator, who, according to Shaked, "sees that as a failure." Shaked sums up the plot thus: "A process of double castration: first the mother vanquishes the son in the practical area, when she marries him off to a woman she chose, and then, by a process of healing, she realizes in the soul what was realized initially in the world of deeds."

The submission Shaked finds in the conclusion of *A Simple Story* belongs to "Kalonymos and Naomi" and to the end of Tirza and Akavia Mazel, more than to the end of Hirshl and Mina. A different reading of the concluding chapter supports a sense that he who laughs last laughs best—and neither Tsirl nor Toyber nor all their hosts are laughing last in this story, but rather Mina and Hirshl; they are laughing, at any rate, behind the closed door of their bedroom.[13]

When all is said and done, Hirshl seems to have learned to love his wife "with both his drives." Since he stopped being only a son, only a brother, only a beloved lad and turned into a husband worthy of the name, in the process he also became a father worthy of the name. The narrator does not seem to view this "sorrowfully" (in Shaked's words), but benevolently. And he grants his seal of approval to Hirshl and Mina's happiness without any irony. Almost.

10 |

A Heart Consumed by Desire

> But the more they afflicted them, the more
> they multiplied and grew.
>
> Exod. 1:12

Even before Hirshl is betrothed to Mina, we learn that "in those days when Bluma turned away from him, his heart turned around. Not that he removed her from his heart, but his heart was consumed with her." Three times the words "his heart" appear here—so that the sentence is all heart. And "his heart was consumed" is a phrase that has a quintessential talmudic source that may shed an interesting light on some obscure areas of the story. The Babylonian Talmud Tractate Sanhedrin, 75, page A, says:

> Rab Judah said in Rab's name: A man once conceived a passion for a certain woman, and his heart was consumed by his burning desire. When the doctors were consulted, they said, "His only cure is that she shall submit." Thereupon the Sages said: "Let him die rather than that she should yield." Then, "let her stand nude before him." "Sooner let him die." Then said the doctors, "let her converse with him from behind a fence." "Let him die," the Sages replied, "rather than she should converse with him behind a fence" . . . as

> Rabbi Isaac said: Since the destruction of the Temple, sexual
> pleasure has been taken from those who practice it lawfully
> and given to sinners, as the Bible says, stolen waters are
> sweet, and bread eaten in secret is pleasant.[14]

Perhaps we may assume that this is the source of the title of Bialik's
story "Behind the Fence." Agnon seems to have taken the kernel of the
torments of the fellow from Shibush whose heart was consumed—even
though the doctors in the Talmud thought the opposite of what Dr.
Langsam thought in *A Simple Story*. (Even though the main issue here
does not depend on any specific interpretation of the word *tina* [resent-
ment], note that *tina* in the Talmud does not necessarily come from the
root *TiNaNa*, which means envy, hatred, anger, or excitement in
Aramaic. But it may come from the root *Tin*, that is, mud or clay.)

At the beginning of the story, Hirshl appears to be someone
whose heart is consumed, someone ruled by an obsession, like the hero
of the ancient story—a person who is incurable "until he [has] intercourse with her." But the Torah, society, and the mother have decreed:
Let him die or go mad, but she will not have intercourse with him.

Hirshl's end seems to be that he is forced to break his thirst
with insipid water from the well of Mina and to give up "sexual pleasure," for ever since the Temple was destroyed, it has been given only
to sinners. He seems to have been sentenced to go mad and not to
approach the stolen waters or the bread eaten in secret of Bluma. What
did Hirshl do? In spite of both the "Sages" and the "Doctors," he followed the divine voice that spoke forty days before his creation and
turned his wife into stolen waters and the mother of his sons into bread
eaten in secret—until he won and found in her the pleasure that was
divested from other souls in *A Simple Story* and in many other stories,
ever since the Temple was destroyed.

A thousand times did Tsirl and Toyber try on earth to take from
Hirshl the hidden taste, as it was taken from Kalonymos and from Tirza
and from Noah in "Behind the Fence." But when they afflicted Hirshl,
he became wiser than they. God in Heaven knows how.

NOVEMBER 1988–JANUARY 1989

CHAPTER 4

Guilt and Orphanhood and Fate

A Reading of *Only Yesterday*

The opening paragraph of *Only Yesterday* is a mosaic of biblical verses inlaid with echoes of poems by the Hebrew poets of Hibat Zion (the Lovers of Zion in Russia in the 1880s) and of Bialik's poem "To a Bird," with a slight whiff of the mid-nineteenth-century Hebrew novelist Abraham Mapu, propaganda clichés of early Zionism, and slogans of BILU, the idealistic founders of the First Aliya. The opening sentence—"Like all our brethren of the Second Aliya, the bearers of our Salvation, Isaac Kumer left his country and his homeland and his city and ascended to the Land of Israel to build it from its destruction and to be rebuilt by it"—includes a fusion of Ezekiel 11:15 ("Son of man, thy brethren, even thy brethren, the men of thy kindred, and all the house of Israel wholly, are they unto whom the inhabitants of Jerusalem have said, Get you far from the Lord: unto us is this land given in possession"), a quotation from Gen. 12:1 ("Get thee out of thy country"), and the popular Zionist song "We came to the Land to build and be rebuilt by It." The use of the first person plural—"our brethren, . . . the bearers of our Salvation," and "our comrade Isaac"—presents the narrator as one of Isaac's friends and makes Isaac a representative of the whole group of "our brethren, . . . bearers of our Salvation."[1] The name "Isaac" (meaning "he will laugh") reminds us that "all that hear will laugh" (Gen. 21:6), while at the same time it alludes to the sacrifice of Isaac. "Kumer" in Yiddish means "the one who is coming," "arriving," but the German meaning of the word also connotes trouble and catastrophe.

The opening paragraph presents the Land of Israel as it glows in Isaac's longings and imagination in a parallelism and a language that are a biblical inlay (the "seven kinds") mixed with Hibat Zion rhetoric ("and the firmament was all blue") and verses of Bialik's poem "To the Bird," with an echo of the fourth glass in the Passover Haggada ("glad at their work and joyous at their rest"), as well as a trace of the paintings of the early artists of the Bezalel Art School in Jerusalem and the enrollment certificate of "the Golden Book" given to contributors to the Jewish National Fund. The Land of Israel is depicted here not as the Delightsome Land of the patriarchs where all hopes would be fulfilled, but as a land where all hopes were already fulfilled, and the days of the Messiah were well under way.

This idyllic opening is countered by two opposing ironies at the end of the paragraph. First, it is hinted that, more than Isaac yearns to leave his native Galicia and live in the Paradise of the Land of Israel of his fancy, he longs to settle in the pastoral Land of Israel and smugly recall his wretched hometown in Galicia. It is as if the biblical phrase were turned around to mean: "by the rivers of Zion there we sat down, yea, we rejoiced, when we remembered Babylon." Right here, the careful reader can discern that the small town is, after all, the measure of all things: from it, Isaac's fancies go to the shadow of the vine and the fig in the Land of Israel, and to it they return. And through the dream of Zionist ascendance to Israel, the dream of social ascendance—the eternal dream of immigrants—emerges, for the first but not the last time. Isaac is not described as "a man who sleeps here and sees a castle in Spain," but as one who sits here and sees himself sitting in Spain and dreaming of the rivers of Babylon.[2]

Second, at the end of the paragraph, over the head of the hero, the narrator winks ironically at the reader: "A man of imagination was Isaac, what his heart desired, his imagination would conjure up for him" (p. 3). That is, the basis of the "pact" between the narrator and the reader is that they both know how the Land of Israel looked at the beginning of the century and how contrary its reality was to the sentimental pictures in Isaac's imagination. Such a tragic irony can work only if the reader actually does know how terrible the reality of the Land of Israel was. That secret pact concluded here between the narrator and the reader is what gives meaning to everything the reader is going to absorb through Isaac's eyes and thoughts. But the narrator is going to violate that pact now and then and upset the "didactic" partnership he himself has offered his readers.

The opening of *Only Yesterday* would seem to be characteristic of the topos of a bildungsroman, the tale of a naïf who has to absorb "a blow of reality" and lose his innocence. Such stories usually end in shattered hopes, and their moral is that a change of place is not a change of luck. (A quintessential example of a bildungsroman is Chekhov's short story "The Schoolmistress," in which the tragic gap is revealed between Nikitin's sublime expectations of married life and the reality he discovers after he is married. Incidentally, in that story, too, the tragic irony stems from the fact that the narrator and the reader know from the beginning what the hero will discover only in retrospect.) But *Only Yesterday* is hardly a typical case. Even though its opening looks like the typical opening of a bildungsroman, it does not reach the conventional conclusion: Isaac does gain knowledge and does encounter pain but does not lose his innocence, while the dog

Balak does lose his innocence and does encounter pain but does not gain knowledge.

|

The second paragraph continues to the end of the first section (pp. 1–2) and describes the small town and Isaac's place in it. Some of Isaac's friends "had already taken a wife and opened shops for themselves, and they're distinguished in the eyes of folks. . . . When they enter the bank, the clerk sits them down on a chair. . . . And others of Isaac's friends are at the university studying all manner of wisdom that sustains those who possess it and magnifies their honor" (p. 3). But none of Isaac's friends have become talmudic scholars or saints, and none have become scientists or inventors, "while Isaac shortens his life and spends his days and his years . . . selling stamps of the Jewish National Fund" (p. 4). Lightly and casually, the angle of vision changes: first a picture of Exile and a picture of the Promised Land in Isaac's eyes, and then a picture of Isaac in the eyes of his fellow townsmen, and then this picture superimposed, as it were, on the picture of the town and its values in the eyes of the narrator. The result is a complex and comic picture: an idle dreamer in a society already emptied of its religious values whose whole world revolves around the lust for lush "practicality." The external form of life in the town is still traditional and religious, while the raison d'être is already materialistic and petit bourgeois. Isaac is considered an eccentric who is wasting his life because he has ostensibly resigned from the general race for wealth and honor.

Parallelism controls the syntax of this paragraph just as it controlled that of the first. But in the first paragraph, it served to emphasize the harmony in the picture of the idyllic Land of Israel in Isaac's heart, while in the second paragraph the parallelism stresses the self-satisfied balance of wealth and honor in the world of the small town. The difference between Isaac's friends "who opened shops for themselves" and his other friends "at the university" is a make-believe opposition: shopkeeping and studying are merely two different entrances to the same parlor of bourgeois "well-being" that brings livelihood and honor. What is seen briefly as a binary opposition ("some opened shops . . . and others . . . are at the university") quickly turns out to be a complementary parallelism.

Isaac himself is thus depicted as an eccentric "loser" who misses out on the "purpose of life," trapped by a childish fantasy about an Arcadia that never existed outside the brochures and pamphlets of

Zionist propaganda. But a close reading of the first, pastoral paragraph shows that even Isaac's imaginary Land of Israel is simply bourgeois wishful thinking. What it contains for Isaac, after all, is neither national renewal nor spiritual exaltation, but mainly the promise of livelihood, serene family pleasure, and upward social mobility. The only difference is that, in the Land of Israel, it is agriculture and not shopkeeping or the university that will lead you to the parlor—the same petit bourgeois parlor. The Land of Israel in Isaac's visions is a shortcut from the low status of the son of impoverished shopkeepers to the heights of a landowning "lord." Even though Isaac Kumer is the first in his hometown to ascend to the Land, he is hardly a revolutionary Zionist, but a conservative, Austro-Hungarian Zionist, a Herzlian Zionist who doesn't care about "saving the world," who wants only to make a respectable living by working the soil.

This is not how Simon Kumer, Isaac's father, sees his son's dreams: Simon wants to "extricate him from his folly and set him up in a shop so he [will] be occupied in trade and become a man" (p. 4). An examination of the chain of clauses in that sentence indicates that the shop is an instrument for trade, and that trade is to extricate Isaac from his folly and turn him into a man. (Without trade a man is not a man? Against our will, we must listen to the subtext, to the language of Simon Kumer's thoughts, which the narrator weaves into his own discourse; hence we must not read "become a man," but rather the Yiddish "may he be a *mentsh*.")

And here is Isaac, soft and submissive, not only refusing to be a *mentsh* but persisting in his rebelliousness and even turning his father's store into a "branch of Zionism," that is, a club for idle chatterers, and thus driving the customers away. Here, for the first time, but not the last, *Only Yesterday* approaches the familiar ground of Agnon's virulent satire in *With Our Young and Our Old.*[3] The narrator, who shifts nimbly from one point of view to another, unreservedly adopts here the voices and positions of the small town and laments that Isaac is spending the days of his youth in idleness. On the very first page of the novel, the reader can pick up the threads of humor, irony, sarcasm, satire, and parody running through the novel. The narrator's agility, avoiding quotation marks and other grammatical and syntactic modulations, enables him to adopt various contradictory positions, alternatively and surprisingly, and to depict a given reality simultaneously from various points of view, as far as a text can be simultaneous. Through quick "cuts," the reader is invited to see the Land of Israel through the eyes of Isaac, Isaac through the eyes of the small town, the small town through the eyes of the narrator, Isaac through the eyes of his father, and the loquacious idle Zionism of the loafers through a view worthy of Mendele Moykher-Sforim. In the eyes of his father, Isaac is a boy who refuses to grow up. His Zionism and the Zionism of those who come to the shop are eccentric. The expression "to split hairs about Zionism" is a concentrated satiric poison, for Zionism, which intended to revolt against the hairsplitting world of the idle, barren yeshiva students, has itself become a matter of barren hairsplitting. Zionism set out to shatter the loquacious and hollow idleness in Jewish life, and itself became idle, loquacious, and empty.

How interesting that a man like Simon Kumer, a downwardly mobile shopkeeper and the descendant of saints and pure men, has no ambition whatever for his son to be a talmudic scholar, or a saintly rabbi, or even a doctor. All he has is petit bourgeois practicality: Isaac should get married; he should open a shop; he should be like all his friends, who are "distinguished in the eyes of folks."

The constant struggle is between two silent, stubborn men who do not raise their voices and never come to open conflict. Isaac, who is ostensibly a rank innocent, does not pack a suitcase in the dark of night and run away to the Land of Israel, like many heroes and non-heroes in and out of literature in those days. On the contrary, he appears to submit to his father's will and becomes a shopkeeper "as was decreed on him from above"—just as Hirshl, his fellow townsman and contemporary, submitted and became a shopkeeper in *A Simple Story*. But Isaac's submission is not submission: he very quickly "turn[s] the shop into a branch of Zionism," drives the customers away, and thus endangers whatever is left of his father's livelihood—and thus makes his father submit.

There is a marvelous economy of text in the first section of the first chapter. Even though *Only Yesterday* is several hundred pages long, the exposition (part 1) takes less than two pages to unfold before the reader the divine Land of Israel, as Isaac envisions it, and—implied with a wink by the narrator—the earthly Land of Israel in its wretchedness at the beginning of the century; the small town emptied of its Jewish spirituality and devoted wholly to materialism and a provincial pursuit of honor; the empty Zionism of idlers and eccentrics and loafers; Isaac's quiet and enthusiastic devotion to his belief; Simon's paternal worries; and the stages of the silent conflict between them. All that—in less than two pages. The pieces are already arranged on the board, and the plot is already spread out before us and ready to start moving. Tolstoy might have taken a hundred pages to do that.

|

Some of Isaac's friends got married and opened shops, and others studied at the university. Both groups achieved a practical goal. And there are idlers who come to the store "to split hairs about Zionism." What does the town lack in this description? It lacks Torah scholars and saints and those who serve their Creator humbly; and it also lacks genuine secular scholars. The world of that small town stands on three things: livelihood, provincial honor, and idle conversation. The second paragraph (pp. 3–4) depicts that world even more sharply. An indirect dialogue takes place between the father and his son, and the narrator—in combined discourse with his character—adopts the voice of each of them in turn; he seems to identify with both, and to mock neither. Like a Jewish incarnation of the struggle between Peer Gynt and his mother, Solweig, here too the dreamer son refuses to help the destitute parent and ends up going his own way and forsaking the languishing parent. And like Peer and his mother, the status of Isaac and Simon has declined from their family's once high place, and they live a wretched life on the fringes of a mocking society.[4]

The town does not follow the Zionists, for the great Torah scholars condemn them as "anticipating the coming of the Messiah," challenging a salvation that will come miraculously and not politically. On the other hand, the heart of the town is no longer with those great Torah scholars and does not negate the Zionists, but the townspeople "are afraid to be counted among the Zionists" (p. 4). At most, they "take the license" (a typical rabbinical expression) to come to Kumer's shop, where they can enjoy both worlds and "split hairs about Zionism" without being called Zionists. The narrator's ironic darts are shot in every direction—at the hairsplitting Zionists and at the Torah luminaries who do battle against a movement that is not a movement at all, but a stagnant puddle. Ridiculous if also touching is Simon Kumer's effort to turn his son into a "normal" shopkeeper. But Isaac himself is not ridiculous: his quiet persistence, which looks like submission, contains a profound internal integrity. His wretchedness contains a willingness to resist all trends. His innocence contains a strong faith that befits the son of the son of the son of the daughter of the daughter of Reb Yudel Hasid of *The Bridal Canopy.*

And what does Isaac do when he "is left alone in the shop"? The boy plays: he sits and counts "the Zionist Shekels he [sells] and [makes] calculations, such as, If every single Jew gives a penny every day to the Jewish National Fund, how many acres can you buy with that small change and how many families could be settled on them" (p. 3). This is the infantile element that will remain part of Isaac until his death and will endear him to Yedidia Rabinovitch, Yohanan Leichtfuss, Sonya Zweiering, and Samson Bloykof, who all "adopt" him as a son. And it is the infantile element that also contributes to his catastrophe, for Isaac, who paints the words "crazy dog" on Balak's back, does that as a childish prank. At any rate, the sarcastic smile hovering, as it were, on the narrator's lips as he depicts the small town and its petite bourgeoisie, its idlers and Zionists and Torah scholars, seems to give way to a forgiving, humoresque smile when he describes the "child" sitting in the shop every day and playing at building the Land, "and the customers keep dropping off." For "[a] man of imagination was Isaac, what his heart desired, his imagination would conjure up for him."

And his father? "When Simon . . . saw Isaac's deeds, he was bitter and depressed and worried. . . . If you haven't seen Simon Kumer, the father of Isaac, . . . you never saw a father's grief" (p. 5). In this we hear an echo of the Talmud: "Anyone who has not seen the rejoicing of *bet hashshoebah* in his life has never seen rejoicing."[5] These linguistic allusions create an ironic "short circuit" when the rejoicing of the *bet hashshoebah* is replaced by the grief of raising sons. And what brings grief to a father raising sons? A son's desire to ascend to the Land of Israel to renew, among other things, the rejoicing of the *bet hashshoebah.* Such is Agnon's ironic tactic. Like Bialik and others of his generation, he evokes the sources only to stand them on their heads.[6]

Isaac is the firstborn son, and his mother died when he was young. Simon Kumer ponders: "A curse has descended on the world, sons do not heed their fathers and fathers do not rule their sons." This sentence about undermining the tradition and violating the laws of nature carefully preserves the ordered and balanced tradition of harmonious parallelism. Thus the stylistic strategy serves the spiritual assumption about the Jewish tradition: its content is rotten from within, yet its external appearance is preserved. The same is true of the descriptions of Isaac's hometown and later on, in the chapters on Meah Shearim in Jerusalem. Moreover, the sentence "A curse has descended on the world" is not presented as a quotation from Simon's contemplations, but as the narrator's voice, combining his discourse with the discourse of the unfortunate father. Once again, humor operates through a frequent and undeclared change of point of view: the narrator, who spoke before in the voice of small-town public opinion and before that in Isaac's voice, now says the opposite in Simon's voice. Here it is not the "Zionists" who are accused of ruining the natural order of the world. On the contrary, since piety has diminished and the hierarchies are undermined and the days have come when sons don't obey their fathers, the way is now opened for all kinds of evil maladies, including Zionism. That is the reverse of the widespread sociohistorical concept of cause and effect in the processes of change in Eastern European Jewry. The small-town world Agnon depicts at the beginning of *Only Yesterday*—as well as in the chapters of Meah Shearim—is a fossilized world, empty within, that ends in assimilation and Zionism and coarse materialism.

"Simon has despaired of getting any joy and satisfaction from his son and has started worrying lest his other sons learn from Isaac's deeds" (p. 5), and he decides to let Isaac do what he wants and go to the Land of Israel, because of many overt reasons and one censored one. The overt reasons are to prevent him from being a bad influence on his brothers and sisters, to keep him from destroying the shop, and to prove to him with his own eyes that the Land of Israel is "a fiction the Zionists made up." And the censored reason is that the draft board is about to come to town and Isaac is a healthy fellow, and Simon doesn't have any money for a bribe.[7] Hence, Simon doesn't despair of his son; on the contrary, he believes that the encounter with the "earthly Land of Israel" will be such a "shock cure" for him that he will return home without birds in his head—and in the process may he become a *mentsh*. Simon's expectation is ultimately not realized—but it is not proved completely wrong either.

The language of this section, where the narrator combines his own voice with the internal voice of the father, is steeped in Yiddish-talmudic logic and traces of traditional texts, for example, "and [he] agreed to send Isaac where he wanted to go" (cf. Abodah Zarah, 1:4). And "there is no prospect for the Land of Israel," where the word "prospect" serves both in its denotative meaning of hope (*toykheles*) and in the sound connotation of practicality (*takhles*), so that the reader is invited to recall that Simon is thinking in Yiddish, even though this is not stated explicitly. The combined discourse here not only combines the narrator's voice with the father's voice—it also combines the overt Hebrew voice with the "subterranean" Yiddish voice. The same is true of the words "at any rate there may be some profit in that"; and "when he sees there is nothing real there, he'll come back to his hometown." The "real" *mamash* (substance) in Simon's thoughts may well be the Yiddish "really" *màmash* (something tangible). And later: "So he'll see with his own eyes that the whole business of the Land of Israel is a fiction the Zionists made up, and he'll remove it from his heart" (p. 5). For the "business of the Land of Israel" is merely a Hebrew cover for the mocking Yiddish phrase *Eretz Isroel gesheft*.

Thus Simon agrees to let Isaac go and even helps him, as "a reluctant man says amen," with the hope that he will be saved from the draft and will return sobered and ready to be "a bourgeois," like a proper Jewish boy. As for Isaac, he goes with hope: "Let Father say what he wants, in the end he will see that my way is the right one" (p. 5). Isaac therefore wins the contest of wills, but he does not win the argument between himself and his father. The argument remains moot, and both contestants believe that the Land of Israel itself will in time settle the issue between them. "The verdict of the Land of Israel" is debated in the rest of the novel and remains ambivalent to the end.

Many fine critics have written about the passivity that characterizes Isaac, his submissiveness and obedience. Yes and no: at least regarding Isaac's excited dream to ascend to the Land of Israel, Isaac's willpower and persistence overcome his father's will and persistence, the town's derision, and even the barren futility of the group of "hairsplitters of Zionism." Isaac does not take money from the coffers of the store and does not flee to the Land of Israel; he fights and wins. The secret strength of the ostensibly weak is what makes Isaac similar to Hirshl in *A Simple Story*.

As we have seen, the central event in Hirshl's life, as in Isaac's, is overdetermined: Hirshl's madness, like Isaac's ascendance to Israel, mutatis mutandis, presents a "heap" of explanations, each more persuasive than the sum of the whole. Hirshl goes out of his mind because of disappointed love, but also because of the inherited madness rampant in his family, and because of the curse an ancient rabbi placed on the family; and aside from all that, he also goes crazy to avoid the draft. Similarly, Simon Kumer helps Isaac ascend to the Land of Israel because there he will recover from his lunacy, and because he is destroying the shop, and so to keep him from influencing his younger brothers—and, contradicting all those reasons, because perhaps, after all, "God sent him to be a sustenance and a refuge for us" (p. 5) (like Joseph in Genesis), and the draft board is also included on the list of explanations.

"So great was the power of Isaac's trust" in his Zionist belief that "even the town wags who make a joke of everything didn't laugh at him" (p. 6). But Simon Kumer's power of trust is not negligible either: even though he doesn't know why he is being punished with a stubborn and rebellious son, he is sure that "everything the Merciful One does, He does for good"—and that Isaac's voyage may be revealed as the finger of God, "a sustenance and a refuge." Even though the father's trust is religious and the son's is apparently ideological, the two are very similar. And "trust," of course, means belief. Basically, the father and the son are believing people with religious souls. For the first time in the novel, but not the last, Zionist idealism is depicted as religious energy diverted to a new channel. Not only are both the father and the son convinced of their belief, each in his own way, but both are graced with a powerful optimism. Since "there is a leader in the capital," everything will end for the best. "Yea, though I walk through the valley of the shadow of death, I will fear no evil" (Ps. 23:4)—Simon and Isaac both inherit this trust-belief from their ancient forefather Reb Yudel in *The Bridal Canopy*.

The structure of Simon Kumer's considerations as he ponders where he can find money for his son's trip (p. 6) is the structure of talmudic consideration, mixed perhaps with the tone of Yiddish argument. Even if I do this, there is still thus and so. And even if I succeed in thus and so, there is still this and that. And even if both this and that, there is still the other thing, and so on and so forth. (As in the Yiddish anecdote: first, I didn't borrow any pot from you; second, I already gave it back to you safe and sound; and, third, the crack was already in it when I got it from you.) The whole section that begins with Simon's trust-belief continues in his amassed doubts and ends with a loan he took at interest that he doesn't know how or when he'll pay back, nor does he know where he'll get the money to pay for Isaac's return "when he sees there is really nothing there" (p. 5)—this entire section depicts a world very close to the world of those hard-working Jews in the satirical fiction of Mendele Moykher Sforim, or in the world of Sholem Aleichem's Tevye the dairyman, with its comic-pathetic travails.

Isaac Kumer is the son of the son of the son of the daughter of the daughter of Reb Yudel Hasid of *The Bridal Canopy*. Three generations, it is told, have lived on the treasures of Reb Yudel, while subsequent generations, including that of Simon Kumer, live in wretched poverty; "no miracle occurred to him, and he didn't find a treasure as his ancestor did. Reb Yudel who had perfect trust in God was paid by the Holy-One-Blessed-Be-He to match his trust," while Simon Kumer, the grandson of his granddaughter, "placed his trust in trade" (p. 5) and hence is not worthy of a miracle. Like Simon and Isaac, the narrator adopts a complete religious position here: there is a Judgment and there is a Judge. There is reward and punishment. As the Talmud teaches, "by that same measure by which a man metes out to others, they mete out to him."[8] Miracles are governed by a strict bookkeeping of divine "points of merit." Justification of the Judgment, belief in reward and punishment, trust that "everything the Merciful One does, He does for good"—all these appear here as a bridge between the world of Reb Yudel and the worlds of Simon, Isaac, and the narrator. The miracle that does not happen to Simon is as much a theodicean testimony to the righteousness of the Creator as the miracle that did happen to Reb Yudel. The position of the narrator here is distant from his position at the end of the novel, when he asks (and is not answered): "And now, good friends, as we observe the adventures of Isaac, we are shaken and stunned. This Isaac who is no worse than any other person, why is he punished so harshly?" (p. 639). Not to mention the torment of Job of God's revelation to Shifra: "The Lord did good to her and spoke with her from her heart and said to her, Don't be a fool, Shifra, all that is done is done from My mind and My will." Adi Tsemakh has noted the profound nihilism in the description of Shifra, who wants an answer from God as God changes Himself into her paralyzed father.

The basis of the suspense in *Only Yesterday* is indeed in its religious tension. Will the initial position of the narrator and his heroes be realized or proved false? Will Isaac's innocence, reminiscent of Reb Yudel's innocence, win him a small miracle? Will the clear religious vision at the start of this "Zionist" novel hold out as it continues and concludes? Needless to say, a similar tension exists in *A Guest for the Night* and other works by Agnon, and even in *The Bridal Canopy*: the miracle that was done to Reb Yudel can be seen as a miracle, but it can also be seen as natural. The ambivalence of the miracle at the end of *The Bridal Canopy* is perfect and puts its seal not only on the conclusion, but on the whole structure of the work.

Simon Kumer goes to the pawnshop and borrows money not only for Isaac's travel expenses, but also for his clothes and shoes. The woolen clothes and the black felt hat indicate that Simon, like Isaac, sees the Land of Israel through the eyes of Bialik's poem "To the Bird," as "a land where spring blooms eternal"; he hasn't any idea of the climate there. Moreover, Isaac "is going to a place where they don't know him and his clothes will show that he is from a fine home" (p. 7). For the first but definitely not the last time in *Only Yesterday*, the belief appears that clothes (and shoes!) make the man, a belief common to father and son. The narrator, in his ironic way, not only adopts this view, he even seems to grant it such profound symbolic validity that, with a little exaggeration, *Only Yesterday* may also be seen as a novel about clothes and shoes, about the substance of something as opposed to its paint, about content as opposed to exterior, about what is written on the skin as opposed to what is inside. It is a mistake to rush to the conclusion that the narrator distinguishes between the "jug" and "its contents," and it is equally mistaken to assume that the narrator does not distinguish between them.

In any case, in a period when—as Isaac and his father know— there are Hasids and Misnageds, Zionists and assimilationists, the pious and the impious, those who deserve a miracle and those who do not deserve a miracle, everything in the world is debatable except one issue: the immortality of petit bourgeois values, to which Isaac and his father attribute universal validity. And they are sure that even in the Land of Israel, despite its Zionism and its Pioneers, a person who wears a good suit will be accepted as being "from a fine home," and that— Zionist revolution or not—it is still better to be thought of as "someone from a good home," especially "in a place where they don't know him," and especially because, in fact, Isaac is not from "a fine home" but is the son of a destitute shopkeeper, almost a lumpen. It is fascinating that Simon Kumer, an observant man, "knows" that the Land of Israel is neither rabbinical (for then he would have bought his son a caftan) nor ragamuffin (for then he would have saved himself the expense of good clothes) but Viennese bourgeois, as Herzl envisioned it, a worthy branch of the Austro-Hungarian Empire. Once again a comic gap appears because of the secret pact between the narrator and the reader, who both know something hidden from Isaac and Simon—that an antibourgeois ethos prevailed in the Land of Israel in the days of the Second Aliya, and the more tattered and threadbare you were, the better; glorying in wool suits and felt hats was ridiculous.

In any case, at the very beginning of *Only Yesterday*, we encounter the forceful impulse moving Isaac to ascend to the Land of Israel. This drive is depicted as more like those impulses prevailing in small-town life than it seemed initially: the townspeople want petit bourgeois "success," "practicality," a good impression. Even Isaac and his father want these. The Land of Israel is merely a social "detour": what Isaac does not have in his hometown, he will surely have there in the Delightsome Ancestral Land, where he will pick up a hoe and make himself an estate, thus becoming a property owner and a big shot, so that all those who have mocked him will envy him. Hence, the traveling clothes Simon makes for Isaac are likened to bridegroom's clothes, and the trip itself is seen as a regrettable, but inevitable, substitute for a "decent" match (p. 6). From now on, playing with the traditional motif, the novel will connect ascending to the Land with betrothal, the Zionist realization with erotic realization. This link appears first to be a comic issue, then a grotesque issue, and finally an issue illuminated by the horrifying light of tragedy.

Assuming that the novel begins in a Galician town in about 1908 and ends in Jerusalem in about 1911, the terrible conflicts that split the Jewish world seem to have reached Isaac's hometown in a moderate and mellowed form. The quarrel between "religion" and "life," the erotic dysfunction that emerged from that quarrel, and the crisis of "faith and thought" as reflected in Haskalah literature and in the literature of "the generation of the Revival"—including all the torments that fill Hebrew literature at least from the time of Reuben Asher Broydes's novel *Religion and Life* (1876) up to the core of Agnon's work—do not seem to torment the "fathers and sons" at the start of *Only Yesterday*. Simon Kumer and his son Isaac still seem able to maintain some "naïve synthesis" between perfect religious belief and petit bourgeois values, between piety and a "bourgeois" felt hat, or between all those and the Zionist Pioneer ascendance to the Land of Israel. That "naïve synthesis," which Isaac will hold onto through hell and high water, in love and disappointment and catastrophe, may very well be the heart of the novel. At any rate, it may be what the author's heart yearns for, even if the narrator describes that synthesis with forgiving and humoresque mockery. Beyond all the irony and parody and sarcasm and sardonic and grotesque tones that fill the novel, the naïve synthesis is left as a desideratum: not achieved but something to strive for. Several characters in *Only Yesterday,* especially Reb Menahemke, the Standing Menahem, should perhaps be reexamined in light of the dream of a naïve synthesis unifying the tragic oppositions between the parts of the nation and the ways of the spirit. Isaac, in his innocence, embodies and even realizes this synthesis to some extent—until the blows of reality or even worse beat him down. This is already obvious in the fact that Isaac goes to the Land of Israel, with his father's half-hearted permission, to realize three wishes: (1) to build the Land and to be rebuilt by it, as a Pioneer working the soil; (2) to realize a petit bourgeois prosperity, in a wool suit and a felt hat, that is, to obtain what the small town refused him and to be "a proper bourgeois"; and (3) to observe the Commandments in the Land of Israel and to avoid profaning the Sabbath and eating forbidden food, which would have been forced on him if he were conscripted into the Austro-Hungarian army. (In addition to these three declared wishes, there is a fourth, which his heart will not reveal to his mouth: to find himself a mate and to reach erotic realization.) Keep in mind that, in Isaac Kumer's day, these three wishes were already considered mutually exclusive in the arena of Jewish history; a bitter cultural struggle that included reproaches, vilification, excommunication, and ostracism was waged over the values behind any one versus the values behind the other two. Armed with the naïve synthesis in his heart, Isaac walks among these drawn swords, noticing neither that they are swords nor that they are drawn. So, until the blows of reality become too hard to bear, the three wishes coexist peacefully in his innocent and pure heart, the heart of a petit bourgeois observant Zionist. When the blows of reality force him to decide between these wishes, Isaac is hurled back and forth, does not decide, and is dismayed and diminished.

"Isaac parted from his father and his brothers and his sisters and all his other relatives and set out on the road. To the disgrace of his hometown, we must say that he parted from it without pain. A city that didn't send a delegate to the Zionist Congress and was not inscribed in the Golden Book of the Jewish National Fund is a city you leave without pain" (p. 8). The narrator's voice expresses what the naïve Isaac recites to himself as he leaves, like whistling in the dark to drive out regrets. The whole novel will tell the readers the opposite. This is the human comedy Agnon displays, and this is his style of humor: conversions, inverted language without quotation marks and without "shifting gear." The text ostensibly passes through the hero's consciousness, lingers there a while, goes on, lingers in other consciousnesses, and continues on its way as the narrator and the reader, on a "wave" of hidden knowledge, agree when to believe what the hero says and when to pick up behind his words what his heart does not reveal to his mouth, or what his mouth denies in its innocence—like the homesickness that gnaws at him even before the journey begins, which he silences "without pain" with the argument that a city that has no delegate to the Zionist Congress and is not listed in the Golden Book does not deserve to be missed. Isaac will construct a complicated system of rationalizations around his feelings, and the narrator will collaborate with him, not trying to contradict them frontally but ostensibly confirming them. He will contradict them indirectly, circumstantially, while seeming to nod his agreement, pretending to respect Isaac's positions, as we sometimes do with a child. This connivance between the narrator and the reader, when the reader is invited to smile along with the narrator behind the hero's back, is possible because the reader has enough information to understand what Isaac is hiding from himself. Of course, this pleasure is open only to the active reader who is willing to play along and execute the "reversal of meaning" wherever he is asked to.

For example, without quotation marks or direct speech, the reader seems to absorb the thoughts of an excited child who has never before left his hometown and is now sitting on a train perhaps for the first time in his life, and not the consciousness of a young Pioneer setting out to carry out a revolution in his life and in Jewish history: "Yesterday he had worried lest there be some obstacle and he wouldn't go. And lo and behold, there was no obstacle and he is traveling" (p. 8). The words "lo and behold, there was no obstacle" do not refer to the train service in the Austro-Hungarian Empire, but to Isaac's childish eyes and capacity for wonder. The quality of the amazed child in Isaac is one of the bases of his charm, described wonderfully by Leah Goldberg. The capacity for wonder is the ability to absorb greatness and treasures in things others see as routine or self-evident or don't see at all. This is the capacity for "first sight" that may have been what Alterman meant by "even an old sight has a moment of birth." The Greeks called this capacity Thaumazein.

The description of Isaac's journey through the Austro-Hungarian Empire is one of the most marvelous descriptions of a journey in literature. Yet Isaac professes to remove his eyes and his mind from the road: "In his ruminations on the Land of Israel, he cleared his mind of every other matter" (p. 8). Ostensibly, he is forgetting the world and everything in it because his spirit is already in the Land of Israel. But in point of fact, he almost forgets the Land of Israel because of the Austro-Hungarian charm revealed to him with the cataloguing detail of a pastoral, all in pairs: mountains and forests, rivers and streams, towns and villages, et cetera. For Isaac, Austro-Hungary is a promised land, a land of desire that he is condemned to "see as a negative"—and that he will long for from the dust and heat of the arid Land of Israel, at moments when he thinks of the Austro-Hungarian landscapes with the same devotion he had felt in Austro-Hungary for the Land of Israel (for example, in book 1, chapter 3). While Isaac is glued to the train window and is all a child's eyes, he professes to be acting like his ancestor Reb Yudel, who "for many a year ere he went up to the Land . . . had his eyes covered with a kerchief because he did not desire to use his eyes more without the Land" (*The Bridal Canopy*, p. 373).

Isaac's eyes are enthralled by the landscapes; and all along the way there is another eye that observes Isaac "gorging himself" on the sights, that of the hidden traveler who accompanies him on the journey; sometimes he weaves his discourse into the hero's meditations, sometimes he even binds Isaac and himself together with the word "we," and sometimes he leaves Isaac and comes close to the reader to maintain the "comic connivance."

"Up close," Isaac ponders the sight of the Jews traveling with him on the train, who are depressed and scared about their business. "He would soon shake off the dust of Exile, like a man shaking something repulsive off his feet" (p. 18). This is indeed the image raised by the Zionist legend: there is a big doormat on the threshold of the Land of Israel, and as everyone ascends to the Land, he "shakes off" the disgusting dust of Exile and enters the parlor clean and new. It is no accident that the reader is invited to look down at Isaac's shoes, which still have the "dust of Exile" on them—it will soon disappear. Shoes will play a big role in Isaac's life and in the plot of the novel. The depiction of the doormat at the threshold of the Land of Israel may echo "put off thy shoes from off thy feet, for the place whereon thou standest is holy ground" (Exod. 3:5). The vision of a "rebirth" while "shaking off the dust of

Exile" is to be cruelly proven wrong: Isaac and his comrades of the Second
Aliya will not be reborn and will not get rid of the dust of Exile. On the
contrary, wherever they turn, they will carry Exile with them, some in a
wool suit and a felt hat, some with the sharpness of a born wheeler-dealer
from generations back, and some in the torments of sin that won't let go
even of someone who has ceased observing the Commandments.

　　This concerns some of the basic questions of *Only Yesterday*,
and perhaps of all Agnon's works: Can a person change fundamentally? Can he "renew himself"? Can he "get up tomorrow morning and
start over from the beginning"? Manfred Herbst in *Shira* wants that
renewal just as much as Isaac Kumer does, when he asks: "What can a
man do to renew himself?" (*Shira,* p. 514). Adiel Amzeh in "Forever"
may succeed in renewing himself—in the leprosarium. Menashe Haim
in "The Crooked Became Straight" "will be reborn"—against his will
and to his destruction. The hero-narrator of *A Guest for the Night* will
attempt such renewal in vain.[9]

|

Isaac Kumer sees Galicia through the window of the train as

> villages and hamlets, cities and towns. Some were known for
> their great rabbis . . . some earned a name with . . . the fruit
> of their trees. . . . And yet other places have neither learning
> nor earning, but do have a Quarrel [between various forms
> of prayer—A.O.]. . . . And another Quarrel, between Assimila-
> tionists and Zionists. The former want to be like all the other
> nations and the latter want to be Jews. . . . And yet another
> Quarrel, between those who want Salvation by miracle and
> those who want a natural Salvation. (pp. 8–9)

　　Thus, in one harmonic paragraph, which is well balanced
with soothing parallelisms, measured and weighted with nouns and
adjectives in every clause, Isaac hovers over the abysses separating the
various branches of the Jewish people in his day. The naïve synthesis
delights in inclusion—and erases the conflicts and clashes involved in
this inclusion. Isaac is easily impressed at one and the same time by the
towns that were famed for great rabbis and the towns that were famed
for great scholars or for fine fruit or for distinguished Zionists or for a
well-known quarrel about prayer formulations or for important rabbinical printing presses. Everything is sublime in his eyes, everything

he takes to his innocent heart (and see also pp. 9–10). And who besides Isaac Kumer can find joy in both the thing and its opposite? If a Jew in those days (and in this time) admires wonder-working saints, he is unlikely to be excited by "the first Maskilim who wanted to rejuvenate our spirit" (p. 11); and if he is enthusiastic about those Maskilim, he is unlikely to be excited about rabbinical printing presses; and if he is delighted with rabbinical printing presses, he won't follow Zionism; and if he is a Zionist, he won't pay homage to the theaters and fountains in the cities of the Diaspora.

The opening of *Only Yesterday* leads the reader astray: it is easy to be tempted to believe that the rents in the souls of the heroes of Broydes and Nomberg and Feyerberg and Berdichevski and Bialik and Brenner and Gnessin, who are Isaac's contemporaries, and the conflicts that have driven them to madness and death do not threaten Isaac's emotional and idealistic virginity—he takes to his heart, with delight, all sides in all quarrels. All have a respectable place in his infantile album of experiences. This is the naïve synthesis. And the narrator? He seems to report on it neutrally and without taking any position. But beneath the report is a good-hearted, almost paternal mockery. And perhaps deeper inside, beneath the paternal mockery, the narrator's soul yearns for this naïve synthesis, throughout the novel, as for the desired Land of the soul, the Garden of Eden before the woman, the snake, and the fruit.

For Isaac, who has not yet tasted sin, all the famous towns on the way are dear to his heart, no matter why they are famous. Here is a small catalogue of various wonders Isaac attributes to the various towns: great rabbis, fine fish, a great quarrel between the Hasids and the Misnageds, a newspaper by Maskilim, a delegate to the Zionist Congress, a quarrel over a minor detail of a prayer formulation. In short, never mind why the town is famous—so long as it is famous, it has a place in Isaac's heart. And indeed, most of the towns the train passes through remind Isaac of fish, arguments, or historical movements, and he esteems them (as we would say today: "They were mentioned on television"), for Hebrew newspapers are the main source of Isaac's education.

And how do the other passengers see Isaac? Once again, the point of view changes, and as for the passengers, "some of them glanced at Isaac, for he had a pin stuck in his tie with the name of Zion engraved on it" (p. 9). Thus, in bridegroom's clothes, with a tie and a stickpin, that petit bourgeois Pioneer goes to work the soil of Canaan.

Isaac breaks up the trip in Lvov, "Lemberg the capital of Galicia," intending "to appear before [the Zionist] leaders and get their blessing before his ascent to the Land of Israel" (p. 10), just like a Hasid on a pilgrimage to the rebbe. Here the comic pact between the narrator and the reader rests, among other things, on the fact that the reader understands that there is more Zionism in Isaac's little finger than in all those chatterbox leaders, for he is really ascending to the Land of Israel, and they will go on playing billiards in the café in Lemberg. That is not how Isaac himself sees things. To consider his ascent more important than the blabbermouths in Lemberg would be a revolutionary awareness, and Isaac is hardly a revolutionary. On the contrary, he embraces the social hierarchy with his whole being, submissively accepts his lowly place in the world, and dreams, at most, that his ascent to the Land of Israel will boost him a rung or two up the social ladder (a house and a parcel of land), compared to his lowly status in his hometown. He certainly does not think ill of the standards of the "Austro-Hungarian" ladder, or of the validity of the social hierarchy in the bourgeois world in general—to Isaac these seem to be the original order of things. Indeed, many, perhaps most, of the Pioneers of the Second Aliya burned with a revolutionary fire, and many of them appear in the literature of the period. Isaac is not one of them. From the beginning to the end of the novel, Isaac is one of the most conservative heroes in Hebrew literature. He stops in Lemberg only to get a blessing for the road from his "Rebbes," as in the annual custom of the Hasids, and like his ancestor Reb Yudel who put on fine clothes and went to see the holy Rebbe of Apta to get his blessing before he set out on his way (*The Bridal Canopy*, p. 10).

When he enters Lemberg, Isaac entrusts his suitcases to the porters and "[smoothes] the wrinkles in his clothes" (p. 9). In a thousand ways, Isaac will repeat this gesture all his life, because clothes make the man, and because if he stands before the Zionist leaders in wrinkled clothing they will suspect that he is not "from a good home"—and who knows, maybe the Land of Israel won't want someone who doesn't look like the scion of a "good family" and isn't ironed and wearing a tie fastened nicely with a stickpin.

The sentence "A big city is not like a small town" (p. 9) is not intended to enrich the reader's knowledge of the world, but to reinforce the comic connivance between the narrator and the reader, behind the hero's back and at the expense of his provincialism and

infantilism. The difference between "Isaac saw monuments and fountains" and "bronze horses stand erect with bronze dignitaries astride
them . . . and stone figures spraying water from their mouths" (p. 10) is
not an informative difference, but a way of shaping the observing
awareness, and as Leah Goldberg has noted, this is the awareness of a
child. Incidentally, here and in other places, Isaac uses the word "dignitary" in an inflated sense: in Isaac's usage, a dignitary is not a minister,
but anyone dressed in "respectable clothes." So many "dignitaries and
lady dignitaries" and so many respectable clothes almost tempt Isaac to
betray the Land of Israel of his dreams for the Lemberg before his eyes,
which is depicted here as a Delightsome Land, a perfect Arcadia.

|

Once again, Isaac is amazed at everything. The reader who is familiar
with the literature of the time knows, and the narrator knows that the
reader knows, that anyone who appreciates "the first Maskilim who
rejuvenated our spirit" no longer believes that "a cemetery full of saints
protects the city." And someone who does believe that the pious wives
of those saints "with their grace overcame the persecution" is not concerned with the monuments in the streets and will certainly mutter
"tfoo" as he passes by the statues. And someone who enjoys the presence of "theater actors" has already lost his awe of "the ministers of the
Torah." And one who is in awe of "the ministers of the Torah" does not
make a pilgrimage to the "great Zionists"—in short, a succinct list of
difficult contradictions that have divided the Jewish people for the past
century or two. But Isaac does not perceive them as contradictions. He
is one of the most anti-intellectual heroes in Hebrew literature, and the
contrasts are eliminated in his heart by the all-encompassing amazement and the naïve synthesis. Just like his ancestor Reb Yudel, Isaac
walks between those abysses and mutters "holy holy holy" on all sides
and isn't harmed (so far) because of his innocence, which protects
him. "Behind all that," in the words of Yehuda Amichai, "hides a great
bliss": a singing and eager affirmation of all the phenomena of life,
especially, of course, an eager affirmation of those aspects that wear
"important clothes."

When Isaac reaches the entrance to the temple itself, "with
several thick glass doors, running one behind another and turning non-
stop, and a boy [standing] between the doors, dressed in blue and gold"
(pp. 10–11), the allusion raises the café of Lemberg to the level of the

vision of the End of Days (cf. Isa. 11:6). He is led inside, where there are "people of stately mien wearing distinguished clothes sitting on plush chairs, reading big newspapers. And above them, waiters" ("above them" because they lean over the guests, and perhaps also because their garb is more flamboyant and flashy), and they are called "dignitaries waiting on the guests" (p. 11). Then, "a miracle happened to Isaac and he started talking" (p. 11). The narrator seems to be joking with the reader when he states that a miracle happens to Isaac, but, in fact, this is no joke—a small miracle did indeed happen to Isaac, the kind of ambivalent miracle that happened to his ancestor. The proportion of the miracle is geared to the person, "the place of Jephthah in his day is like Samuel's in his," and if a "dignitary" hadn't come and taken him in, Isaac would have stood there to this day.

Isaac's adoration of the splendors of the café in Lemberg, that charming description of a villager in the temple smitten with shaky knees and humility, does not end as it started. At first, Isaac "began shriveling and shrinking until nothing was left of him but his hands, and he didn't know what to do with them" (p. 11). He will not experience such awe even when he enters the Land of Israel, even when he arrives in Jerusalem, even when he stands before the Western Wall. And it is not by chance that he will not, for here stands Isaac, among the gilded chandeliers and the blaze of lights and gleaming marble tables and "people of stately mien wearing distinguished clothes," in the holy of holies of the petit bourgeois dream, in the very heart of the Austro-Hungarian promised land. Isaac's religious soul kneels in love and awe before its internal purpose. Even though he is thoroughly Zionist and Pioneer and full of scorn for Exile—nevertheless, his soul prostrates itself, as at the giving of the Torah at Mount Sinai, in that place where the greatness of the bourgeoisie joins the splendor of Zionism's leaders.

Returning to the miracle that happened to Isaac: as in *The Bridal Canopy*, here, too, the reader does not have to accept the miracle as overt divine intervention in natural laws, a kind of heavenly hocus pocus. A miracle is whatever a person sees as a miracle; sometimes a miracle is a glass of water to a weary soul, sometimes it is a rare encounter. Many miracles happened to Isaac as he started out: a miracle that there was no mishap and the train left on time; a miracle that he found "a dignitary" who took him into the café; and, of course, a miracle that "happened to Isaac and he started talking" to the group of leaders (p. 11). And not only did one follower stand up and talk and the whole group of leaders listen to him, but those leaders are the idols of his youth; until yesterday he adored their pictures in his room, like singers and actors and athletes in another generation, and here they are sitting "big as life" in front of him, who until then had not seen a living leader. And Isaac "sat and feasted his eyes on them" (p. 12). And what are the deeds of "our leaders" in the café? According to Isaac, they sit day and night and "discuss the needs of the nation." According to the comic connivance between the narrator and the reader behind Isaac's back, they are "fat, stocky people in shirtsleeves" who spend their days playing billiards in the back room of the café. Once again the comic connivance is helped by quick cinematic "cuts," as the camera angle shifts quickly and without warning, and the pictures seem to dissolve into one another. Here is Isaac as the activists see him: a childlike, embarrassed provincial, a pesky groupie, a gullible fool. And here are the activists as Isaac sees them: a group of holy and pure men who serve as priests in the splendid temple of Zionism. And here they are as the narrator shows them to the reader: a group of fat, cynical idlers, "their heart . . . as fat as grease" (Ps. 119:70). Isaac is too innocent to play the role of the boy who reveals that the emperor has no clothes.

When Isaac begins unfurling all his problems before the activists, a situation almost Balzacian or Dickensian develops: a village fool confesses to a group of charlatans and pretenders. The picture is supposed to progress according to the familiar, set pattern of a bildungsroman. The provincial, like Pinocchio tempted by the cat and the fox, should emerge deceived and exploited, but sobered.

But this conventional pattern is not realized, neither here nor as the novel continues. Isaac does not sober up and does not discern the deception. As is usual among Hasids, he wants a blessing for the road from his "Rebbes"—and he gets a blessing and a pat on the back and even "letters of introduction to their comrades in Palestine." (The description approaches the world of the venomous Agnonian satire in *With Our Young and Our Old.*) Throughout *Only Yesterday,* the narrator behaves with sarcastic or satiric ruthlessness toward "the mighty," the pretentious, and the pretenders, just as he is forgiving and compassionate and humorously tolerant of the humble of the world, the mute of soul. Here there is a profound closeness between Agnon and Brenner, beyond all differences of style, literary temperament, and artistic position. Isaac, who goes himself to the Land of Israel, is described, unlike "our leaders," almost as a hidden saint, a Zionist Lamed-Vovnik, one of those on whom the (Zionist) world stands but who is unaware of that. Certainly those leaders are unaware of it—even though they sense "something." And when they sense that "something," a fascinating change takes place in the power relations. What began as an amusing scene, the tale of a valiant soldier Schweik, who on his way to the battlefield innocently pays excited homage to a gang of counterfeit generals who have never smelled gunpowder in their life, ends with "a repair of hearts": at first, the "generals" are eager to get rid of that little pest and get back to the billiard table, but in the end they forget the billiards and thirstily drink in his words. And wonder of wonders, Isaac doesn't give up his innocence, but the greasy-hearted leaders give up their cynicism for a moment.

Thus, Isaac has the power to melt hearts and revive dead souls. This is the major miracle on a day that is all miracles: something of Reb Yudel Hasid's soul beams from Isaac's personality and cleanses (for a moment) the seat of the scornful. It is as if the narrator has chosen to fool even his partner, the reader, who thought in his innocence that soft Isaac was clay in the hand of the potter before the activists. It turns out that it is Isaac who controls that scene, he who tints it with his emotional tone, and not vice versa—in decided contrast to the conventional pattern of the bildungsroman, in which the innocent is deprived of his innocence. "Our leaders" treat Isaac to coffee and cake such as he has never tasted in his life, and Isaac tastes and enjoys, but meanwhile he is secretly calculating that the price of the coffee and cake add up to one-thirteenth of the price of planting an olive tree in the Herzl Forest. This discovery neither sullies his innocence nor makes him ponder the manners of his leaders: "Yet our comrade Isaac didn't disgrace us, and didn't drink more than one glass, and didn't eat more than one piece of pastry, even though he was hungry and had never seen such fine pastry as that in his life" (p. 13). The first person plural in that sentence connects the narrator, the hero, and the reader, as well as the narrator, the hero, and the Pioneers of the Second Aliya, into one "bourgeois" bundle of sons of good families who "don't disgrace us."

Slowly "the hearts of our . . . leaders [are] stirred by . . . Isaac," and they decide on the spot that "even they might ascend"—the narrator seems to exchange a smile with the reader over Isaac's shoulder—"to see what was going on there in Palestine . . . and would have their picture taken with him as he walked behind the plow" (p. 13). The sword of irony unsheathed here is completely invisible to Isaac: "How happy Isaac was when he imagined himself standing among our leaders and our chiefs and the photographer is taking a picture of them together" (p. 13)—a photo to be sent home to his town to show them that the "despised and no-account" fellow rose to greatness in the Land of Israel. Somehow, in the café of Lemberg, a barrel of honey is not sullied by a drop of tar, but a barrel of tar is sweetened by a drop of honey for a moment: "the heart of our leaders is stirred" so that they abandon their billiards and drink in Isaac's words and even write him letters of introduction to their colleagues in Palestine. Thus Isaac emerges a winner from that struggle, just as he emerged a winner from the struggle with his father, just as he will succeed in overturning the heart of a group of embittered Pioneers in the café in Jaffa, and just as he will melt other stone hearts and bring water out of the emotional rock in many hard people. Perhaps, all in all, Isaac Kumer is not as soft and delicate as we tend to see him. Perhaps he inherited from Reb Yudel some of the Hasidic miraculous ability to repair hearts, to increase innocence in the world. When the encounter in the café in Lemberg concluded, the foolish Hasid had almost become a Rebbe himself and the counterfeit Rebbes his Hasids—and neither side noticed the reversal.

|

As his journey continues, between Lemberg and Przemysl, Isaac ponders: "How many cities there are in the world. There must be a need for them" (p. 14). A ridiculous childishness encounters a genuine religious profundity here. The essence of it is that "everything the Merciful One does He has done for good," that is, the existence of a thing, the occurrence of an event, indicates the greatness of the Creator and His goodness, for nothing is done in vain and nothing exists for no reason. Just like Reb Yudel, Isaac affirms the entire Being not because he claims to understand or wants to understand the reason for it, but because he believes that "there is a leader in the capital," and so everything is for the good. This is the wholesome assertiveness of a person who truly believes.

Moreover, the entire world, the world of the Holy-One-Blessed-Be-He, is understood here as a kind of Austro-Hungarian Empire—great, varied, abundant, flourishing in the harmony of unity within multiplicity. God Himself is depicted as a kind of Emperor Franz Josef, a forgiving old man with whiskers who nourishes and supports everyone and does good to all his subjects, different as they are from one another. Austro-Hungary is exalted here (e.g., pp. 16, 17, and later) to a symbol of the order of the cosmos and the rule of divine Providence. This is also how Musil, Broch, and Josef Roth—each in his own way—depicted it; and even in Kafka, the laws of the state are likened to the laws of the universe, albeit in an unharmonious way. Isaac's vision here may continue the custom of the talmudic explanation of God's ways by means of a parable of a flesh-and-blood king (as, e.g., in Pesakhim 75: "Seeing that you do not do thus before a king of flesh and blood, is it not all the more forbidden before the Holy-One-Blessed-Be-He"). So that Galician fellow who immigrates to the Land of Israel out of Zionist ideology, under the influence of Zionist poets and Zionist slogans, seems basically more religious than many observant Jews in his hometown and more than many observant Jews who will turn up their noses at him in Meah Shearim in Jerusalem.

In Przemysl, Isaac presses against the train window, fascinated by the colorful uniforms of "army commanders, generals of legions of several nations with different collars and colors" (p. 14). This is not a summit meeting of the commanders of the armies of Europe in the train station of Przemysl, but simply soldiers waiting on the platform who stir Isaac's inflated admiration.

The words "like those we saw in our hometown" (p. 17) lead us to try to distinguish at least five kinds of "we" in *Only Yesterday*. There is the first person plural that embraces the whole Second Aliya, including the hero and the narrator (as in the opening sentence of the novel). There is the "we" of the narrator and the reader, in a secret partnership, a circle the hero cannot enter (as in "May you never know such things, good friends. Isaac would have despaired" p. 65). And there is the "we" of the narrator as writer who takes a rhetorical tone common among lecturers and writers, as in the closing paragraph of the novel, when the narrator promises to continue the plot in *A Parcel of Land*, the proposed sequel to *Only Yesterday* that Agnon wrote and decided to suppress—apparently for good reason.

And there is also the participatory "we" of this or that scene in the novel when both the hero and the narrator are present (as in "Embarrassed and ashamed, we stood on this earth we had come to work and preserve" [p. 58]). And there is the "we" of sons of decent families (as in "Our comrade Isaac didn't disgrace us, and didn't drink more than one glass" [p. 17]), and "we artists," when the narrator includes himself, the painter Samson Bloykof, and other artists (as in "When Isaac knocked on the door, Bloykof flinched and shook, and he cursed and insulted him in his heart as we tend to do with anyone who comes to divert us from our work" [p. 219]).

Even in Przemysl, the naïve synthesis protects Isaac's naïveté, and he won't sense the depth of the rents in Jewish life. On the one hand, Przemysl has made many Jewish hearts skip a beat because of its holiness, its rabbis, and the holy books printed there. On the other hand, it also excites every Austro-Hungarian patriot and everyone interested in politics because of its place as a strategic key city, an important fortress, a famous site of historical battles. But for the most part, someone whose heart is taken with the Jewish holiness of Przemysl has nothing to do with the army or other "gentile excitements," and vice versa, while Isaac synthesizes everything in his naïveté.

Indeed, in a certain sense, that synthesis will exist in Isaac's soul to the day he dies. But he nevertheless will not avoid the torments of rupture experienced by the heroes of Feyerberg and Nomberg and Berdichevski and Brenner. Even if Agnon longed for the naïve synthesis, artistic truth won and the rupture triumphed over the synthesis. "Repair" of the rupture will not be realized in *Only Yesterday*; it will be postponed to the messianic days of *A Parcel of Land*.

"The train moves on and on and Reuben doesn't go where Simon goes and Simon doesn't go where Levi goes, but this one goes to this place and that one to that place" (p. 15). Who will utter those secrets? How does each one in that enormous mob remember his destination? Why don't they get confused? This is the virtue of wonder, if only we had it. Someone who has not lost this virtue doesn't need to run to the Himalayas or to the peaks of the Andes to seek excitement, for everything is full of excitement and every moment has a wonder. But, in Agnon's terms, "let us return to our issue." Isaac and the hidden traveler accompanying him like a shadow and observing him observing the world reach Vienna. The description of Isaac's hours in Vienna is one of the most forgiving and moving comic descriptions in all of Hebrew literature. The Vienna railroad station is full of lords and ladies carrying gifts to the king. The lords and ladies, of course, are all the splendidly dressed passengers. And the "gifts for the king" are their beautiful bags and suitcases. Vienna is not completely foreign to Isaac Kumer: it is the heart of the Zionist world as well as the heart of the bourgeois world, and those two worlds intersect. According to Isaac: "Maybe here in this place where I'm standing now Herzl stood" (p. 19); and that is also a typical "Hasidic" excitement. Only the emperor's palace might rival the place where "Herzl stood" for Isaac. If the world resembles the Austro-Hungarian Empire, then Vienna resembles Jerusalem and the Emperor's palace is the Temple, and the height of splendor of the Temple—as Leah Goldberg has shown—is "the gatekeepers garbed in red and wreathed in loops and stripes, with many buttons sparkling on their clothes" (p. 19). The apotheosis is apparently "sparkling," and Isaac is like the native won over by glass beads, for in his childish eyes, all that glitters is gold. And perhaps all the comic absurdity in the character of Isaac is connected with some historical vision of his creator: if not for childish surprise and wonder and amazement, there would not have been a Return to Zion. It was not just skeptical intellectuals and certainly not activists steeped in billiards, but excited and gullible children who ascended, and it was they who established the beginning of the Return to Zion. "And if he had stayed there longer, he might have seen the Emperor. . . . But we didn't wait, for we were in a hurry to travel" (p. 19). Here, too, the "we" includes Isaac and "the hidden traveler," a kind of spirit of the story who clings to Isaac all the way and yet observes him from the distance of years. Incidentally, two or three sentences after "But we didn't wait, for we were in a hurry to travel," the pedagogical "we" of the narrator as writer reappears: "We don't know if he went there on purpose or not" (p. 19). What is fascinating is how easily the text shifts back and forth between an intimate closeness that collapses the narrator and the hero, on the one hand, and an epic or ironic distance between the two of them, on the other.

Through the window of the train descending from Vienna through the Tyrol to the port city of Trieste, Isaac thirstily drinks in the pictures of the Austro-Hungarian idyll, the reflection of the neat and regular and perfect cosmic order (p. 20). Needless to say, the "prologue," Isaac's journey, is not an "introduction" but the essence of the matter: Isaac is going to the Promised Land and leaving behind another Delightsome Land. In the Land of Israel, horrors and disappointments and catastrophe are in store for him. From there, from "the Land of Zion and Jerusalem," he will often miss the original Delightsome Land, a land flowing with milk and honey, "a land whose stones are iron, and out of whose hills thou mayest dig brass" (Deut. 8:9—the biblical verse is applied to Austro-Hungary in an expansion of

the "catalogue" in section 10 of *Only Yesterday*). Isaac sees the land of
the emperor as rich in species. It is described in a biblical language and
in symmetrical biblical rhythms. It is less the abundance that wins
Isaac's and the narrator's heart than the harmony, a varied system of
climatic, agricultural, political, and economic balances, including natural resources that complement one another, and minerals and vegetables and fruit whose increase creates a perfect "symphonic" unity.
The religious apotheosis behind this description reaches the reader
through a combination of two awarenesses that interweave with no syntactic or stylistic warning, with no paragraph break: the prophetic religious awareness of "the child" and the perspectival, relativistic, and
"restoring" awareness of the narrator, "the hidden traveler." Through
Isaac's calflike wonder at buttons and train tunnels, the narrator injects
excitements in clear contradiction to the Zionist thesis that controls the
surface of the novel. Beneath the explicit rejection of the Diaspora is a
strong love of the deep and pastoral beauty of the world of the emperor.
Throughout their voyage, Isaac and the narrator often violate the
"Thou Shalt not Covet" of Zionism. The abundant detailing of the
names of mountains and cities and villages and rivers and quarries and
plants is clearly opposed to what is in store for Isaac in the sands of Jaffa
and among the ruins of Jerusalem. Only once, in the first part of the
chapter "Days of Grace" (p. 78), does the Land of Israel get an almost
"Austro-Hungarian" description. Thus there are two "Delightsome
Lands" in the novel, each a reflection of the other.

On the deck of the ship about to take him to the Land of Israel, at night
in the port of Trieste, Isaac has an erotic awakening. Perhaps it is the
sea or the warm air or the Italian atmosphere that causes it. Isaac
changes his clothes (he saves his best clothes for the day he comes to
the Land—"to greet the bride"). He lies alone on the deck "by the light
of the stars in the firmament and the voice of the waves in the sea"
(p. 23), and he gets excited for two overt reasons, and especially for one
covert reason. First, never in his life has he lain down alone, but—like
all poor children—has slept in the same room as his father and in the
same bed as his brother Yudel. Second, never in his life has he slept
outside like rich boys who go on camping trips. And the third, implicit
reason: as the sailors sing Italian songs in the distance, "the moon
[rises] from the dark water and the black waves [sway] silently. . . . All

that [is] heard [is] the sound of the waves lapping the boards of the ship" (p. 23). The tone, the pace, the shape—everything here is steeped in repressed eroticism. (Sonya too, when the sexual instinct overcomes her, is described as "licking her lips" [p. 129].) And censored visions of girls immediately arise in Isaac. Between the lapping of the waves and the swaying of the water, he lies alone and dreams not of the Land of Israel but of his hometown, even though it hasn't produced a delegate to the Zionist Congress and even though he "parted from it without pain" (p. 7): "The street lamps have been lit by now . . . and girls are strolling between the marketplace and the post office, and students are escorting them, and maybe the girls are thinking about Isaac, because he went to the Land of Israel" (p. 24). And further on: "Never in his life had Isaac paid any heed to girls," for he is a fine and modest fellow by nature. But the rest of the passage contradicts its beginning:

> If his passion struck him, his heart carried him to the fields and vineyards of the Land of Israel. As he came to the Land of Israel, he saw a well in a field with flocks lying nearby, and a big stone lies on the mouth of the well, and it takes the strength of more than one or two men to roll it off. The village girls came there to water their flocks. And Isaac rolled the stone off the mouth of the well. They watered their flocks and returned to the village. The whole village was amazed, How did they manage to get back so fast today. And the girls said, We chanced upon a young man from Poland who rolled the stone off the mouth of the well, just as you pull a cork off the mouth of a flagon. And they said to the girls, Where is he, why did you leave him there? Call him and he shall dine with us. And they went out to call him and bring him with great honor, and a few days later he married one of them. Or perhaps this was how it was: Arabs were there and didn't let the girls draw water from the well. Isaac chanced by there and drove out the Arabs, and the girls filled their ewers and told their fathers, A fellow from Poland saved us from the Arabs. And they said to the girls, Where is he, etc. (p. 24)

This passage, which blends Isaac's explicit Zionist dream with his hidden erotic dreams, is vital for a correct understanding of the novel and its hero. It seems to be merely the continuation of the picture of the Land of Israel as it appears in Isaac's visions in the opening paragraph of *Only Yesterday*, a picture composed of biblical chapters, songs, slogans, and propaganda. In fact, it is much more than a continuation of that picture. The Zionist Arcadia promises everyone who comes to it both advancement in social status (house and estate) and, as is now revealed, an erotic shortcut and a response to the distress one doesn't admit ("Never in his life had Isaac paid any heed to girls") even though it gnaws ("If his passion struck him"). In *Shira*, there is a description that parallels and complements this description of the modest Isaac and his erotic distress.[10]

Just as Isaac Kumer, son of a destitute shopkeeper, has almost no hope for upward mobility in his hometown—so he has almost no possible channel for erotic fulfillment. In his hometown, he "falls between the stools": not a Torah scholar married off by a matchmaker, and not yet—and never will be—a student who dares to accompany the girls on their evening stroll "between the marketplace and the post office."

Beneath its ideological and national promise, the Land of Israel, the Delightsome Land, also contains a promise to rise in the social scale (an estate, bourgeois life) and an erotic shortcut: as soon as his feet touch the ground of the Land, he will turn into a man and will easily roll the stone off the mouth of the well that "takes the strength of more than one or two men to roll it off," or else he will drive away a whole gang of Arabs. Either way, with the new powers granted him, Isaac will open the blocked well for the girls, and in exchange an erotic well will be opened for him. In "The Ascent and Death of Isaac Kumer," Boaz Arpali writes: "More than enslaving himself to a realization of the Zionist dream, the hero enslaves . . . the Zionist dream to the realization of his personal wishes, both overt and covert."

The sources of Isaac's vision, of course, are the tale of Jacob and Rachel in Gen. 29, and the story of Moses and the daughters of Jethro in Exod. 2. In the small towns of the Diaspora, a fellow achieves his purpose through a matchmaker or by wooing as a student, and Isaac can aspire to neither of those modes. But in the Land flowing with milk and honey, who knows? As soon as a fellow comes of age, his friends immediately arrange a stone on the mouth of a well for him or hire a few Arabs to hinder the drawing of water, and the fellow rolls the stone away and drives the Arabs away and rescues the girls and is immediately invited to a feast, and "a few days" later he descends to his garden and eats choice fruit. This is the custom of the Land of Israel, unlike the custom of Babylon. This is the erotic utopia, here in the Delightsome Land of the forefathers, all hopes will be realized; and this utopia should be presented to the reader when the plot leads Isaac from the envisioned magic mountain to the erotic vale of tears of "our brethren of the Second Aliya, the bearers of our Salvation."

Along with thinking of the girls in his hometown and the girls drawing water in the Land of Israel (who, of course, are proper daughters of Israel who observe the tradition and say such things as "The Lord sent us a fellow from Poland"), Isaac also thinks about his father's house. For the first time, an issue arises that will not let go of Isaac until his end: guilt about his family, mixed with homesickness. Isaac remembers the only pillow in the bed and how his father gave it to him, for his trip. Over and over his regrets, erotic stirrings, and guilt feelings about his father's home all come together in Isaac's thoughts.

The fall from the sublimity of dreams to the absurdity of disappointing reality is the movement of the novel in general and the logic of certain scenes within it. Isaac's ardent night visions—removing the stone from the mouth of the well, expelling the gangs, fame and marriage—end in a burlesque awakening: "a cold shower," a stream of water, wakes him, when the sailors begin washing the deck. Isaac wakes up and recites the morning prayer, stretching it out, "since all the days on the train, he hadn't put on Tefillin. . . . After he [fulfills] his obligation to God, he [takes] out bread and sardines and [sits] down to eat" (p. 26). For a moment, Isaac's piety looks like Isaac's Zionism: both follow the petit bourgeois norms rooted in his soul. He stretches out the prayer as befits a decent shopkeeper, "settling his debts" with the Lord as if the Lord were a wholesaler, and perhaps adding interest. Isaac sees the commandment to lay Tefillin not as something between himself and his God, but as a tax to be paid every morning—and if he is late, he will be in arrears. It is interesting to compare this with Jonathan Orgelbrand's oblique reply later in the novel, when he compares prayer to a debt owed the bank and deduces from the comparison a strict pattern of behavior.

Isaac travels "alone on the ship," that is, alone on the deck, at a cheaper fare. The other passengers are "lords and ladies" who live in cabins. In his solitude, Isaac thinks about his ancestor Reb Yudel Hasid, who ascended to the Land of Israel in a rickety sailing ship. Isaac compares himself to his great-great-grandfather, and this does not make him arrogant because of the perfect ship he is sailing on, but rather humble because he lives in a generation that is not worthy of a miracle. The covert clash between the world of the fathers and the world of the sons lives on in Isaac's heart, for he believes with complete faith in the possibility and existence of the miracle. What doesn't he believe? Only that he himself is worthy of a miracle. And he doesn't sense that small miracles may already have happened to him from the beginning of his journey. There is a connection between the censored erotic awakening Isaac experiences at night and his thoughts about Reb Yudel in the morning. Even in his night visions, he hopes for a miracle—for the strength of Samson to be revealed in his muscles, for without that the stone cannot be rolled off the mouth of the well, the Arabs cannot be driven off, and there is no bride. The humor in the description of Isaac's romantic scenario at the well in the Land of Israel is misleading. Again the narrator seems to operate the comic connivance between himself and the reader, who knows very well that the Land of Israel of shepherds and flocks might exist only in Arab villages and in the songs of the Pioneers. In fact, the narrator assumes the reader knows that the erotic problem of small-town boys like Isaac is serious unto death—or unto madness. In "Scroll of Fire," "Fligelman," "Mahanaim," "Kalonymos and Naomi," and "Bereavement and Failure," there are descriptions of pious small-town boys who set off on journeys from God to woman. They have lost God, and they have not yet reached woman but are lost on the way. This may be the most common subject in the so-called "literature of the Revival," even though there isn't much revival in it. But there is an abundance of repressed longing combined with gnawing guilt that emanates from a puritanical religious education. If not for the comic form, Isaac could be placed in the group of fellows separated by the river of perdition from the girls in Bialik's "Scroll of Fire," and he could find several comrades in torment among the heroes of Nomberg, Berdichevski, and Brenner. But Isaac is protected by the naïve synthesis, and the tone of the story is softened by the comic connivance, allowing Isaac to cling to his extreme optimism: there, in Arcadia, in the ancestral Delightsome Land, the delight the heart does not reveal to the mouth will be realized, too.

With the words "Between sky and sea travels this ship we're sailing to the Land of Israel" (p. 28), the presence of the hidden traveler accompanying Isaac on his journey is suggested by the use of the first person plural. Soon after, on deck, Isaac meets a couple of Jews, an old man and woman, who are also ascending to the Land of Israel. This is the first in a series of what Gershon Shaked calls "fateful encounters," each one shaping Isaac Kumer's fate. This meeting seems to happen completely by chance and is even rather amusing when the old man and the old woman dissociate themselves from Isaac, who belongs to "the sect of Zionists" (like "the sect of Sabbatarians"), those "who want to strip the Land of its holiness and make it like all other lands" (p. 28). Isaac, on the other hand, sees the old people—who are traveling to the Land to be buried on the Mount of Olives and thus to spare themselves a long underground journey to salvation when Messiah comes—as those who "came only to add dust to the dust of the Land of Israel" (p. 29). Isaac presumably did not formulate that venomous expression but was quoting from some Zionist polemic he had read, for Isaac does not have even a trace of malice of his own.

After a distancing and a new entente, the old man asks Isaac if he has any relatives in the Land of Israel. "Said Isaac, What do I need relatives for, all the Children of Israel are comrades, especially in the Land of Israel. And the old man smiled and said, In the Sabbath blessing, say that and we shall answer Amen, but on all other days it's hard to make it without a relative, especially in a new place" (p. 29). The couple tell Isaac that they, on the other hand, are going to their married daughter and their granddaughter in Jerusalem. This "theoretical" argument between the old man and Isaac on the issue of whether all Jews are comrades, especially in the Land of Israel, or whether that should be regarded as a desideratum and not an existing reality, indicates a reversal of positions, as it were. Isaac, the "modern," takes Scripture literally, while it is the pious old man who divorces Scripture from its literal meaning and takes the sober and realistic side of the argument. Isaac's position, not the old man's, is the authentic religious position: Isaac accepts Scripture literally and believes it. In the debate, Isaac appears as the proxy of Reb Yudel Hasid. It is fascinating that this debate will continue—in Isaac's heart—throughout the novel, when experience throws its weight sometimes on one side and sometimes on the other. Sometimes Isaac humbly ponders how right the old man was, and sometimes he boasts to the figure of the old man (whom he has thoroughly internalized as a father figure) that he, Isaac, is right, and in fact a person does not need relatives because "all the Children of Israel are comrades" here in the Land of Israel. The occurrences of the debate throughout the novel overlap precisely with the ups and downs in Isaac's life, until the paradoxical determination comes: the old man and his family will finally be Isaac's only relatives in the Land of Israel, but this family relationship will not save him from his fate—it's a stalemate.

Before Isaac boasts to the old man that all the Pioneers in the Land of Israel are his comrades because of their common ideal, the narrator intervenes and directly addresses the readers in the present tense: "Look at Isaac, his hands are as delicate as a maiden's, but they are eager to do any work. And when the ship reaches Jaffa, he'll go to a village and pick up a hoe and work. Too bad the ship doesn't hurry as fast as his heart" (pp. 29–30). The good-hearted comic mockery the narrator aims at his hero is quite different from the venom he devotes to the Zionist activists of Lemberg. Nevertheless, the comic connivance prepares the reader for "the blow of reality" in store for Isaac about the character of the Land and the mat on its doorsill that helps everyone who comes there "to shake the dust of Exile off his feet," and about the hoe waiting for everyone in the village, and certainly about the girls he chances upon at every well. Meanwhile, the words "his hands are as delicate as a maiden's" hint at the nature of the relations between Isaac and some strong people like Rabinovitch, Leichtfuss, and Samson Bloykof, and also perhaps at his relation with Sonya, who has hair on her upper lip (p. 131). The provincial petit bourgeois also bubbles up here in this Pioneer eager for the hoe, "already seeing himself hob-nobbing with the notables of the New Yishuv" (p. 30) because of the letters of introduction from the leaders in Lemberg.

Meanwhile, the food Isaac brought along for the road turns moldy, and Isaac almost dies of hunger because he is ashamed to appeal to the old man—whether or not all Jews are comrades—"for Isaac was the son of fine citizens who would rather die of hunger than ask for charity" (p. 30). All he can do now is hope for a miracle—and the (minor) miracle does indeed occur, along with the second fateful encounter: the assistant chef, not a Jew, takes pity on him and gives him "bread and cheese," and, from now on, he supplies Isaac with food. Are the bread and cheese and other food kosher? Not likely. It is fascinating to observe how easily Isaac (and the narrator) pass over the hurdle of kashrut without crises and punishment after death, without thunder and lightning. It is also fascinating to compare that "unbearable lightness" with the torments of other heroes in Hebrew literature, who experience desperate inner conflicts before they commit a sin—from Kalonymos in Berdichevski to "Hedgehog" in Yehoshua Knaz's

Heart Murmur.[11] Indeed, the religious distress is not canceled but only postponed, and it will strike Isaac hard—at a later stage and in special ways.

In exchange for his food and, as if by chance, so as not to be ungrateful, Isaac becomes the assistant chef's helper and agrees to paint the whole kitchen. This encounter becomes fateful because, "by chance," Isaac picked up a paintbrush and that brush will never leave him. This painting will paint Isaac's life in the Land of Israel and even contribute indirectly to his catastrophe. Several other fateful encounters are in store for Isaac along the way: with Yedidia Rabinovitch, Yohanan Leichtfuss, Samson Bloykof, and last but not least—the dog Balak. One of the hardest philosophical and theological questions raised by *Only Yesterday* and other works by Agnon is the meaning of "the hand of fate." In *Shira*, the narrator speaks of "a man and woman touched by the hand of God, which the faithless call the hand of destiny." And later in that novel: "The gods who mock each other . . . did what they did . . . the gods took charge, brought Shira home, and brought Herbst to Shira's door."[12] Indeed "fate" is conceived as predestination, as a preordained decree. And sometimes a deterministic view emerges here: the iron laws of society, status, and psychology dominate all human acts. And there are places in the novel where destiny bursts forth in its third, most threatening sense: a cruel fate, an oppressive destructive force that mocks human beings and brings catastrophe down on them. In his study of *A Simple Story*, Dov Sadan says: "Behind the precise psychological explanation, the veiled face of another explanation peeps out at you, and if you remove its calming veil you'll see the horror of Fate."

Is Agnon's fundamental position in this novel—and in his work in general—a deterministic position, or a predestined position, or a fatalistic position? I will not undertake to answer this question. To use Dov Sadan's words on Agnon in another matter: "You don't know and you wouldn't know even if the author published a declaration about it." In any case, two fateful encounters happen to Isaac on the ship, one with the grandparents of Shifra, who will become his wife, and the other with the paint bucket that will provide him with a livelihood almost all the days of his life in the Land of Israel, just as it will contribute to his death. Thus the first link is forged here in the meticulous chain of causation that Isaac will follow to his end.[13]

"Our ship reached Jaffa," and in the very first paragraph of section 17 of the book, Isaac receives the first blow of reality, just a tap: "A

Jew arrives in the Land of Israel, leaps off the ship and kisses her soil, in the joy of weeping and weeping for joy [but] until a doctor came to examine the passengers of the ship, no one was allowed to leave" (pp. 33–34). Thus the biblical and traditional pattern cannot exist without the slight delay of a bureaucratic reality "with no prooftext in the sources." When Isaac sees his acquaintances, the old couple, whose daughter has come to greet them, he envies them and feels orphaned. In the first round, therefore, the old man's practical wisdom ("it's hard to make it without a relative") overcomes Isaac's idealistic wisdom ("all the Children of Israel are comrades, especially in the Land of Israel").

Along with Isaac's fateful encounter with the old couple, and along with the fateful series of circumstances that lead Isaac to start painting on the ship, we must emphasize the appearance of the fateful adjective "orphaned," which is repeated twice here in the same paragraph. "He began imagining that the old people were telling him, Come with us" (p. 34). Indeed, at the very beginning of the novel, we are told that "[a] man of imagination was Isaac" (p. 3). But back in his hometown, his imagination carried him to the Land of Israel of Pioneers and comrades, while here, even before he sets foot on the ground of the Land, his imagination is already carrying him to the foster home of an Orthodox family that is thoroughly and purely Diaspora. The orphan already wants to go home. He is already seeking parents. It is only a slight exaggeration to say that throughout *Only Yesterday*, Isaac will go from one foster parent to another.

When the Arab porters swoop down on Isaac—"one snatche[s] his sack and one [takes] his valise and another one pull[s] him" (p. 35)— he immediately "assume[s] that they [have] been sent for him to ease his entrance into the Land of Israel, and he [says] to himself in rhetorical figures, Our Mother Zion sent her sons to greet their brother who has returned to her." He almost presents to the porters the letters of introduction from the Lemberg activists, "so they would know that they weren't mistaken about him" (p. 35). The comic misunderstanding delays the blow of reality that threatens to land on Isaac when he arrives.

|

Does Isaac Kumer "represent" the Second Aliya? Does *Only Yesterday* intend to be a "novel of the Second Aliya"? And is there any sense in these sociological questions, which concern the "Zeitgeist" on the one hand, and a great and unique work of literature on the other? If a computer were asked to create a composite character embodying the characteristic sociological profile of the people of the Second Aliya, the product would not be Isaac. Isaac is a naïve believer among ideological revolutionaries, a Galician among Russians, a childish man among intellectuals, a conformist among rebels, a "feminine" sleeping beauty among tormented lusty men, a petit bourgeois among conscious ragamuffins. Nevertheless, Eli Schweid was right that "if Isaac Kumer represents the Second Aliya, he symbolizes it in the rare and correct meaning of a symbol: he is not the most average, but the most consistent." In any case, this Galician baby imprisoned among Russians clearly ascended to the Land of Israel without an ideology, without a party framework, without a political program or "platform." In a generation in which every thinking fellow had opinions and every Pioneer was almost a trend in himself or a splinter of a party, Isaac is a "Herzlian Zionist" in his dream of finding Austro-Hungary on the soil of Canaan, and he is a "general Zionist," not in the party sense of the term, but in the more innocent sense. Isaac's Zionism doesn't stem from an analysis of the national situation or from a diagnosis of historical processes, or from a political strategy of the ingathering of the exiles; it is an "emotional Zionism." Just as he has no ideological preferences, so he has no personal program. Not once has he asked himself where he would spend the first night or where he would go in the morning, where he would live, which villages he would go to, what branch of agriculture he would work in. Isaac's Zionism is not an ideal but an impulse. Perhaps, in some respect, it is reminiscent of the journeys of migrant birds or the return of salmon to their spawning grounds: an activity of an internal sense, like a genetic instinct, which impels and guides him from his hometown to the Land of Israel. Perhaps this is Agnon's meta-ideological view of the return to Zion. Perhaps not. It's hard to know.

In his visions, Isaac sees himself, very simply, lingering for a moment on the doorsill of the Land of Israel to "shake the dust of Exile off his feet," immediately picking up a hoe and starting to work the soil, and in the evening sitting comfortably on his estate with the wife he won as a prize for his heroism at the well and with his sons "like olive shoots," taking a bourgeois pleasure in everything he had not acquired in his hometown—especially honor, for he is "hobnobbing with the notables of the New Yishuv." This is a strange and touching picture, a picture of a Pioneering lord or a bourgeois Pioneer with his feet in the Land of Israel and his face toward the shtetl and the great impression he will make there. He doesn't bother to collect concrete information in advance about the conditions of life in the Land of Israel or what a new immigrant needs, or about prices, climate, clothing, housing, and such. Almost like Reb Yudel in his day, Isaac flows from his hometown to the Land of Israel because of an innocent and excited impulse, a religious energy that shifted from the synagogue to Zionism and from the dream of the coming of the Messiah to the dream of building the Land.

|

Book 1 is titled "A Delightsome Land," while the title of the first chapter is "On the Soil of the Land of Israel." There is a descending order here, from the sublime to the prosaic, and the Land of Israel will soon descend to the level of Palestine. These titles mislead the reader into thinking that everything that preceded book 1 was merely a technical prologue that doesn't count among the chapters of the book. There could be no greater mistake: The Prologue, the introduction to Isaac, his father's house, his hometown, and his family tree are the foundations of the book. The journey across the Austro-Hungarian Empire allows the tragic clash between one Delightsome Land and another, and between one region of longing and another, between a Paradise on earth and a Paradise of dreamers.

Therefore, Isaac Kumer's first encounter with the Land of Israel is based on the model of the comic misunderstanding that inoculates its victim against tragic disappointment. In old-fashioned movie comedies, foolish suitors would appear, eager and virginal, and, when mocked by the girl of their dreams, who was sharp and hardly virginal, they interpret all scorn as desire and every humiliation as a promise of yielding. In the same way, Isaac "interprets" the porters in quest of baksheesh as brothers "Our Mother Zion sent," and in the same way, he will later do what a fellow of his religious education can do so well: interpret and reinterpret recalcitrant reality until it fits into a determined pattern of consciousness.

Thus, Isaac stands "on the soil of the Land of Israel he had yearned to see all the days of his life," rocks below him, a blazing sun above him. "Isaac's flush is an enveloping flame and his sinews an ardent fire . . . inside a case of fire and a pool of boiling water" (p. 39). From the sensual verb "yearned" to the "case of fire and a pool of boiling water," there is a subtle parody of the erotic union in which the virginal bridegroom is stunned by the heat of the bride, a heat above and beyond his strength and temperament.[14] Isaac cannot and will not yet see things as they are, lest he be forced to ask, "Is this Naomi?" (Ruth 1:19) or to discover to his distress that "in the morning, behold, it was Leah" (Gen. 29:25).

Afterward, he is taken to a house, and Isaac intends to present the letters of introduction given him by our leaders in Galicia "to show the landlord that he wasn't mistaken about him. The landlord wasn't mistaken about Isaac, but Isaac was mistaken about the landlord. This house was an inn and the landlord was an innkeeper and all his efforts with Isaac were simply to be paid for room and board" (p. 40)—another comic misunderstanding like that of the shlemiel lover who cannot and will not recognize the stratagem of a clever and disreputable girl. What follows is guided by the same sort of misunderstanding, with Isaac refusing to sober up lest his world collapse. He repeatedly defends himself from the blows of reality that descend on him because he interprets reality through exegesis and allusion until it yields to his expectations. "The ironed shirt he donned in honor of the Land sits on his heart like a soaked matzo and the hat rains salty dews down on his face" (p. 41). Isaac's exterior increasingly embodies the figure of the solemn and ridiculous lover who won't recognize that he is deceived. Reb Yudel Hasid's genes seem like antibodies protecting Isaac from disappointment. He lovingly accepts torments and justifies the harsh sentence of "All that the Merciful One does, He does for good." Thus Isaac is rescued from the blow of disillusionment, and thus he will go on being rescued from the blows of reality many more times. When filthy, hot, deceiving, and ugly Jaffa is not at all like the Land of Israel of his excited visions, he pushes the Land of Israel back a few kilometers: "Today I'll get to the settlement and I'll go into the forest and dwell in the shade of a tree and no sun in the world will overcome me" (p. 41). And the narrator immediately adds: "An imaginative man was Isaac and he imagined that the people of the settlements had planted forests to dwell in their shade" (p. 41). When he gets to the settlement and there is no forest and he is forced to notice the degeneration of the settlers, he immediately pushes the "real" Land of Israel back again and locates it in the Galilee. There, in the Galilee (where Isaac will never go), there the proper reality exists, the one he imagined in his youth and at the beginning of the novel.

Just as Isaac repeatedly pushes the Land of his love beyond the horizon so as not to be disappointed by it, so will the author push his

Delightsome Land beyond the horizon and promise the reader in the final sentence of the novel (p. 142) that thus far he has shown us nothing but the vale of tears, the vestibule; soon we will be invited to the parlor, to the perfect Land of Israel, to *A Parcel of Land,* where "our brothers and sisters . . . work the earth of Israel for a monument and fame and glory." For both Isaac and his creator, their perfect wedding night with the perfect Land of Israel is not called off because the bride is ugly but only postponed until tomorrow and the day after tomorrow. In fact, a profound religious spirit is again operating here: ugly reality neither cancels nor refutes messianic visions but keeps them as a song for the future. At any rate, it is an ancient Jewish concept that every messianic vision translated into the present tense and the present time is false messianism, while true messianism always belongs to the grammatical and emotional sphere of the future. The core of the Jewish messianic idea is apparently its fixed, paradoxical attachment to the future: "I will wait every day for him to come"—and the first emphasis, "I will wait," precedes the second emphasis, "every day," and even channels it.

As soon as Isaac leaves the inn "to look for a cart," an emphatic contrast is drawn between, on the one hand, the enchanted, idyllic landscapes of Austro-Hungary, where Isaac's route wound through a soft embrace of mountains and villages, vineyards and forests, orchards and snowy peaks, and, on the other, the sandy, parched, and blazing harshness of the Land of Israel. Isaac's first encounter with the landscape of the Land is shaped as a parody on the dissolution of materiality: Isaac achieves a melting of materiality, not from great ecstasy, but from a sunstroke.

The direction of the novel, like the direction of migrating birds, as in Bialik's poem, is from the cold Diaspora to "the warm, beautiful Land." From now on, the emotional direction is the opposite: from the hot desert toward home, to the rivers of Galicia, to the Austro-Hungarian expanses of lawn, to "all that glitters—is gold" in the palaces of Vienna, to the shtetl, to the father's house, to the girls accompanied by lucky students at dusk "between the marketplace and the post office." This basic and persistent tension between two Delightsome Lands, two Lands of Desire, is one of the marvels of this great work.

"God took pity on him and he didn't lose his head" (p. 41). And perhaps that divine pity is also a kind of small miracle, one of those miracles that have already happened to Isaac and will happen to him again. Nevertheless, the entire description—heat wave, filth, camels, sweat, Jews standing and "splitting hairs"—that description is very close in spirit to that of the authors of "the brutal truth" of the Second Aliya, Brenner and Aharon Reuveni. And in this vein is the scene in which Isaac comes on a gloomy and despairing group of unemployed workers, who mock him and his naïve and florid virginity ("the sun gets hot from patriots like you" [p. 42]). The entire group—in its despair, its cynicism, and the bitterness surrounding it—seems to have come from a description by Brenner or Reuveni. Here, Isaac gets a blow of reality that appears harder and more stunning than all its predecessors—and it seems that he will no longer be able to avoid its implications, as he has done so far, by moving the doorsill of "the real Land of Israel" farther, beyond the present vale of tears. Isaac treats "his new friends" to lemonade and coffee, for tomorrow he will go to the village, where there is no need for money because "all Jews are comrades." One of the workers presumes to "pierce Isaac's virginity" and shock him with a description of the Land of Israel as it really is. What happens in Isaac's heart as he hears the worker's horrifying words (p. 43) is a comic gem of selective hearing—Isaac hears and doesn't hear, takes in and doesn't take in, and through his quasi-religious filters, the speaker's tidings of Job turn into sweet Zionist music. This may be one of the most poignant moments in the novel. The worker tells Isaac that he should get out of the Land while he still has his soul (and his money), because the workers are starving for bread, Zionism is dying, and the ideal has failed. What Isaac hears is a Hebrew worker speaking in a pleasant Hebrew language about many villages and about Hebrew laborers and about schools being built and about a Land that is burgeoning with activity.

Behold this wonder: what happened in the confrontation between Isaac and the "stocky" leaders at the billiard table in the café in Lemberg happens here, too, in the wretched café in Jaffa. It is not the clever and the cynical who corrupt the soft soul of the naïf, but the delicate naïf who manages miraculously to renew the lost naïveté of the cynics. Here, too, perhaps we can say not only did "a miracle happen to Isaac," but on the contrary, he himself once again performed a small miracle. Perhaps the convention that has become so routine among readers and critics of *Only Yesterday*, that Isaac is a "weak figure" or "lacks character," needs to be reexamined. In two cases he has succeeded—and he will continue to succeed—in impressing his exquisite stamp on a vociferous group of people who seem much more aggressive than he, and who initially intimidate him. In both cases he has succeeded—and he will succeed again—in "painting" a determined and dominant crowd with the colors of his soul, while the reader expects Isaac to stand before these resolute men like a lamb before its shearers and adapt to them. The wonder Reb Yudel Hasid performed in *The Bridal Canopy*—reviving the naïveté in several hearts whose naïveté had been lost—can also be performed by his great-great-grandson Isaac, lower than grass in *Only Yesterday*. Like his great-great-grandfather, it can almost be said that Isaac also was graced with the magic ability of a holy fool who changes human beings without lifting a finger, just by his presence; this is the holy fool as we know him both from Russian literature (the *Yurodivy*, God's fool) and from several Hasidic tales.

|

In the second chapter, titled "Tells a Little and Slurs Over a Lot" (p. 46), Isaac comes to the agricultural settlement. From the description here and further on, the agricultural settlement is clearly Petach Tikva, and the time may be spring 1908. ("The springtime isn't over yet and he's already hot," one of the workers says about Isaac [p. 42].)

"Who can describe Isaac's joy"—as "who can utter the mighty acts of" Israel? (Ps. 106:2). And further on, with the words "best man," the motif of the shlemiel bridegroom, head over heels in love, reappears; what is in store for him under the wedding canopy is a great disgrace because he is blind to the real, perverse nature of the bride. (The motif of the Jew as bridegroom and the Land of Israel as bride is common in ancient writings, as well as in modern literature and Zionist slogans.) This is a comic variation on the theme: the bridegroom thinks that his problem is finding best men, while the narrator seems to wink at the reader over the hero's head, for the narrator and the reader know that the problem isn't best men, but the bride.

"Isaac entered the home of a farmer" (p. 46), and before his eyes stands the vision he has seen ever since his youth in his hometown, the embodiment of the dream of the Jewish landlord dwelling on his own land. It seems to blend the Pioneer ideal with the petit bourgeois yearning, the biblical-Zionist idyll with the Austro-Hungarian happiness: a farmer sitting on his porch, enjoying the trees spread out like a fan and the sun laughing in the windowpanes, and sipping a cup of tea with sugar (from the way he sips the tea, he obviously comes from

Russia). The Garden of Eden and the gemütlichkeit the Land of Israel promised Isaac from afar are firm and abiding, and here they are, right in front of his eyes—but the entrance is blocked to Isaac as it is blocked to the other ragamuffins who want to work as day laborers. "Thou shalt see the land before thee; but thou shalt not go thither unto the land" (Deut. 32:52). That bourgeois farmer, and his neighbor, and his neighbor's neighbor, all treat Isaac with polite coldness or brutal coarseness. Nevertheless, the farmer's wife behaves differently: "she [shakes] her head in sorrow for the Jewish fellows" (p. 47). Perhaps once again Isaac has succeeded, in his mysterious way, in touching the stone heart and melting it? In any event, he "straighten[s] his tie" (for who will hire a farmhand whose tie is a little crooked?) and "[goes] to another house," and he wipes his shoes lest he bring dust inside and make the owners think he doesn't come from a good home, and he enters the yard and finds a splendid house with a bell hanging on the door—a real colonial estate. Isaac's "spirit [is] humbled, as are small people who come upon a big house" (p. 47). "Wiping his shoes" is a conjunction of motifs, including Isaac's previous assumption that when he entered the Land "he would shake the dust of Diaspora off his feet the way you shake off something disgusting." Isaac's diminution on entering the house re-emphasizes the triumph of the social hierarchy that Isaac accepts all his life as part of the rules of the world; when he ascended to the Land, he dreamed not of changing or exploding that hierarchy, but of climbing up it a bit. The Land of Israel once again puts him in his place. Simon Kumer was apparently right when he saw more clearly than his son that "the whole world is Austro-Hungary," and so he took care to dress his son "as the son of a decent family." And the old man on the ship was right and Isaac was wrong when he hoped that "all the Children of Israel are comrades, especially in the Land of Israel."

And now another fateful meeting takes place, also marked by shoes, and the shifting scales again lean toward "all the Children of Israel are comrades": Yedidia Rabinovitch enters the novel with his crooked sandals hanging on his shoulder to save their soles. Isaac and Rabinovitch look for work in vain, but they find one another—Rabinovitch immediately takes a paternal-virile position, and Isaac gladly accepts the "feminine" role and, without any contradiction, the position of adopted child, too. Isaac's dejection in the scenes of seeking work, his naïve submission when he is thrown out of every house and even when he suffers abuse (he is sent to knock on the door of an abandoned house)—all that reminded Eli Schweid of the innocent, tragicomic submission of the dog Balak to someone who treats him well and pets him and then kicks him out.

Later, the sunset seems to remove the Land of Israel from Isaac and to fix it again in the romantic distance, the realm of yearning on the horizon, a land seen only before you, indeed "crowned with trees and gardens," indeed flourishing and even bourgeois, but avoiding "her bridegroom" and refusing to give in to his wooing.

Rabinovitch invites Isaac for a cup of tea in his ruin: "The host put his hand on the guest's shoulder and said, My house is your house" (p. 49). This parodic gesture, a typical Charlie Chaplin ritual, indicates Rabinovitch's spiritual foundations, beyond all clowning, which are just as petit bourgeois as Isaac's. Over and over, the narrator calls Rabinovitch a "bourgeois"; over and over, despite his bare feet and poverty, he demonstrates the manners of a bourgeois—and thus his beginning hints at his end. Even though Rabinovitch and Isaac are as different from one another as Don Quixote and Sancho Panza, or—closer—Reb Yudel and Neta the carter, they are still close in the "bourgeois" foundation of their personalities.

In the debate Isaac constantly conducts in his heart with the figure of the old man from the ship, the situation, therefore, is a stalemate: Isaac argued that in the Land of Israel, a person doesn't need relatives because "all the Children of Israel are comrades," while the old man maintained that "it's hard to make it without a relative." When they debarked from the ship, Isaac felt the torments of orphanhood, and the old man was winning. Now, on his first night in the agricultural settlement, comes a stranger who offers him shelter, and so do the fellow's comrades, and Isaac is winning. And that unspoken debate between Isaac and the figure of the old man will continue throughout the novel, until Isaac's marriage with that old man's granddaughter brings that quarrel (and Isaac's life) to a paradoxical conclusion.

The nocturnal conversation between Rabinovitch and Gorishkin (Book 1, chapter 2, section 3) consists of bitter, cynical humor, beyond despair; and Isaac, as usual, absorbs it selectively. This time, too, his filters protect his Zionist virginity from the blow of reality threatening his naïveté. Isaac is like a prudish yeshiva student who comes on some obscenity and isn't offended because he doesn't catch it.

Isaac and his comrades are not hired as farmhands the next day either and, in addition, are insulted and humiliated by the contractors, the representatives of their Jewish employers. At the beginning of the chapter "In the Labor Marketplace," a small but fascinating change is indicated in the convention the novel has obeyed so far. The opening of *Only Yesterday* has unfolded as a realistic social-psychological novel in the best tradition of the nineteenth and early twentieth centuries. At this point, the realistic convention cracks for the first time, and another convention emerges—indeed only a small curiosity at the moment—a surrealistic-satiric one that will become overwhelming with the appearance of the dog Balak. Here, right after the "air sighs" from a whip lash, the class-conscious pondering of the mare Fatima appears, while the donkey expresses proletarian-revolutionary-anarchist views and even considers a terrorist act against the rotten establishment.

At the end of this difficult scene, when the narrator says: "Embarrassed and ashamed, we stood on the earth we had come to work and preserve" (p. 58), he uses the first person plural as if he is an eyewitness, one of the humiliated workers who stand there with Isaac and his other comrades—unless "we" means the narrator and his hero; unless the intention is "we of the Second Aliya," or perhaps "we," the Children of Israel, in that day and time. Indeed, behind the first person plural sometimes assumed by the narrator, a kind of "chorus" operates, not one specific voice. In the chapter "In the Labor Marketplace," there is sarcasm toward the activists, irony toward Zionist rhetoric, a satirical and "Galician" settling of accounts with the "Russians," and tolerant humor mixed with restrained pathos toward the hero and his worker comrades.

Just as he did with "our leaders" in Lemberg, and the old man and the assistant chef on the ship, Isaac tries unwittingly to impose the role of father on Yedidia Rabinovitch and to be accepted as a son.

The feudal mare and the proletarian donkey in the chapter "In the Labor Marketplace" are merely a brief and slight deviation from the realistic-mimetic rules the text accepts. But that irregularity is a harbinger of the future direction of the novel—from realism to surrealism and fantasy, from Balzac and Dickens and Thomas Mann back to Cervantes, or, according to Eli Schweid, Meshulam Tochner, and Hillel Barzel, "toward Kafka." There is an unresolved tension in this work between Agnon's documentary-memoirist impulse and mimetic force and his metaphysical, theological, and grotesque impulse. *Only Yesterday* takes its place between, on the one hand, *The Bridal Canopy* (a Cervantes-type work that conducts a clear dialogue with Don Quixote) and, on the other, *A Guest for the Night* (controlled by mimetic, historicist, memoirist impulses), the grotesque *Book of Tales*, "Edo and Enam," and *Forever* (all oriented toward the metaphysical and the theological). Hence, *Only Yesterday* marks a crossroads in Agnon's work.[15]

Since the "bride" has not yielded to Isaac, and since he can't find work, he escapes to the clearly childish way out: "Out of idleness and out of grief and out of lack of food, Isaac's strength wore out and he got sick" (p. 61; and cf. with the place of illness in "The Way Out" by Y. H. Brenner). When he recovers, Isaac at last absorbs some of the blows of reality that the walls of his innocence and devotion have deflected. When he does absorb them, he does not go on tramping forward toward the "real Land of Israel" (in the Galilee?) but "load[s] his belongings on his shoulders and [goes] to Jaffa" (p. 63). Unwittingly, Isaac Kumer's retreat has begun—a small step, a first step, on the road whose hidden direction is back home. What his father, Simon, imagined would happen to him—"he'll see with his own eyes that the whole business of the Land of Israel is a fiction the Zionists made up . . . he'll come back to his home" (p. 5)—has indeed begun to come true. *Only Yesterday* seems to turn at this point toward the familiar and proven channels of a typical bildungsroman—but only ostensibly.

With Isaac's return to Jaffa (p. 62), the "messianic" part of the novel comes to an end. Isaac will no longer move "forward," toward "the real Land of Israel beyond the horizon," but backward, toward the Diaspora he came from. A messianic impulse, almost a messianic instinct, uprooted Isaac "out of [his] country and from [his] kindred" (Gen. 12:1) and took him across Austro-Hungary, flowing with milk and honey, "a land whose stones are iron, and out of whose hills thou mayest dig brass," and carried him over the sea and led him to the Land where he had hoped to be reborn, purified from "the dust of Exile," to the bosom of a biblical life, which in fact is merely an ideal refinement of the secret Austro-Hungarian charm. It is as if the days of the Messiah are a kind of fusion of the Song of Solomon, bourgeois manners, the seven kinds of fruits in Israel, the kingdom of the Austrian Kaiser, a stone rolled off the mouth of the erotic well, and a decent wool suit.

On his return to Jaffa, after Isaac vainly seeks work from Makherski and Makherson and Makherovitch, who have come here straight out of Agnon's *With Our Young and Our Old* and *The Book of the State*, his feet carry him to the port, as if they were homesick. At the port, Isaac, dazed by hunger, has a fantasy that seems to be taken right from the treasury of folk tales, a tale of a slave who rescues his master and, in exchange, wins half the master's wealth and perhaps also the hand of the master's daughter. Just as in his fantasy about rolling the stone off and chasing away the shepherds, once again Isaac sees himself in his imagination as graced with supernatural powers (for in fact, he is not a biblical hero, and he doesn't even know how to swim, so the heroic tales he imagines, like his Zionism, involve some rebirth, some removal from himself). How is the fantasy about rescuing the master different from the fantasy about a position as an "agricultural lord" or the fantasy about the shepherds? The latter two are integrated into Zionist salvation, while the former is really about Isaac's salvation from Zionism: with the money the lord will give him for saving him from drowning, Isaac dreams not of buying himself a farm like those he saw in Petach Tikva, but of becoming a merchant and coming and going at the port of Jaffa "on business" (p. 63), a merchant whose wealth allows him to look down on "all the activists of the Yishuv together." And as always, right after the fantasy comes a sober and skeptical statement from the narrator: "But miracles don't happen to every person, especially not to a fellow like Isaac, who isn't worth it to the Lord to do him a miracle even in a natural way" (p. 64). Note that the narrator, who pours buckets of cold water on the head of his fantasizing hero, does not deny the possibility of a miracle but only doubts that Isaac is worthy of one. Not only does the narrator believe in the existence of miracles, he even reconfirms the traditional hierarchy prevailing in the world of miracles.

"[Isaac's] heart became the home of thoughts for . . . naïve people like Reb Yudel Hasid his ancestor. . . . Isaac raised his head . . . and peeped into the cave and said, But here there is no treasure. And he laughed at himself for expecting to find . . . two or three pennies to buy him some bread" (p. 64). Reb Yudel Hasid, in *The Bridal Canopy*, crouched down at the mouth of the cave and found a great treasure in it. Isaac, according to the known rule "The authority of Jephthah in his day must be respected as that of Samuel in his," prays for "a proportional miracle" and is disappointed and will even laugh at himself and his expectations. But after he mocks his expectation of a tiny miracle, a certain miracle does indeed happen to him: he falls asleep and wakes up to see an old man bending over him, "holding a green pot with a paintbrush in it" (p. 65). Afterward, when Isaac, in despair, becomes a Hebrew painter in the Land of Israel, the miracle of Hanukkah echoes in the narrator's language: "Who can describe Isaac's joy" (p. 65). As always, with joy, guilt inevitably comes. The awareness that he is not a real painter but only a make-believe painter or "a smearer" gnaws at Isaac. Over time, a deeper guilt eats at Isaac that the craft of painting isn't Pioneering like the craft of building the Land or working the soil, for it does not produce something from nothing and doesn't create anything new—like the commandments of Zionism—but only covers something old in new "garb." There is a proximity between painting and covering up, just as that craft is close to the motif of clothing, which envelops a person in an embellished identity that covers the truth (as Isaac's destitute father hoped, like Isaac, that new clothes "[would] show that he [was] from a fine home"). Isaac, who ascended to the Land to "build and be rebuilt by it," ends up coming to the Land to "paint and be painted there." Is Agnon hinting here at a broader remark about the internal nature of the Zionist revolution? A suggested contradiction of the hope the hero expressed at the beginning of the book to be reborn by ascending to the Land? As in: changing place is changing color—is that a substantive change? Someone whose soul is rooted in Diaspora may hide under new garments or under a coat of new paint, but isn't that only a change of the jar and not of its content?

In any event, Isaac is haunted by guilt, despite his good luck and the miracle that happened to him, because in this craft, he is a painter who isn't a painter, and even if he were a painter, he is a Pioneer who isn't a Pioneer. These guilt feelings are added to the guilt he feels toward his father and his brothers and sisters, because his journey made them even poorer than they were, and he abandoned them to their poverty and doesn't help them even when he can. As the novel continues, these feelings of sin join the sin he sinned against Rabinovitch, and the sin he sinned against Sonya, and the Torah prescriptions he has violated, and the hump of guilt on Isaac's back keeps puffing up—until Balak comes along and takes on his back the burden of Isaac's sins, like a scapegoat dog, including Isaac's sin against Balak himself. In any case, Isaac does not work the soil of the Land and does not build the Land, as he should have done, but only covers it—and himself—with fresh paint.

By the second page of *Only Yesterday*, both the hero and the narrator pay attention to shoes and clothing. There is almost no character in this novel, including secondary and minor characters, who is not portrayed in terms of his clothes and shoes. Hence, the motif of covering up and painting oneself seems to be only the continuation of the motif of clothes and shoes. Can we derive any conclusion from this combination of motifs about the narrator's views of the entire Zionist revolution? Does the contrast between clothing and painting on the one hand, and planting and building on the other, express a general intention? The answer to these questions is suggested in one of the most amusing encounters in the novel, when Isaac Kumer meets Hemdat, the alter ego of the young Agnon, in Sweet Foot's hut: "Hemdat was friendly to Isaac, even though he wasn't comfortable with the craft Isaac practiced, for there is something misleading in it, since painters are wont to embellish ugly things" (p. 397).

In chapter 4, "Work," Isaac appears arrogant and indulgent, almost euphoric, now that he has found a good apartment and a good livelihood and is radiating a comfortable bourgeois life. The narrator still treats his hero with tolerance and humor, for this is a "rich man" who owns one rickety chair and may someday be rich enough to acquire another rickety chair, and the reader can certainly "pity" the poor boy who never slept in a bed by himself and has suddenly risen to relative greatness.

The strange passage from the sublime (arrogance and comfort) to the ridiculous (dejection and nightmares) is apparently connected to the tangle of guilt feelings that accompany Isaac from the start and grow stronger as his situation improves. In both versions of Isaac's recurring nightmare, he sees himself doing what he does while awake: painting walls and seeking a father. In both nightmares, the "father"-artist abuses him or punishes him, either by slipping the ladder out from under him and making him fall, or by filling "his brush with paint and [throwing] it in his eyes and [blinding] him" (p. 71). And in the waking nightmare, Isaac sees himself as a mule turning the mill wheel with blinkered eyes "until he wears out his soul and dies" (p. 71), and thus he foresees a precise and terrifying vision of the fate in store for him.

Just as Isaac sought and found a father figure in the old man on the ship, and perhaps in the assistant chef, and certainly in Rabinovitch, so he wanted in the dream and found in waking a father who is also a craftsman: Yohanan Leichtfuss, whose name means "light foot," that is, one to whom God has granted light feet, and whose nickname is "Sweet Foot." This man is revealed to Isaac in the synagogue of the artisan's center, drunk, wallowing in his vomit, while everyone sneers at him. It is Isaac, of all people, that chameleon who takes on the color of his surroundings, who doesn't join the sneering rabble. On the contrary, this time, as in the café in Lemberg and as with the group of despairing workers in the café in Jaffa, Isaac has enough quiet internal strength and integrity to make himself an exception, to go against the current and separate himself from the crowd mocking the drunken man. Isaac behaves like a Lamed-Vovnik, as befits the grandson of the great-grandson of Reb Yudel Hasid. Indeed, Isaac returns to Leichtfuss the favor the assistant chef and Yedidia Rabinovitch did for him.

But the first revelation of the connection between Isaac and Leichtfuss is completely different from the pattern of their later relationship: on the day they meet, it is Isaac who supports and protects Yohanan. Those roles will soon be reversed.

These two—Yohanan and Isaac—look like complete opposites: Leichtfuss is an authoritarian, arbitrary, bohemian person who loathes all conventions; women and dogs always obey his orders; his employers pay him homage; and he rules over everything around. The women "who make pilgrimages to him" save him the trouble of wooing and free him from "the erotic curse" that hovers over Isaac and Orgelbrand, the curse "In the sweat of thy face shalt thou find a womb." Leichtfuss is free from the full load of erotic suffering that descended on the heroes of the Second Aliya, and what Isaac doesn't dare even dream of falls like ripe fruit into Leichtfuss's lap. Isaac is an erotic "beggar" who bows to a woman as to a heavenly creature—and Leichtfuss is an erotic "rich man" who treats the whole feminine gender with scorn. The secret of Sweet Foot's strength is the eccentric nonchalance that exempts him from all obligations; the basis of Isaac's weakness is that from childhood on, he has walked around in the world like a person who is always in debt, who keeps trying in vain to settle his debt but, to the day he dies, won't succeed. Leichtfuss is a colorful character, and Isaac Kumer is a total "square." It is hard to recall a literary hero "squarer" than Isaac. (In terms of E. M. Forster's famous distinction in *Aspects of the Novel* between the "shallow characters" and the "rounded characters," we may also speak of "square characters"—perhaps the most difficult type to embody in literary form.)[16]

In any case, Yohanan Leichtfuss is the first illustration of a strange and embarrassing rule that operates as an iron law in *Only Yesterday:* he who controls dogs controls women and controls his own fate.[17] He who cannot control a woman or a dog is abused by fate. This monstrous law hovers over the chaos until the end of the novel. Baruch Kurzweil has noted it, and Adi Tsemakh has discussed it, emphasizing that Sweet Foot enters the novel lying drunk in the synagogue—thus determining his attachment to the two conflicting worlds of the novel, the world of "the light-footed" (and light-headed), and the world of belief and prayer. Moreover, whenever he likes, Sweet Foot can keep all the Commandments—as when he was in Jerusalem (book 3, chapter 13, section 3)—or he can transgress without being racked by all the torments and temptations that torture Isaac. Thus, Leichtfuss's whole relation to his parents and to his parents' house is in clear contrast to Isaac's sin against his father's house, one of the causes of his torments. Adi Tsemakh goes so far as to see Leichtfuss as a chosen of God, despite his satanic nature—or because of it. Even a reader who doesn't want to go all the way with Adi Tsemakh to his brilliant and bold "two-tiered midrash" can agree that one of the sharpest instances of insolence against Heaven and theological irony in *Only Yesterday* and all of Agnon's work centers in the character of Sweet Foot.

What connection does Isaac seem to have with Leichtfuss, his complete opposite, and what can Leichtfuss find in Isaac? Leichtfuss realizes offhandedly all that Isaac dreams of: he built himself a house with his own hands and planted a vegetable garden and lived from the fruit of his toil just like the childish vision Isaac had in his youth, before he ascended to the Land of Israel and before he discovered that here, a person doesn't "take himself" a field and "take" a hoe or "take" a shepherdess from the well. Isaac's childish fantasy was realized by a man with a strong, almost autistic willpower, who succeeded in realizing "all the hopes." On this side of the barricade stand all the shy dreamers and disappointed lovers—Hirshl and Kumer and Nahman and Fligelman and Feierman and Hagzar and Bialik's bright-eyed young man. On that side—against all of them—stands Yohanan Lightfoot, chuckling, who established a Pioneer settlement in the sand dunes of what would eventually be Dizengoff Center, a "home for one man," and is settling the wasteland and bringing bread out of the earth as he brings water out of the erotic rock. According to Aristotelian concepts, Leichtfuss is either an animal or a god, because he is not dependent on the society of humans. And yet, even that isolated artist, that Robinson Crusoe of the sands of the future Tel Aviv, needs a group of admirers, and Isaac is portrayed in chapter 5 as Sweet Foot's groupie. According to the most stereotypical pattern, Isaac fills the "feminine role": absorbing and admiring. Indeed, we can discern a veiled foundation of latent homosexuality in the relations of Yohanan and Isaac, especially in Isaac's dream: "Isaac lay on his bed and thought . . . about Sweet Foot and about that day . . . when Isaac brought him to his room and lay him on his bed and they had become friends" (p. 412; and cf. the extensive description on pp. 446–49). Nevertheless, Leichtfuss apparently finds Isaac more than just another two-legged lapdog. He seems to locate in Isaac that childish element, quick to admire, refusing to grow up. This element is considered a necessary component in the personality of a creative artist—even though it is not a sufficient component. "Sweet Foot" is also graced with that trait—and with creative originality and complete self-confidence, traits Isaac doesn't have a trace of.

Moreover, in different ways, the two friends demonstrate integrity. Each in his own way is a naïve and wholesome man and does not lie to himself. Thus Isaac finds himself a father for a while, and Leichtfuss finds himself an admiring and childish son for a while. Despite the contrast between the "father" and the "child," the closeness between them is clear, and it is shaped by the ability to be amazed or surprised at the root of their souls.

One paragraph at the end of chapter 5 and one at the beginning of chapter 6, "Days of Grace," indicate the recurring shifts in the novel and its hero from euphoria to dejection and back, for no apparent reason. The beginning of "Days of Grace" presents one of the few idyllic descriptions in the novel—one of the most amazing in Hebrew prose. In this chapter, the Land of Israel almost overlaps the Land of Israel Isaac envisioned in his youth, when the narrator empathizes and explains that "a man of imagination was Isaac." And for a moment, the Land of Israel seems to fulfill Isaac's childish imaginings and refute all of the narrator's skepticism.

As in A Simple Story, The Bridal Canopy, and "The Sign of Pisces," Agnon reaches some of his epic climaxes in Only Yesterday's descriptions of food and drink. The fruits of the Land are described here through Isaac's eyes, and Isaac's eyes are filled with wonder and amazement. Isaac sees the "choice fruit of the Land" with the eyes of his ancient forefather, who was amazed to see the wonder of wonders even in what others saw as everyday things. For example, in The Bridal Canopy Reb Yudel Hasid marvels at the sight of the light of day: "When he finished his prayer, he looked at the world . . . and marveled at the great light spread by the Holy-One-Blessed-Be-He in His grace, Who adorned His world with it" (my translation—B.H.). And now, six generations later, like a reincarnation, here are Isaac's words of wonder at the sight of the sea: "That water that can cover the land, schoolchildren play in it and aren't afraid" (p. 78). Here is Reb Yudel's whole and profound reverence: "Throughout that time he never gave over repeating the verse in Proverbs, 'the eyes of the Lord do watch in every place.' . . . If a man does a deed it must assuredly be for good, seeing that otherwise he would not be aided in the doing" (*The Bridal Canopy*, p. 288). And six generations later, here is a similar reverence in Isaac's mouth: "The eyes of the Lord wander throughout the Land, and when He wants to, He bestows a good taste even to the thorns of the hedge" (p. 80; and cf. Deut. 11:12, "the eyes of the Lord thy God are always upon it"). Such associations between the two characters, as well as the ascent to the Land of Israel, indicate the deep affinity between these works.

As for the narrator, in that idyllic chapter, "Days of Grace," he is careful, as usual, to delineate a thin, subtle line between Isaac's admiration and his own sobriety. The section praising the "eyes of the Lord" continues in the narrator's first person plural, which may be in his own name and in the name of his hero and perhaps in the name of the whole Second Aliya: "And it seems to us that we really are in a Delightsome Land" (p. 81). The narrator's careful reservation ("it seems to us") cools the hero's religious and Zionist ardor.

|

Isaac's gradual abandonment of religious precepts and his neglect of religious practices is fascinating (book 1, chapter 6). Isaac appears to be different from all the heroes of the literature of the "Generation of the Revival" because he is spared the tragic crisis of faith. In Feyerberg, Berdichevski, Brenner, and others, deserting the Commandments is an incurable trauma; while Isaac seems to slip painlessly from keeping the Commandments to not keeping them, from being in the synagogue to being in the (relatively) permissive Pioneering Land of Israel. Isaac shifted but wasn't uprooted. He slipped down but didn't rebel.

But as the novel continues, it becomes clear that "the unbearable lightness" in Isaac's passage from a religious existence to a secular one only seems so. In fact, the religious distress in *Only Yesterday* is very close to the religious distress described in the works of Feyerberg, Berdichevski, Bialik, and Brenner: guilt and dread and doubt, sin and punishment, orphanhood, erotic repression and erotic depression, incurable tension between reverence and Eros—all this will also explode in *Only Yesterday*. The idyllic path from a religious existence to a "permissive" existence, like the idyll of the Delightsome Land in the chapter "Days of Awe," is not an idyll, but an idyllic delusion, a desideratum and not a reality (see the essays of Baruch Kurzweil and Jacob Katz on this point).

There may be some internal logic in the fact that it is precisely when Isaac Kumer stops observing the Commandments—including the supreme Zionist commandment to build the Land and work the soil—that the Land of Israel appears to him as a Garden of Eden full of fruit. He bites hungrily into all the fruit of the garden—except the fruit of the tree of knowledge, which is waiting for him in the next chapter.

"Isaac was different from most of our comrades in two things, he didn't belong to any political party and he didn't court girls" (p. 83). Isaac is portrayed as an ideological virgin and an erotic virgin: an ideological virgin by virtue of the "naïve synthesis," and an erotic virgin because he has left the world of the matchmakers and has not yet entered the world of those who court, has not yet found the biblical wells with the girls who shepherd flocks and draw water.

|

"Isaac had no better days than those"—that line with slight variations will be repeated over and over ("good were the days," "good were those days, and better than the days were the nights"), like a recurring anthem, until it suddenly explodes. Isaac supports himself with his work and enjoys the choice fruit of the Land and lives in a room all by himself and envisions—as expected—the jealousy and amazement of the townspeople, like his younger brother Yudel, when they come and see him in his greatness (book 1, chapter 6). Isaac even has six shirts made for himself—but he postpones fulfilling his intention to send a little money to his family rotting in poverty in the small town. To the day he dies, Isaac will not send them one penny, and to the day he dies, he will be afflicted with guilt that gnaws at him for not helping them.

With the revolution that occurs in the life of Rabinovitch, who despairs of Pioneering and manual labor and returns to be the merchant he is by nature, and as "was decreed about him from above"—the narrator's voice toward Rabinovitch changes along with the reader's attitude toward this character, as controlled by the text. Tolerant humor gives way to biting sarcasm. Rabinovitch was not "born again"; his bourgeois manner and his talent "to get by" in any situation were evident even in the days when he walked around the Land with his sandals twisted on his shoulder to save their soles. But back then, he was sincere, and now he is merely pretending and paying lip service to the ideas he has already betrayed. It is a mistake to think that the narrator mocks Rabinovitch because he has deserted the ideals: he mocks him precisely because he seems to go on professing the very same ideals (book 1, chapters 6 and 7). It is not selling clothing, Rabinovitch's new livelihood, that is portrayed as a loathsome profession, but the hollow Pioneering rhetoric that accompanies it: "and from agriculture and commerce the Land will benefit" (p. 92). Agnon's irony involves an imaginary seriousness, an ostensible identification with the lying excuses of the victim of the irony: the narrator plays a credulous fool, and with a wink, he repeats the hypocrite's deceiving arguments—while integrating his own expression into the speaker's expression, as if he is repeating his words with a nod. For example, the narrator, feigning honesty, adopts the terminology of Rabinovitch, who has not "abandoned" or "forsaken" the Land and has not "descended" from it: "it happened that Rabinovitch left the Land" (p. 91). It happened. It was not deliberate. Perhaps he only went down to the kiosk to buy cigarettes, and "it happened" that he went astray and found himself in Europe. And similarly: "I better go to Europe where I'll learn something I won't learn in the lands of the Levant" (p. 92). With a word, the Land of Israel and the Glorious Land and the Delightsome Ancestral Land become simply one of the "lands of the Levant"—in the mouth of a person who still sees himself as a Pioneer and even boasts of sacrificing himself on the altar of promoting the clothing trade in the Land.

The character that parallels Rabinovitch, Mittelman (meaning "middleman," "mediator"), is also a former ragamuffin Pioneer who despaired of the hoe. He went to Alexandria, Egypt, and was promoted from a lowly shop clerk to his boss's brother-in-law until he turned into a kind of "shoes of the State," whose "hand extends over the whole land of Egypt"—a Saint Joseph of the shoe trade. The metamorphosis of Mittelman and the assumed metamorphosis of Rabinovich constitute a sharp anti-Zionist contrast to the Zionist ingredients of the novel: those who come to the Land to be reborn, to produce a Hebrew worker from the Jewish merchant, "as the wonder of the butterfly born from the worm" (Alterman), wind up back in the bosom of the Diaspora bourgeois world. And they do it in old-fashioned Jewish ways: someone whose clothes are nice and whose shoes are shiny and whose tongue is smooth won't get lost.

When he goes, Yedidia Rabinovitch leaves behind two "deserted wives," Isaac and Sonya. (They are mirrored later in the characters of the two ex-wives of the marvelous musician Vittorio Godswill—Mira and Masha—who become inseparable after the man abandons them.)

Sonya Zweiering (Sonya "Double-Natured") says of Rabinovitch, in a mood of cynical bitterness, that "in a year or two, he'll return with his boss's daughter, whom he got from her father along with a dowry" (p. 106). As for the narrator, he does not necessarily identify with the Pioneering ideals, nor does he necessarily condemn Mittelman and Rabinovitch for betraying those ideals. Hypocrisy, false piety, and the hollow "pose" stir Agnon's mockery just as they kindled Yosef Haim Brenner's wrath.

Reading between the lines, it is obvious how much Isaac envies Rabinovitch for his descent to Europe, which stirs in Isaac (and in the narrator, who is integrated in his discourse) "thoughts of transgression"—the words spoken in the first-person plural (book 1, chapter 7) by the narrator.

Isaac's longing for bourgeois Europe, for the Austro-Hungarian Garden of Eden (book 1, chapter 7)—a longing that leads him to a tempting vision of stowing away on Rabinovitch's ship back to his native land—constitutes a precise negative image of the idyllic-ecstatic opening paragraph of the novel. Isaac longs here in almost identical terms for the landscapes of his native land. Thus, there are two Delightsome Lands in *Only Yesterday,* so similar they seem to be formed on the same idyllic-arcadian model. In both, "the secret of pastoral charm" is blended with "the secret of bourgeois charm," and both charms turn into one desired brew. The child (Isaac) whose "father" (Rabinovitch) abandons him is filled with a strong yearning to go home. There, in the realm of gemütlichkeit, everyone "sings" and everyone sits comfortably and at ease in some padded existence that— when you were in the small town in Galicia—looked ready and waiting for you in the Land of Israel; and now that you are here in the Land of Israel, it seems to be there, overseas, calling to you to return home to the Austro-Hungary you left behind. The Promised Land of Isaac Kumer's visions is connected not with a change of character or with a change of profession, but with a change of place, with purchasing a ticket to the Garden of Eden "over there." Yet, Isaac is not "torn between two homelands"; he is basically a poor boy who dreams of social, economic, and erotic success—the three forms of success he sees as forever intertwined. Therefore, the Land of Israel Garden of Eden and the Austro-Hungarian Garden of Eden are revealed as two in one, always slipping away to whatever side of the sea you are not on when you fantasize. The erotic subject, the Zionist subject, and the status subject all come together under one petit bourgeois wedding canopy.

Sonya Zweiering is a modern girl, a graduate of a Russian gymnasium, an experienced flirt. While Isaac, "like most of the fellows of Galicia in that generation, . . . was excellent and modest" (p. 90). The female image controlling Isaac's emotional life is the ideal of his mother, who died when he was small. She "appear[s] to him as on Yom Kippur, wearing white garments, her voice full of compassion, [or] . . . sometimes part of her appear[s], like a white hand stretched out to him . . . and it [is] clear to him that there [is] no woman in the world like his mother. And since his mother died, another woman who would come take her place would be modest and pious as his mother" (pp. 90–91). The operative words in this passage are "would come": Isaac, Sleeping Beauty, is waiting for the prince on a white horse to come wake him up with a kiss from his erotic sleep. Like Hirshl in *A Simple Story*, Hemdat in "Hill of Sand," Jacob Rekhnitz in "An Oath of Faith," and Manfred Herbst in *Shira*, Isaac is waiting for a pure and virginal savior whose "clothes [are] always white," bride-white (or sick-white, as in the opening of "In the Prime of Her Life"), and even though she may tarry, he and every other one of these heroes "anticipates every day that she will come."

And later: "Ugly sufferings [do] not afflict him, the frailties of human beings [don't] hurt him, by virtue of his mother who was perfect in her qualities. And even when his faith slacken[s], his modesty [does] not." Erotic realization depends not on taking initiative, but on waiting for the mother's reincarnation ("another woman would come in her place"), and the spouse will have to embody the continuation of the personality of the white, perfect, virginal-regal mother, whose "voice was full of compassion." This suggests that Isaac, like Hirshl in *A Simple Story,* is blocked sexually and yearns for both the thing and its opposite. On the one hand, he wants to blend with the feminine-maternal ideal, and thus, as Bialik says: "You are too pure to be my mate / You are too holy to sit with me / Be a God and angel to me / I will pray to you and worship you." On the other hand, he yearns for sensual realization. Sonya Zweiering may be the least appropriate woman in the world to fill the regal-maternal role. Yet, for a short time, she seems to find some stimulus, some sharp novelty, slight and amusing, precisely in the game that Isaac "invites" in her. She responds and seduces the "excellent and modest" fellow until her caprices are sated and she is ready for another kind of treat.

Despite the clear contrast between the image of Isaac's virginal-regal mother in *Only Yesterday* and Hirshl's fleshly and controlling mother in *A Simple Story,* the mother in each work is the decisive presence in her son's world. Moreover, one in her pure angelic nature and the other in her libido, both have a castrating impact on their sons. It is interesting to compare the "milk" and the "meat" mother figures in Agnon's works with other mother figures of both kinds in Hebrew literature since Agnon—including *Past Perfect* by Yakov Shabtai and *The Book of Internal Grammar* by David Grossman, as well as mother figures in works by Jews in other languages, from Kafka and Isaak Babel to Saul Bellow and Philip Roth. Such a comparison might explain how figures of "the white mother" and "the red mother"—even though they are opposites—inflict similar torments on their sons.

Rabinovitch blows a farewell kiss to Isaac and kisses Sonya goodbye, and the air of the ship is filled with grace: "And the world was white and fresh . . . and something throbs in the air like something a man's soul yearns for" (p. 95). Along with that yearning, Sonya enters Isaac's life, and she "looks like . . . a sick lad" (p. 95)—like a lad and not like a maiden. Because of her short hair? Because of her shape? Or perhaps because the excellent and modest Isaac is allowed to look at a lad and is forbidden to look at a maiden? Or because of a hidden and secret tendency in him (and in her) to exchange roles? In any case, from now on, the entire pattern of relations between Isaac and Sonya is a comic reversal of the stereotypes of male and female roles. And with Rabinovitch, Sweet Foot, and Sonya, almost from the first moment, Isaac tends to embody both a "feminine" role and a "childish" role.

The reader first met Rabinovitch through the twisted sandals he carried on his shoulders to save their soles. And now he appears in patent leather shoes, and his future can be read in the tale of "his twin," Mittelman the shoe king. During the farewell, Sonya climbs onto Rabinovitch's shoes with her shoes to kiss him, a ceremony that upsets the order of anarchic intimacy. Rabinovitch disappears from Isaac's view, from Sonya's view, and from the reader's view when he bends over and wipes the dust of Sonya's shoes from his patent leather shoes with a silk handkerchief. Before his ascent to the Land of Israel, Isaac believed that at the gates of the Land of Israel was a doormat, and that everyone who comes from Exile shakes the dust of Exile off his shoes like a person shaking off a disgusting thing. And here, paradoxically, not as he enters the Land of Israel, but as he leaves it does Rabinovitch shake off of his sparkling shoes both Sonya's love and the dust of the Land of Israel. Both the Land and the woman are revealed in retrospect as ephemeral, minor youthful adventures in the orderly life of a respectable merchant. Wiping the shoe is also Rabinovitch's erasing: erasing the olives and the tomatoes and the hoe and the *Young Laborer* and manual labor and the entire Second Aliya. Rabinovitch's wiping his shoes even before Sonya is out of his sight and before he is out of her sight indicates that their relationship was merely a passing flirtation.

But Isaac Kumer cannot clearly discern the emotional temperature between his friend and his friend's girlfriend—if he could, he would have been spared great torments. Once again, the narrator and the readers exchange a wink behind the hero's back—and at his expense.

As in *A Simple Story* and in Agnon's "Other Faces," and "The Doctor's Divorce," relations between the sexes are expressed by the precise, "tropistic" detailing of body language. Body language becomes the main channel of conveying feelings and emotions, while verbal dialogue is fragmented, hinted at, and sometimes even muttered with the weight of internalized shyness and repression.

|

Sonya and Isaac sit "in silence" in the little boat returning them to the shore from the ship that Rabinovitch departed on (p. 95). This is almost the first time in the novel that an event is conveyed from a consciousness that is neither Isaac's nor the narrator's. Earlier, there was sometimes a hint to the reader of how Isaac looked to the activists of Lemberg or to the old couple on the ship, for example, or of the opinion of the mare Fatima about the Pioneers of the Second Aliya. But here, for the first time, we encounter the internal delivery of a sequence of consciousness that is not Isaac's, but is Sonya's, perhaps because her role is more important than that of Rabinovitch and Leichtfuss, or perhaps because this is the only way the reader can grasp something Isaac could not see—like the fact that Sonya Zweiering is a very experienced girl who is tired of love affairs, or that the rings in her name, like the rings in a tree trunk, indicate years of experience. Her first lover was her father's journalist friend, who removed his rings before he embraced her, and the list includes Rabinovitch, whose minor place in Sonya's heart is revealed to the reader by her thoughts about him. As she parts from him, a parting she sees as final, Sonya isn't thinking of him at all or of her relations with him but is privately browsing "comparatively" in the album of lovers and of men available in Jaffa. She concludes that what's available is too meager and desolate for her. Thus, the reader receives a sufficient explanation for why a "great" girl like Sonya pays heed to "inferior goods" like Isaac. Through her thoughts, Sonya is reflected to the reader as a person with a stunted emotional life. Her former lovers and the candidates whose qualifications she considers do not stir strong feelings in her—no admiration, no longing, not even indignant disappointment—but, at most, a slight disgust.

"Sonya jumped out and climbed up onto dry land as quick and vigorous as a lad. . . . Behind her Isaac got out with the help of three sailors" (p. 96). This is the second time in this chapter that Sonya is compared to a lad, while Isaac is again portrayed as a helpless beauty. Even before the relationship begins, this comic episode captures the role reversal, everything that is to be between Sonya and Isaac, and all that will never be and can never be between them.

"Sonya shook her dress and smoothed its wrinkles" (p. 96). From here to the end of the chapter, the reader should keep his eye on Sonya's hand, where the narrator's eye and perhaps Isaac's eye, too, are stuck. Isaac strictly censors everything his eyes see and his ears hear, and he even censors Sonya herself so much that he sees her not as a girl but as a lad. And yet Sonya dances almost a coquettish dance, a sexy dance, in front of Isaac, that included sniffing the fresh jasmine and throwing it behind her back ("Is that what would be done with Rabinovitch?"), lifting her leg and raising the hem of her dress (while polishing her shoes), and the brushes "the shoeshine man . . . spat into . . . and dipped" (p. 118). Incidentally, "the shoeshine man" portends exactly what Isaac will also do with his "brushes" when the time comes to paint the dog Balak—and the two scenes are similar in several fascinating details (cf. book 2, chapter 14).

Sonya's devotion to the ceremony of polishing her shoes, as the uncomprehending Isaac stands by, seems to express a final ritual of severance from Rabinovitch. Just as he "shook the dust" of Sonya off his shoes a short while ago, so she, after smelling the jasmine flowers and throwing them behind her back one by one, wipes the traces of Rabinovitch off herself, as if to say, Whatever you can do, Rabinovitch, I can do better, either polishing my shoes or "fooling around." Thus, in the language of gestures and signs whose significance she certainly is not aware of, Sonya ends "her conversation" with Rabinovitch and starts her business with Isaac, who stands next to her stunned. He inadvertently passes his hand over his forehead and peeps into his hand, as if seeking the kiss that Sonya stamped on Rabinovitch's forehead when she stood on his sparkling shoes.

Sonya's first words to Isaac might have put off another man who was less dazed: "Those are going out and others aren't coming, and the Land is growing empty" (p. 96). Of course, this is neither the opening of a demographic symposium nor an ideological lament. Sonya is like a person who enters a crowded and bustling café and mutters that there is no one here, meaning that there isn't a man left who is worth looking at, and new ones aren't coming in. Isaac isn't offended because he has no idea what she means.

After the two of them pass by "sailors scurrying to houses of pleasure," among other things, Sonya wisely starts laying a basis for the code of communication that she and Isaac will use from now on, the only channel open to her to get close to Isaac without driving away her prey prematurely: "Next Saturday we'll get a letter from Rabinovitch." As an experienced woman, Sonya senses Isaac's naïveté and virginity, so she assumes the role of "the continuation of Rabinovitch" for Isaac—otherwise, he would have fled from her immediately. Sonya's words "we'll get" create the basis of a partnership and grant a context and seal of approval for another meeting, after next Saturday. Moreover, her words also refer to the fact that Rabinovitch is far away from here and will be far away on Saturday, too, so "permission is granted." All that, along with her jokes about Gorishkin, who mistakenly thought that, when Rabinovitch left, his turn with Sonya had come, are not only calculated manipulative messages, the product of a sharp chess-playing mind, but also signals Sonya broadcasts to Isaac from a half-conscious source to an even less conscious receiver, a message sent at frequencies Isaac cannot receive—at any rate, not with his intelligence.

Sonya's inclination to trap Isaac takes shape in her body and her heart, while she may not understand the reason for every one of her movements and words. But the subtle and detailed text enables the reader to pick up more than the two characters do. This is a masterful portrayal of the connection evolving between two souls, one who is completely unconscious of what is going on and one who has only a dim grasp. One is very childish; the other, despite her experience and manipulative talents, is also childish. The text here is so saturated and "dense" that the narrator does not need any "direct communication" with the reader and never uses the "hotline" he employs in other places in the novel to convey the meaning of events to the reader's awareness at a level the protagonists cannot rise to. The narrator "falls silent," and, on the basis of what is put before him, the reader can restore the sequence of emotions—emotions and not considerations— that motivate Sonya in this scene. Yarkoni left. Rabinovitch left. In Jaffa, what is in store for her is only the repulsive Gorishkin, waiting his turn. But here in front of her is a young and good lamb—and here is also the means to "show" those fellows, to stun them or to punish them.

As she gossips to the dazed Isaac about the people close to her— all of them protagonists of Agnon's story "Hill of Sand"—she incidentally signals to Isaac that this one disgusts her and that one nauseates her, traditional signals of female encouragement. But Isaac cannot pick up the signals: he "[shrinks] before Sonya. All his answers [are] simply yes or no. . . . Even though she isn't important to him, she is important because she is his friend's girlfriend" (p. 97). For the first time, but not the last, this system of defense against his feelings and his passion operates in Isaac: from now on, he will excuse all his meetings with Sonya as meetings with "the emissary of a man like him"—and he secretly appoints Sonya Rabinovitch's "emissary," so that his friendship with his friend obligates him to be friendly with his friend's lady friend. Nevertheless, to the day he dies, Isaac will never get rid of searing guilt for the sin he committed, as it were, against Rabinovitch, and for violating the Commandment "Thou shalt not covet thy neighbor's wife."

Isaac walks around "dazed" at Sonya's side. And "since he wasn't used to women, he walk[s] carefully as if she [is] the daughter of lords and dukes. This behavior amuse[s] Sonya and annoy[s] her"

(p. 97). She asks mockingly: "Is this how you act with a woman back in Galicia? Isaac lower[s] his eyes as he blushe[s] and [says], Never in my life did I talk to a woman, aside from my mother and my sisters" (p. 97).

The end of the affair—Sonya's decision to throw Isaac out of her life—is already inherent here, even before it begins: the fact that Isaac treats Sonya "as if she [is] the daughter of lords and dukes" will make Sonya feel disgust and revulsion toward him, because it opposes "the male convention" that attracts her and was common in Jaffa society in those days. But all that will be disclosed only in the future. For the time being, Isaac's confession of virginity excites Sonya. She doesn't yet have such a specimen in her album of lovers, and his downcast eyes and blushing face and erotic inexperience tempt Sonya so much that her body responds for her: "She look[s] at him and close[s] her eyes. She straighten[s] the two points of her collar and passe[s] her hand over her heart . . . [and] with the flowers in her left hand, Sonya point[s] . . . and [says], Here's where I live" (p. 98). This is a clear and detailed announcement in body language, but Isaac doesn't understand this language and Sonya herself may not register what her body is saying.

And what about Isaac? He who hoped to "shake off . . . the dust of Exile" as soon as his feet touched the soil of the Land, and with a magic wand to change from an erotic lamb to a young lion, expelling gangs and rolling heavy stones off the mouth of wells? Isaac acts strictly according to the dictates of the religious and class code planted deep in his soul: because Sonya is "respectable" and he is "simple"; she is at the top of the communal ladder (a Russian girl) and he is at the bottom (a Galician); she is an educated girl from a good family who graduated from the gymnasium and he was only a poor *heder* boy; she is an angelic creature (a woman) and he is a flesh-and-blood creation (a man); she is Rabinovitch's girlfriend and he is Rabinovitch's tool bearer. For all these reasons, he "shrink[s]," "walk[s] carefully," in short— he knows his low status in the world and lies lower than grass.

|

"Let us return to Isaac. Eight or nine days hadn't passed before Isaac chanced to meet Sonya" (p. 101). After all, the two of them almost arranged to meet after Saturday ("Next Saturday we'll get a letter from Rabinovitch" [p. 96]). In *Only Yesterday,* the word "chanced" should definitely be understood not as deriving from "chance" in the sense of opportunity, but as deriving from "time" in the sense of "fate." There are no "incidental" meetings in this book; fate operates in everything; similarly, Gershon Shaked has noted the importance and meaning of "rendezvous" in Agnon's work.

Isaac and Sonya meet, and from Isaac's point of view, their meeting is possible and forgiven only because "a picture postcard [arrives from Rabinovitch], a sign that he is thinking of us" (p. 101). Sonya, with her sharp sense, carefully maintains the "tacit agreement" and pretends that Rabinovitch and only Rabinovitch is the justification for her meeting with Isaac—as if Rabinovitch's name is a kind of "area code" the two of them have to dial before they make contact with one another. Sonya also carefully presents Rabinovitch's letters and post-cards as if they were addressed both to her and to Isaac, and even when she attributes nostalgia to Rabinovitch, she connects herself to Isaac in his longing: "A sign that he is thinking of us." Thus she includes the two of them, Isaac and herself, in a kind of "association of those deserted by Rabinovitch," and their meetings are camouflaged as regular meetings of that association. Moreover, when she emphasizes that Rabinovitch "is thinking of us," it is as if she presents the permission and blessing of the distant Rabinovitch for her meetings with Isaac.

Envious and mocking, Sonya delivers a lecture to Isaac on the dizzying rise of Mittelman, the king of shoes, Rabinovitch's "double," and as she does, she drags Isaac to the workers' club, where "an intelligent person [can] find tea and a newspaper on a winter night." She doesn't care about the newspaper—she, it seems, is one of the intelligentsia of tea (p. 103).

Sonya tells Isaac of the greatness of Dr. Schimmelmann (whose name means "a moldy man"), who is setting up a Tanakh group (the enlightened Sonya says "Bible" and not "Tanakh"). The doctor's Bible is modernized, and he succeeds in raising the old-fashioned Prophets to the sublime level of "people like you and me." In Schimmelmann's version, the Prophets are much more than simply the chosen of God—they were real journalists, "the orators of their period," and the prophecies are not simply visions but rise almost to the heights of investigative reports in a local newspaper.

Sonya's admiring remarks about her spiritual hero Schimmelmann introduce an amusing comic perspective and indicate the composition of one of Agnon's strategies of humor: between the lines, the narrator invites the reader to laugh at this fool, Schimmelmann, who "speaks like a prophet and researches like a professor" (p. 119). Thus, the narrator secretly and tacitly implicates the reader in a mocking revulsion toward Sonya's intellectual world, a shallow and hollow world "narrow as the world of an ant," filled with vain ideas, famous names, and fashionable calflike admiration. Sonya seems to embody a first omen of what will be called being "in" on the local scene. And here is Isaac in his innocence, naturally awed by the depth of the meditations and the height of the thoughts of this intellectual woman: "Words like Sonya's a person doesn't say unless he has thought about them a lot. And someone who can think like that is endowed with great wisdom" (p. 104).

While the narrator thrusts a sarcastic stiletto into the shallow and fashionable character of Sonya and splits her "guru" apart with his mockery, he treats Isaac's shortsightedness and amazement at hearing the empty blather with forgiving paternalism and humor. (Incidentally, Sonya's shallow and pretentious character here and in other places in *Only Yesterday* is reminiscent of the character of Yael Hayyot in "Hill of Sand" — there too the lover's eyes are unable to see the emptiness of the woman he admires.)

Once again, the dramatic irony common in Agnon operates here: the narrator and the reader understand what the hero does not see, laugh at what the hero takes with abysmal seriousness, chuckle together at what the hero admires. Over the heads of his protagonists, the narrator broadcasts intellectual, ideological, emotional, and erotic signals they cannot intercept, while the reader is invited to be amused that he is given, all together, both the right message and the hero's jammed reception that leads to incorrect or sometimes touching responses: "Now that he heard Sonya talking . . . things . . . were like a new teaching to him; . . . it's nicer to hear things from a living person, from a young woman, than to hear them from irascible speakers" (p. 105). And here, incidentally, Isaac admits to himself for the first time that Sonya is a young woman — and not only an emissary or a terminal of the distant Rabinovitch.

If Isaac's intellectual world can be defined as a "naïve synthesis," it is tempting to say that Sonya's intellectual world (as on pp. 103–4, and elsewhere) is a "nonnaïve synthesis": Sonya is involved in the Pioneering effort and in the experience of the Land of Israel without being involved in them. She knows her way around. She can quote what some activist said, and she is an expert in local gossip. She knows the "right people" and goes around in the "right places." All sides in all arguments seem weak to her—she sticks her nose into all of them a bit, and on every issue she can chatter fluently but without emotional obligation or intellectual preference. She knows everything, and she is a little contemptuous of everything, as fashion dictates. If only some "Mr. Shoes" or "Mr. Clothes" would come along and take her away from here to Europe, to "the big world," she would follow him without a backward glance. The sources of her livelihood are an allowance sent her by her father from Russia and some temporary work as a substitute kindergarten teacher. She revolves around the edges of the theater. At the moment, Isaac is for Sonya "what there is." She enjoys his solemn and eager attention to every word she speaks, just as Rabinovitch and Leichtfuss enjoyed his innocent admiration.

> Isaac didn't join any party. It's enough for Isaac that he's a Zionist. . . . As the son of poor, wretched, and ineffectual parents, Isaac grew up in a world where all people are conditioned and stand from their birth in the place where their fortune put them, higher ones on top and lower ones on the bottom. If success favors a person, he rises. The more he's favored, the more he rises. And the idea that people can change the laws of nature . . . was not only inconceivable to him, he even poked fun at it. Back then in his hometown he made fun of the socialists.

This is a fascinating paragraph, for one thing because the narrator almost completely gives up the distance between himself and his hero and presents the essence of a credo. Pioneering, revolutionary Zionism not only wanted to bring Jews from Exile to the Land of Israel, but also to change them fundamentally, to cultivate in the Land "a new Jewish person" in a new, equal, and classless society. Isaac (and the narrator) are not concerned with any of that. Even though Isaac is excited by the opportunity for "a new beginning," for Pioneering and working the soil, he is fundamentally a conservative fellow who accepts the class hierarchy of bourgeois Austro-Hungary without any reflection or rejection. Austro-Hungary is considered a cosmic model, hence eternal and indestructible: the Delightsome Land of the Jewish homeland on the soil of Canaan must be built not only in its image and according to its pattern, but also as a kind of metaphysical creation (as indicated by the words "laws of nature," which appear in the combined discourse of Isaac and the narrator).

Here, too, Isaac is revealed as an instinctive "Herzlian" Zionist or a "general Zionist," who, for some time, unfortunately comes upon members of Po'alei Tsion and "The Young Worker" who profess to be tempted by "the laws of nature." It is no accident that Isaac Kumer does not reach the level of agricultural worker, despite his religious-messianic excitement, in the style of Reb Yudel, on his visit to Eyn Ganim. And it is no accident that Isaac at last "slips" into the bosom of the Old Yishuv in Jerusalem: Isaac's Zionism—instinctive and not intellectual—is a Herzlian Zionism that longs to establish a polite, new Vienna in the Land of Israel. But in complete contrast to Herzl, Isaac also has a religious and joyous component inherited from Reb Yudel, so that his ideal Land of Israel–Austro-Hungary should also be steeped in "Yiddishkeyt." In short, the fellow who rebelled against the world of his Galician town and departed his father's home and ascended to the Land of Israel to be a new person is revealed—under a thin layer of Pioneering–Land of Israel paint—to be an outstanding and loyal representative of his town, his father's house, and his empire. According to Isaac, the desired change is not, God forbid, annulling the social ladder or turning it upside down. On the contrary, the social ladder is considered one of "the laws of nature." The desired change is that he will find himself rising and climbing up the ladder, leaving the others behind and maybe even secretly enjoying their envy. (It is interesting to compare this with the deeply childish credo of Hirshl [*A Simple Story,* p. 10]: "There were those who claimed that the whole problem with the world was its being divided into the rich and the poor. Indeed, that was a problem. Certainly, though, it was not the main one. The main problem was that everything was so painful.")

This is Isaac's implied credo, and almost immediately afterward, a figure appears (in Sonya's words) who realizes that credo, and who will be portrayed as Isaac's "ideal I": Rabinovitch's room is now inhabited by Mr. Jonathan Orgelbrand (whose name means "God granted him a burning organ"). This gentleman secretly hopes to take Rabinovitch's place in Sonya's bed, just as he has taken his room. This Austro-Hungarian clerk, far from the life of laborers and Pioneers, is condemned to an incurable erotic sterility. Isaac will frequently cross paths with Orgelbrand, who is both a parallel figure and another candidate for a father figure. His bourgeois prosperity makes Isaac jealous, his manners are delicately European, yet his organ burns and is not extinguished.

In book 1, chapter 8, Sonya and Isaac's conversation is once again about Rabinovitch. It seems to be a simple conversation between two people extolling the virtues of an absent mutual friend. In truth, in its subtext, Sonya sends Isaac a sharp signal: I am free; Rabinovitch won't come back, and if he does come back he won't be angry, and if he is angry, so what, his place in my life was quite limited from the start, and now it is all over. Isaac both receives and does not receive this message, and both replies and does not reply in the subtext of the conversation: Rabinovitch will surely return. You have to wait for him and remain faithful. The two of us have to remain faithful to him. At most, as an expression of our faithfulness, we, you and I, can meet from time to time and "unite" with Rabinovitch's "memory," or "bring up the outlines of his figure together." Sonya replies both openly and in code: even if Rabinovitch does come back, he surely will bring with him "his boss's daughter whom he received with a dowry"—and you and I are free and clear. Isaac answers this, mostly between the lines, that Rabinovitch "is loyal as gold" and has descended to Europe only to return as a prince and take Sonya as his princess in the chariot of gold she deserves.

The comical aspect of these exchanges is latent in the fact that the woman and the man once again exchange roles attributed to each of them by the stereotype. The woman pleads with the man to hold out his hand to her because there is no obstacle, while the man defends himself on behalf of the values of modesty and loyalty and insists on not touching her and on reminding her that she is not free. Since none of Sonya's coaxing works, "she place[s] both her hands on his as a gesture of reconciliation. Isaac blushe[s] and drop[s] his eyes, as if, in the touch of Sonya's hands, there [is] some affront to Rabinovitch's honor. She glance[s] at him and [is] puzzled" (p. 107). She is puzzled because she has already tasted various and strange men in her life, but never such a pleasant and modest virgin, and she seems increasingly fascinated by this sleeping beauty who blushes and lowers his eyes at the touch of a woman's hand on his for the first time since his mother died—and he thinks he blushes only because of the offense to Rabinovitch.

|

Desolation, desperation, and painstaking artificial rejoicing prevail in the workers' club. The whole description is very close to parallel images in the work of Brenner and Reuveni and in the memoirs of Shlomo Tsemakh, Shlomo Lefkowitz-Lavie, and other members of the

Second Aliya. But Agnon also unfurls a broad humoristic gamut here: a sardonic mordancy toward Gorishkin, the narrator's mortal enemy; a warm and compassionate humor verging on repressed pathos toward the working fellow wasting away with hunger and disease; a parody of Ossip the anarchist, that Lenin who was destined from birth to lead a world revolution and is somehow trapped in remote Palestine like a beached whale; an absurd humor in the two inseparable ex-wives of the marvelous musician Vittorio Godswill; a Platonic mention of Madame Tsina Dizengoff; buffoonery in the shape of Falk Spaltleder and the poet Tshernipolski; and a loving humorous caress for Yosef Aronovitch, editor of *The Young Laborer.* Incidentally, a great rule in *Only Yesterday* (with a few exceptions) is that whomever Agnon appreciates—Aronovitch, Brenner, Gordon, Simha Ben-Zion, Malkhov, and a few others—enters the novel under his real name and sometimes even wins a "stylistic concession," a partial exemption from the unifying stylization Agnon spreads over most of his characters. Aronovitch, Brenner, and Gordon get special permission to speak in *Only Yesterday* almost as they spoke or wrote in real life.

The chapter "In the Workers' Club" emphasizes a grotesque aspect of the Second Aliya: many Pioneers, it turns out—a greater number than those who came to the Land to build and be rebuilt in it— came in fact "to write and be written in it." All kinds of Gorishkins ("bitterman") and Pizmonis ("songman") and Tshernipolskis ("black polish," and a swipe at the poet Tshernikhovsky) sit and dream not exactly about building the Land, but about the praise and success that will fall to their lot as the authors of the great novel on the building of the Land. At any rate, in the workers' club of *Only Yesterday,* there are four or five writers, several activists, some eccentric peripheral figures, one or two local belles, and a naïve and very eager painter who behaves "like a petit bourgeois on a holiday." Into the midst of all these comes a single unemployed worker, who is hungry and sick.

|

"Has he really not spoken with a girl in his life, or is he just saying that to make himself interesting" (p. 115), Sonya wonders to herself, and thus she exposes not Isaac's soul but the face of her own social circle, the one revealed in the workers' club, where men (and women) say such and so, appear such and so, solely to "make themselves interesting."

"For no reason, as we people of the Land of Israel say" (p. 115), Sonya parted from Isaac even before they came to her house. Although the narrator includes himself in "we people of the Land of Israel," under that ironic sentence is its absolute negation: no leaf falls to the ground "for no reason." A causal and fateful network is spread over every living soul in this novel and is already spread at Isaac's feet. This is the causal network that connects the old couple he met on the ship to the ship's assistant chef who gave him a bucket of paint and a brush to the dog Balak, who would not have suffered what he did and would not have done what he did if not for the old couple and the assistant chef and the brush. The narrator who says here, as if in astonishment, "without any reason" is the same one who will say the veiled words "Not every day are a man's actions in his own hands" (p. 125) and "But the open wish is undermined by the hidden cause" (p. 128).

"A few days later," Isaac does meet Sonya, and he has a ready-made excuse, for he has received a letter from Rabinovitch. Sonya reads the letter, and the narrator lets her emerge for a moment through the stylish wrappings and say "ohhh" about that Rabinovitch who went to metropolitan Europe where he found nothing but bad wine in Brindisi and sailors fighting over a whore (p. 116). And she immediately adds, opening the door wide to Isaac and freeing him from every trace of worry: "At any rate, our Rabinovitch isn't willing to fight over a girl" (p. 116). At long last, Isaac gets that Mack truck of a hint and drops his head in embarrassment; yet Sonya doesn't turn her face away from him, and he is even more embarrassed. "But his embarrassment was divided, half of it tremulous and half of it rejoicing" (p. 116).

Like the scene in the café in Lemberg, and like the scene in the despairing workers' café in Jaffa, this scene is also made up of quick "cuts," and the reader is invited in turn, at every sentence or two, to see Sonya through Isaac's eyes and Isaac through Sonya's eyes and the two of them through the narrator's eyes. Sonya leads Isaac for a walk like a pet dog, and Isaac is constantly impressed by her importance: "Passersby ask how she is. Some of them are teachers, some of them are writers, some of them are clerks. And though they are noted people whose name you find in the newspapers, she replies to their greetings rather casually" (p. 116). Sonya's indifference to these famous people raises Isaac's admiration of her to the skies. And thus, softened and ripened, she brings him at last to her room.

Isaac's eyes wander over the room, first to the windows as if he's seeking an escape hatch, then over the furniture; finally they stare at Sonya's bed, "covered by a colorful blanket embroidered with a yellow dog carrying a stick in his mouth" (p. 117).[18] The box under the bed is also yellow. Just as in the closeness of Sweet Foot and his dog, here too the dog "leads" to Eros. More precisely, the dog leads to erotic vigor and erotic control and discipline. Yellow is the color of hatred. And a stick is not only a famous and quintessential phallic symbol, but also a tool for beating.

"Whatever he saw in the room, he saw only by short glances, split into several details" (p. 117). Those glances are enough to present Isaac with a new and uncensored Sonya, far from the "sick lad" Isaac forces himself to see in her at their first meeting. This is a Sonya who "hides her secret," a Sonya who "stands erect," a Sonya who "brings her dress to life," a Sonya whose "dress gambols on her, as if it too were alive" (p. 117)—perhaps one of the most pungent and refined erotic descriptions in Hebrew literature.

Now the text presents a full list of Jaffa belles, most of whom are familiar to the reader from "Hill of Sand" and "An Oath of Faith," all of them more beautiful than Sonya but without her sexuality. The description of Sonya here is reminiscent of nurse Shira, "the one he called Nadia . . . her name was actually Shira" (*Shira,* p. 4; and cf. the description there, pp. 3–4). Like Sonya, Shira is a combination of small defects that do not diminish her attractiveness but indeed enhance it. (Incidentally, the same is true of the blemishes of Toni Hartman for her husband, Michael, in "Other Faces," in the sentence that begins: "He looked at her and saw her as he had not looked at her and had not seen her for a long time.") And if that is not enough, the narrator calls on Sonya's father's friend, that dirty old man who taught her Hebrew and who removed his rings before he embraced her, to testify to her sweeping sexuality. Just as in Agnon's "The Doctor's Divorce"—"the story of a man whose mistress forced him to marry her. He went and gathered for the ceremony all her lovers who had lived with her before her marriage"[19]—in precisely the same way, the narrator gathers here the shade of every one of Sonya's lovers the first time Isaac comes under her roof: the Russian journalist, Grisha, Yarkoni, Gorishkin, and Rabinovitch. "Sonya passe[s] her right hand over her head and smoothe[s] her hair. Her hairdo is masculine" (p. 118). And even though her hairdo is masculine—perhaps because of that—"when Isaac saw Sonya on the sea, she looked like a lad, now he sees her as a maiden whom our comrade Rabinovitch liked" (p. 118). "Our comrade Rabinovitch" is attached to the word "maiden" without a comma, to indicate Isaac's panic and his internal flight from what his eyes see and his flesh feels. The very same thing happened a moment before, when "Isaac sits before Sonya, because he is the friend of Rabinovitch who is Sonya's friend" (p. 118). These are Isaac's last barricades.

From now on, the masculine maiden presents to the feminine-virginal lad a precise and detailed dance of seduction: it is the tiny tropisms that build the sensual density in this paragraph. In nature, it is the male who performs the seduction ritual to win the favors of the female. Here, it is Sonya who bends down under the sofa and stands erect on tiptoe, walks around, unpeels, and once again leans over and stoops. Obviously, whatever Isaac "saw in the room he saw only by short glances, split into several details."

And from dance to food: not only does Sonya offer Isaac oranges but she also peels the oranges for him, lest he is too shy to peel them himself. And not only does she slowly remove the orange peels, but she also agrees to open and slice and offer the orange. In that peeling and slicing, as with the apple of Eve, there is a pungent element of seduction, as well as a certain maternal instinct that Isaac apparently stirs in Sonya's heart. She longs to feed the shy, hungry child, and to satisfy him. This impulse does not contradict the erotic message but rather intertwines with it, as if to say: Don't worry, I agree to do what you are afraid of or don't know how to do, and you can remain passive, and you don't have to understand what's being said, either. In the middle of this oedipal scene is Sonya's promise of abundance: "Eat, Mr. Kumer, eat, said Sonya softly; there's a lot here" (p. 118). Isaac opens up—or is opened up—and tells Sonya about his "first time," about the first and only emotion for oranges he had experienced so far, an emotion connected—of course—to the angelic figure of his mother. The orange, which serves here as a distinct erotic "conductor" between Sonya and Isaac, also serves as a connecting object between the only two women in his life so far. The whole scene might be called "The Love of Oranges."

Of course, in the subtext, Isaac and Sonya exchange messages they are not conscious of, and thus the great charm of this "dense" fragment. Isaac responds hesitantly, fearfully to Sonya's seduction of oranges, as if to say: Don't give me too much lest you won't have any left for yourself, as happened to my beloved mother, who gave all she had and so we lost her. Thus Isaac makes Sonya his mother's heir, and the erotic orange combines with the orange of childhood latent in his mother's death. Everything is woven here into an intense and delicate texture: the puritanical childhood where love is doled out in scant portions, the religious idealism, the figure of the mother as angel and also as obstacle, the orange of pleasures, the mother granting without reckoning until she is destroyed and doesn't exist, Isaac's "first time" in its full oedipal sense, and also the great contrast between the Land and Exile. An embarrassed conversation begins between Isaac and Sonya, ostensibly about the prices of fruit and vegetables there as opposed to here, a trite and insipid subject. But in fact, when Sonya emphasizes that there, in Exile, potatoes are cheap and oranges are rare and hard to get, while here it's the opposite, and anyone who wants an orange just has to stretch out his hand and take whatever he likes—she is signaling to Isaac that what is absolutely forbidden in Exile is permitted and easy and common in the Land.

Everything is connected in this scene to the comprehensive system of motives with its center in the ceremony of peeling the orange and slicing it, and the pleasure of eating it in Sonya's room, under the eyes of the embroidered yellow dog with a stick in his mouth, who "lies" silently on Sonya's bed like a dreadful Cerberus guarding the gates of Hell. Nevertheless, the emotional, motivational, erotic, and associative abundance in this chapter is all disguised masterfully behind a banal, embarrassed conversation about the price of oranges, which are a thousand percent cheaper in the Land than they are in the grayish Exile bound to potatoes. As Sonya suddenly says to herself casually, when she recalls what the priest's wife told her: "Sometimes you find perfect wisdom in simple speech" (p. 119). And what does Isaac do after the sin of the orange he committed with Sonya? Once again, cautious movements flicker like signals indicating what's going on in the depths: Isaac wipes his hands "and pick[s] up a Bible from the table," like a person hurrying to be purified from his sin and rushing to repent. He was fed an orange, was tempted and ate, wiped himself, and "ran" to the Bible.

|

"The moon stood in the sky and the citrus groves were fragrant and the sea uttered its voice, not the voice of mighty waters, but the voice of a quiet humming" (p. 119). This sentence, like many sentences in *Only Yesterday*, is made of three linked parts and two opposing parts ("not . . . but"). The five links are well balanced, almost rhythmic (seven to ten syllables in each one), with a penultimate ending to the first two links and an ultimate accent on the last three. This is the general texture of the novel: a harmonic, calm weave presents a stable, orderly world, even when it is horrible. The language is very sensual: each of the five links appeals to one of the senses—the first to the sense of sight; the second to the sense of smell; and the last three to the sense of hearing. The negated connotation, "the voice of mighty waters," leads the reader from one sound—"The Lord on high is mightier than the noise of many waters, yea, than the mighty waves of the sea" (Ps. 93:4)—to another, "a still small voice" (1 Kings 19:12).

A detailed examination of a single sentence of landscape description, therefore, can indicate that the whole text of *Only Yesterday* is steeped in fragments of atmosphere as much as in descriptions of overt and covert human contact.

Nature often serves as a metaphor for frames of mind. When Isaac walks on the nocturnal paths in the sands of Jaffa on his way back from Sonya's room, even the moon acts like Sonya and plays a coquettish game with him: "The moon played by itself. It hid between the clouds and shone through them" (p. 120). Since Sonya created in Isaac a kind of sexual orange conditioning, the oranges in the nocturnal grove he passes on his way also coax him to pleasure, as if reminding him that this is no town in Exile; here his desire can be found in abundance, and here the abundance is permitted, stretch out your hand and touch it, and the owner of the grove won't scold you. The owner of the grove in this description is none other than Rabinovitch's "representative," who allows Isaac to enjoy the fruit of his grove.

Isaac's envy of Rabinovitch a few weeks before because of his trip to Europe and the Austro-Hungarian nostalgia that assaulted him when his friend traveled, disappear as if they had never existed because the "owner of the grove" came out "and allowed" Isaac his orange grove.

Chapter 11, "Mutations and Permutations," opens with Isaac returning from work, putting on his best clothes, and going for a walk—or more precisely, deceiving himself that he is only going for a walk. "By chance," Sonya comes toward him, "her light shirt flutters over her heart and a new hat is on her head, a girl's hat that gives her face the bloom of a handsome girl. She too went out early, just like Isaac" (p. 125). Isaac does not yet allow himself to make a date with his friend's girlfriend, and they have to wait for a letter from Rabinovitch to give them a pretext for a meeting of "those deserted by Rabinovitch" or else to arrange to meet without arranging to meet and to anticipate and go out at the same time and "bump into" each other in the street and start with the requisite "area-code dialing": What does Rabinovitch write?

A wonderful example of a "sentence of retreat" appears in their conversation, a sentence that starts with Isaac and Sonya but turns hastily in the middle to the figure of Rabinovitch to receive a seal of approval for the communication between these who meet: "Great was Sonya's joy when she found Isaac, for a letter had come from Rabinovitch" (p. 125). Or "Isaac was fond of those hours when he strolled with Sonya and chatted about Rabinovitch. If Rabinovitch isn't here, his mate is" (p. 126)—this too is a perfect "sentence of retreat." And so is this: "Isaac Kumer and Sonya Zweiering walk together because he is Rabinovitch's friend and she is Rabinovitch's girlfriend" (p. 126). In the first example, the sentence is turned and retreats with the word "for"; in the third example, the sentence retreats with the word "because." Incidentally, at the beginning of the book, long before Isaac meets Sonya, the narrator used a "sentence of retreat" to shape his hero's censorious awareness: "And then again, Isaac began musing on girls, and not because he was fond of them, but because of his sisters" (p. 25).

The seemingly honest narrator is willing to contribute supporting evidence for Isaac's position, even though it isn't true. Thus, the narrator says: "Since they came upon one another, they . . . went for a stroll" (p. 125). As usual, he goes along with the white lie Isaac tells himself to avoid the tragic, Brennerish confrontation with an awful tangle of puritanical, religious, cultural, class, and—especially—oedipal prohibitions: Rabinovitch is like a father to Isaac, and Sonya is like . . . a mother.

"For Sonya was a girl from Russia and read Russian stories that make troubles endearing and make the poor precious. But Isaac was a Galician fellow from a poor family who were ashamed of their poverty" (p. 127). This is how the narrator, Isaac's defender, explains Isaac's tendency to lie a little bit and prettify his father's house for Sonya, as well as to improve his class "pedigree" a little. But the contrast contained in this paragraph cannot be reconciled. It is a time bomb that will destroy the contact shaping up between Isaac and Sonya, and the collapse of that contact is already indicated. It is the contrast between, on the one hand, a Tolstoyan-Narodnikan, antibourgeois, "discarded" romanticism that is fond of the poor and especially of ragamuffins, as in the song: "Tattered are we, in rags are we," or "whether I have bread or not, what's the difference"; and on the other hand, a petit bourgeois romanticism whose bases are "pedigree," "practicality," and "respectability." This profound contrast between Sonya's education and values and Isaac's is the source of "the comedy of errors" that is revealed in the pages that follow. Isaac, the uneducated, childish, rustic son of a destitute shopkeeper, charms Sonya as he is and stirs feminine, maternal, and "Narodnik" emotions in her, for he grants her a nice opportunity "to descend to the masses." Isaac, who doesn't understand any of this, irons and embellishes and "paints" himself to be worthy of a "match" with a lady whose value in the class stock market "is out of his price range."

But the more Isaac irons and improves himself for Sonya, the more he loses his charm in her eyes. As his "exotic" attraction as a pauper, as an authentic "peripheral lad," fades away, the decree is inevitable: "The open wish is undermined by the hidden cause" (p. 128). In the long run, there can be no synthesis between the man of the naïve synthesis and the woman of the nonnaïve synthesis.

|

One more searing flicker of guilt for his sin against "Thou shalt not covet"—and Isaac and Sonya become lovers. Out of Isaac's guilt, the dog Balak will be born, who is the embodiment not only of Eros in this novel, as many critics think, but also of all of Isaac's sins: for his "sin" of deserting his family and not bothering to support them and transgressing against "Hide not yourself from your own flesh"; and for his sin against Zionism, for he came to work the Land and to build it, and he found satisfaction in covering it—and his life—with a layer of paint; and for his sin—in his eyes—against Rabinovitch and Sonya, for he transgresses against "Thou shalt not covet" and "Thou shalt not commit adultery."

Isaac only seems different from most of the tormented heroes in the generation called, for some reason, "the Generation of the Revival," those miserable wretches who abandoned God for a woman and for love. They did not attain love, and they lost God, and they ended up lost from both faith and love. They are the fellows of the "Scroll of Fire" and Bialik's other poems, the heroes of Feyerberg, Nomberg, Berdichevski, Brenner, and others, heretics haunted by sin, licentious men devoured by inhibitions. Isaac only seems different from those heroes, whose lives were made a hell by torments of love and sexual distress. The dog Balak will show that, despite their differences, Isaac is the taciturn and childish brother of Jeremiah Feyerman, Ezekiel Hefetz, and others.

The description of Isaac and Sonya's " wedding night," when the lamp is lit and not lit, and Isaac sits and reads a book of tales that are fiction or not fiction, and the door is open or not open, and Sonya suddenly appears with "her tongue . . . between her lips as if she were licking them" (p. 129)—this description is a gem of subtle and precise shaping, a sketch that hints at the consummation of physical love between a virginal, erotically illiterate male and a female professor of love (and, to borrow an image from the previous chapter, the first love-making of an orange and a potato). Isaac's thoughts and feelings are expressed in restrained sentences, sentences that play the innocent, as Isaac tries not to understand what Sonya wants. He is polite with her and yet is ashamed of his politeness, until finally he gives in and lies on the bed, solely for orthopedic reasons: "since it is more comfortable to lie down than to sit with no support, he stretche[s] out on the bed" (p. 129) and waits for Sonya "to come" and have her way with him. Here, too, is a comic reversal of the stereotypical role of the man and the behavior "reserved" for the woman. But this is not the main issue; rather, it is the "operative paragraph," which starts with the words "Her hands inflamed his hands and his heart" (p. 130) and ends with a striking oedipal emphasis on the words "his mother," stressing the fact that Sonya's kiss "was not a virgin kiss" (p. 130). And incidentally, the one expression of the delicacy in the description is that it refrains from saying that Sonya was not a virgin and is content to say only that her kiss was not virginal.

The depiction of the wedding night of Isaac and Sonya, with her "double ring," stresses the profound religious infrastructure of *Only Yesterday* and its hero. Sonya comes to Isaac's room disheveled, enflamed, her tongue, etc., and conquers Isaac's stunned body. As expected, she is the active one, the conqueror and "predator," and he—as usual—is passive, so obedient and submissive that he grants Sonya "the kiss that had been preserved in his mouth ever since the hour his mother died" (p. 130). Yet Isaac also works a small miracle, like the miracle of the coffeehouse in Lemberg and the miracle of the coffeehouse in Jaffa and the miracle of the group of workers in the settlement. Once again, the spoon of honey sweetens the barrel of tar. Once again, that excellent and modest Lamed-Vovnik manages to "paint" the act of love with the tint of his purity and innocence. It is he, the inexperienced, and not Sonya, who has already had many men and has "a tongue between her lips," who calls the tune of the lovemaking. Sonya only seems to be dominant in this scene. It is not Sonya who breaks through the fences of Isaac's naïveté, but Isaac who renews at that moment something of Sonya's forgotten naïveté. All that happens between them happens with delight, à la Isaac, and not with the voluptuous licentiousness that Sonya brought to his room.

After midnight, when Isaac escorts Sonya home, nature—as usual—takes on a metaphorical role and hints at what has happened in Isaac's bed: "the sandy ground of Jaffa, by day it digs underneath you and by night it appears like fine silk. The sea is fragrant and its waves rock pleasantly" (p. 130). Thus, the sand and the sea and the waves become erotic relay stations. But Isaac's dread of sin and his guilt feelings don't relent; he sees the light of a distant ship and immediately recalls Rabinovitch, "Sonya's boyfriend," and calms himself with the thought that Rabinovitch is certainly not on that ship.

The next day, when Isaac meets Sonya, he feels two shames: "one, that he had disgraced Sonya and two, that he had disgraced their friend" (p. 130).

In chapter 12, we are told that "Isaac changed his ways. He began to be fussy about his clothes" (p. 131), and so on. The honeymoon is still going strong. Isaac finds in Sonya or imagines that he finds in her "a mother and a sister," and Sonya finds in Isaac an infant to quench her maternal thirst and a lover to torment with her female desires and "a disadvantaged pauper" to chill her Tolstoyan ardor. Just as Isaac seeks a father figure in many of the men in the novel, so he moves from one mother image to another. But, already, "the open wish is undermined by the hidden cause": the more Isaac endows Sonya with the charming intentions of a petit bourgeois housewife, the less he embodies the masculine image she wants.

The scene in Café Hermon (book 1, chapter 12), one of the wittiest feuilletons in the literature of the Second Aliya, once again emphasizes—among other things—the depth of Isaac's tendency to ingratiate himself. For example, Isaac feasts his admiring eyes on "famous people all Zionists talk about" (p. 133), and he is sorry that the Zionists of his hometown can't see him "in such honor." He worships Sonya, "who converses with these famous people, and even with the writers, as if they were her friends. Before Isaac ascended to the Land, he had to make do with pictures of the writers, and today he sees a living writer" (p. 133), like Simha Ben-Zion, whom Isaac admires especially for his suit and his poetic cravat. He also sees a living social activist, like Meir Dizengoff, "wearing a light jacket buttoned up to his neck, and on his head is a hard black hat" (p. 133). This adherent of well-known men, this fervent groupie, "asks himself, Can it be that these people sipping lemonade are the ones you read about in the newspapers?" (p. 162). This is the spiritual world of the Hasid who sits forever in his small hometown and worships the holy picture of the Rebbe and now has made a pilgrimage and sees the Rebbe alive and in person and is amazed to see that the holy Rebbe sips lemonade like everybody else. Once again, Isaac's amazement or wonder is obvious, for good or bad. For example, a pious Zionist must not profane the holy and say that Meir Dizengoff is a fat man. Therefore, the narrator weaves his voice into the voice of the hero and states piously that "Dizengoff sits down on a willow chair and his body fills the seat" (p. 134).

Isaac gradually "paints" his past, his family, and his father's house so as to see himself as a "match" worthy of Sonya. Nevertheless, he is gnawed by guilt for not doing anything to relieve his family's severe poverty, and that feeling is intensified by his father's letters. Yet, even when he can afford to send support to his family, he invests every "extra penny" in things to reinforce in Sonya's eyes his image as the son of a well-to-do family and "a fellow from a good home." In fact, that is what makes him ridiculous in her eyes: "Of all the craftsmen in Jaffa, nobody is dressed like Isaac" (p. 137).

Isaac's behavior is emphasized in the contrast between him and one of his "idealized doubles," the respectable official Jonathan Orgelbrand, who, since childhood, has borne the yoke of supporting his distant family. At first, he supported his father, and now he "spends most of his money on various relatives who are no longer related to him" (p. 122).

Isaac becomes a supercilious and sybaritic fellow and is even satisfied with his work, as if he had forgotten his sin against the ideal of building the Land and working the soil. The excuses he uses to justify to himself his painting and his job are reminiscent of the transparent pretexts of Rabinovitch and Mittelman, Pioneers of fine clothes and fine footwear. Isaac's pretexts emphasize the symbolic contrast between "building" and "painting," between "we came to the Land to build and be rebuilt there," on the one hand, and "to paint and be painted there," on the other.[20] A suggested and fateful vision emerges here: Isaac, whose "hand is as light as his soul and his soul is as light as his hand" (p. 138), jests and paints funny "pictures." The narrator himself seems amazed that Isaac, "with nine measures of grief poured over his face" (p. 138), is joking. And he explains that "human beings are wont to change, like those walls he is painting" (p. 139). It is as if one series of the decisive questions of the whole work is casually asked here: is painting or painting oneself considered a change? If so, is it an imaginary change, or an essential change? If we say that the wall he was painting was changed essentially, then according to the simile in that quoted sentence, human beings can also change their nature. But if painting or painting oneself is merely "a change of coat," then this rule applies to both the imagined and the imaginary, to walls and to human beings—including Isaac Kumer. The next time Isaac jests and paints "funny paintings"—on the dog's skin—he will participate with his own hands in a revolution of the wheel of fate and will set in motion a decisive link in the chain of circumstances that leads to his own dreadful end.

"By now Isaac has forgotten the purpose of his ascent to the Land of Israel" (p. 139). This sounds like the mocking excuse that justifies the activists of Lemberg, but more than that, it reveals the nakedness of their hypocrisy: "At first, the Land of Israel was the end of all ends for them, yet when they saw that the end was distant and hard, . . . they traded the distant and hard for the close by and easy" (p. 12). From a religious perspective, as soon as a person forgets the end, it doesn't matter what he does and doesn't do. If the narrator weaves his voice into Isaac's voice when he justifies himself—"In every single thing, a Jew carries out his mission" (p. 139), so "there's no difference if he plows and sows or mixes paints" (p. 170)—once again there seems to be almost "no difference" between Isaac's excuses and Rabinovitch's excuses and the excuses of the Zionist activists in Lemberg. The internal argument Isaac conducts with the old man on the ship is renewed, in which Isaac assumed a perfect religious position on the issue of "all the Children of Israel are comrades," while the Orthodox old man defended a realistic and pragmatic opinion. Isaac, who supports the Pioneers who are poorer than he, practices what he preached in that argument.

Isaac takes his mind off his father's letters because "they muddy the spirit" (p. 141). Every evening, after he comes home from work, "he has to prepare for Sonya" (p. 141). Of course, this Isaac who "prepares" himself is ridiculous, preening in the ragamuffin-Pioneering Jaffa of the Second Aliya for Sonya, "who is fond of the poor and values poverty" and loathes middle-class propriety. But because Isaac and Sonya are still on their honeymoon and the story is still taking place in an erotic Paradise, the narrator's humor toward his hero is still tolerant. Yet the erotic Paradise has a dog (as does Sweet Foot's Paradise), peeping out of Sonya's blanket. Once again the novel emphasizes the strange connection between Eros and a dog, and between control of dogs and control of women. Women make pilgrimages to Leichtfuss and "sit" with him until he tells them, "Thus far, my sister, from now on, this man wants to scratch his foot" (p. 73), and they take off and then creep back to him. With women as with the dog, Leichtfuss follows a custom of amused mastery (book 1, chapter 5). This issue re-emerges in the figure embroidered on Sonya's blanket of the yellow dog carrying the stick. And it has a somnambulistic continuation in the episode of Isaac returning happy and good-hearted from his lovemaking with Sonya and meeting an Arab guard (book 1, chapter 12).

The guard is "a poor and wretched Arab who has nothing but his dog" (p. 141). He tells Isaac that his previous dog, which was stolen from him, had a hide as brown as a doe's. And the humble Isaac assumes a superiority with him: "Brown skin you want? Tomorrow, you'll have a brown dog" (p. 172). Or a red one. Or another color. The stunned guard sees Isaac as the owner of a harem: "a kennel of dogs you have?" (p. 141). And Isaac, arrogant and smug as a two-bit Leichtfuss, chuckles at him: "Not even the tail of a dog do I have" (p. 141). The guard asks if Isaac conjures up dogs by magic. Isaac replies: "I can make you a green dog" (p. 141). But what Isaac means by "make" is not "make" but only paint, and the whole episode is fascinatingly close to the core of the novel—the contrast between making and painting, between renewal and ostensible renewal. One day, again in a moment of excessive haughtiness, Isaac will realize this jest and "paint" a dog. The amusing conversation between Isaac and the Arab guard is another harbinger of the episode of Balak.

As the two of them are laughing, Isaac also tells the guard about a silk dog carrying a stick in his mouth—the dog on Sonya's blanket. The guard says: "Such a dog doesn't bite and such a stick doesn't beat" (p. 141) and also "I would take the stick out of the dog's teeth and hit the dog with it" (pp. 141–42). To which Isaac replies with an envy that may or may not be feigned: "Who is like unto you? You even hit your own women" (p. 142). The guard says: "He who is worthy of the stick gets beaten" (p. 142), and once again the two of them laugh. Thus, Isaac himself does make the dark and embarrassing connection latent in *Only Yesterday* between control of a woman and control of a dog— and by implication, between lack of control of a dog and lack of control of a woman. The guard, who is one of those who "even [hits his] own women," stands here along with Sweet Foot, while Isaac stands outside: he is not a man to take the stick from between the dog's teeth and hit the dog; he is not a man to force women to do his will. In the erotic realm, too, Isaac is merely a painter, and his stick doesn't hit, but at most smears paint on the skin. He mistakenly thinks that Sonya is his because he has "marked" her with his brush and paint. On the very next page, he will discover that a brush is not a stick, and paint is not control, and he himself is far from being Leichtfuss. Power relations prevail between men and women in many, if not most, of Agnon's works, and they approach sadomasochism in "Another Face," "The Doctor's Divorce," "An Oath of Loyalty," "Hill of Sand," *A Simple Story,* and *Shira;* in another way in "Edo and Enam" and "Blemished Ovadia"; and even more in "The Lady and the Peddler." Frequently, in Agnon's works, the stick is in the hands of the woman. In most of his works, the men are "the fair sex," while the women are depicted as the strong sex.

A few days before "Sonya changed her ways with Isaac," he still fantasized about her as if they were bride and groom. As at the beginning of the novel, when Isaac sat in Galicia and dreamed of how he would own an estate in the Land and how the fellows in his Galician hometown would be jealous of him—now he sits in Zion and imagines their envy of him there when they find out that he has made a "high" match with an educated girl who "studied at the gymnasium." The target audience of his aspirations has been and remains his family and the people of his hometown. His internal wish has been and remains the classic petit bourgeois wish: they should all burst with envy. His main pleasure in Sonya is that he can "run and tell the boys" in his hometown. Fortunately, Isaac doesn't compare pictures of family bliss in his imagination, but pictures of the envy of his hometown at the sight of Sonya's photograph, which he is about to send them "so folks would see," and lest the covetous should say that Isaac won her only because she was defective. Therefore, he is about to "teach a lesson" to all those who mocked him in his hometown, and to prove to them that indeed in the Delightsome Ancestral Land all hopes are realized—including the erotic hope and the hope of upward mobility. Hence, he perceives the honorable "match" with Sonya as a combination of erotic achievement and social achievement. Just like his fantasy in Lemberg about the group picture of him and the famous activists, a photo he would send home so the whole town would "burst with envy," here, too, the fact emerges that at the head of Isaac's (hidden) springs is not building the Land or even realizing love, but the petit bourgeois ladder of a rustic town; and to his dying day, Isaac dreams of climbing that ladder, from a deep pit to a high roof, either in the agricultural settlement or in Meah Shearim.

|

In chapter 13, perhaps because of superstitious fears of this number, "the good days" end and "the days that [come] after [are] not good." The narrator explains what happened: "Blessed is he who had his first kiss with a maiden whom others had not yet kissed, and woe to him who kissed a maiden whom others had already kissed before him" (p. 143). And right afterward, without noticing the contradiction, the narrator adds: "For no special reason, Sonya changed her ways with Isaac" (p. 143). An overdetermination of causes, the interweaving of various points of view without distinguishing them with quotation marks or phrases like "he thought" or "in his opinion"—tactics that have already served more than once for comic purposes in *Only Yesterday*— this strategy becomes subtle and sophisticated. "For no special reason, Sonya changed her ways with Isaac"—this, of course, is the feeling of the shocked Isaac. "Blessed is he" who gave his first kiss to a virgin, and "woe to him" who kissed one who is not a virgin—that is the socio-psychological explanation the narrator places as an obstacle before the reader who is more experienced than Isaac but unable to understand the presence of fate in *Only Yesterday* and unable to discern the rule of a force that is neither social nor psychological, and that dictates everything.

Perhaps this is the sequence: Sonya changed her ways for no special reason—in Isaac's opinion. According to psychosociological wisdom, Sonya changed her ways with Isaac because she is experienced and he is inexperienced, and perhaps she got fed up with his childishness. Or because she went slumming to look for an authentic proletarian delicacy, and found a small and sycophantic shopkeeper unpalatable. According to an even more internal logic that operates in the novel, Sonya changed her ways with Isaac because Isaac cannot take the stick out of the yellow dog's mouth and use it as Leichtfuss would. And perhaps, through all those layers of explanation, vague and menacing as a distant dog's bark in the dark of night, peeps fate—a judgment of sin and punishment or simply a joke of horrors "full of sound and fury, signifying nothing."

|

Isaac comes home from work, straightens up, and preens for Sonya—"Come my beloved to greet the bride"—and Sonya doesn't come. In a sharply ironic context here, there is an echo of "the way of a man with a maid," one of the "three things which are too wonderful for me, yea, four which I know not" in the Book of Proverbs (30:18–19). Like a man who despairs of waiting, Isaac gets up and goes to Sonya. Just recently, he appeared all shining and exultant as a bridegroom, recently he joked with the Arab guard as if his success sprouted for him the wings of Leichtfuss, and now the colors of pride are peeled off him and he is once again a Hasid steeped in magic who puts his trust in all kinds of incantations and amulets. "Sonya is sick, Sonya is sick, Sonya is sick, Isaac said, like someone muttering incantations over an illness . . . Sonya isn't sick, Sonya isn't sick, Sonya isn't sick, he repeated three times against those three times he had said before" (p. 144).

|

How pathetic is the rage of a weak man. Isaac's rage is peeled off him and reveals the real hue of his soul: a hue of submission and obsequiousness, awe, and acceptance of the judgment for "the sin he committed."

As for Sonya, she mocks him mercilessly when she again sticks her sword in his most painful place: his feeling of inferiority. "Anyone who knows the first thing about logic knows that there is nothing without a reason" (p. 145). Thus she crushes Isaac even more than at the beginning of the scene and reminds him of his ignorance, and thus she again unwittingly stirs some vague and dark echo from the deepest cellars of the novel, the question of cause and effect.

The moment the arrogance of a smug shopkeeper-bridegroom is peeled away, Isaac once again becomes the character who touches the heart of the narrator and the reader—but not of Sonya. This naïve and innocent boy, struck for no sin he has done, volunteers to Sonya—who is spitefully absorbed in a mania of darning stockings—to paint the new chair she has bought. As if he says to her: if you don't want me as a lover anymore, perhaps you'll keep me as a private painter?

Then, Mme. Puah Hoffenstein, the garrulous patroness of Ossip the anarchist, appears in Sonya's room. Her appearance stirs a repressed cowardly rage in Isaac. Hoffenstein, like the perfect lady in "Hill of Sand," is a wicked caricature of prudish and narrow-minded bourgeois banality (she is also like the characters who populate Hanoch Levin's plays).[21] In Hoffenstein's presence, Isaac is completely emptied and seethes in silence. Isaac would pour all the wrath he cannot aim at Sonya on the head of Hoffenstein, if that Lamed Vovnik were capable of pouring wrath on a living person. She makes his blood boil because she embodies a scathing caricature of himself, but he, of course, does not understand that. She threatens him because she is a distorted and dumb metonymy of his own figure, and because he senses that what wafts from her might also waft from him and provoke Sonya's hatred.

Ossip the Anarchist, Hoffenstein's lover, is a parallel character to Sonya, just as Hoffenstein parallels Isaac. Ossip, like Sonya, winds up in the Land not willingly and not for his own good, but to avoid the czarist police in Russia. The two of them disseminate Russian revolutionary phraseology. Both of them fall into the hands of mates who stifle them with petite bourgeoisie. (Hoffenstein controls her revolutionary so much that he once demeaned himself and polished his shoes for her sake—but he took revenge on her: "as he left her house, he rubbed one foot on top of the other and soiled them" [p. 146]. It is interesting and perplexing that Agnon says the same thing, almost word for word, about Yosef-Hayyim Brenner in his essay "Yosef-Hayyim Brenner in His Life and His Death." Ossip's act is a reprise of Sonya's act of putting her shoes on Rabinovitch's patent leather shoes, and of Rabinovitch's act of quickly passing his silk handkerchief over his shoes [book 1, chapter 7].)

Thus, Isaac is banished from Paradise into the dark of night. In one of the most painful parts of the novel, Isaac walks around in the dark, muttering fragments of Sonya's and Hoffenstein's phrases in a deconstruction of the text, as if to extract from the components of the conversation what is behind the conversation. From the depths, from the religious infrastructure of his personality, the justification of the judgment erupts: Isaac justifies his own punishment and lovingly accepts torments, as befits the grandson of the great-grandson of Reb Yudel Hasid—for the sin of the first Adam, and for the sin he sinned against Rabinovitch, and for the sin that he didn't learn logic, and for the sin that he sinned in his love. Yet, like the first Adam in the Garden of Eden and several other men, Isaac also attributes the sin to Eve, who tempted him (book 1, chapter 13). Perhaps more than any other section in *Only Yesterday,* this sleep-walking-dream monologue reveals the depth of Isaac's dread of sin, his justification of the judgment, his innocent childishness bound irrevocably to his religious belief in the existence of reward and punishment—a pure and perfect belief—and when all is said and done, it is this belief and not Zionism that is at the root of his soul. When the blow comes, he closes himself in his room and winds himself in his sheet and draws out the *She'ma* and is punctilious about it, something he hadn't done as long as "the days were good." The torments renew and reinforce his belief, as they had with his grandfather's grandfather.

As despair overcomes him, Isaac decides to try his luck with Sonya once again and goes to her with good intentions, to forgive her for her cruelty and to get her out of her embarrassment: "He felt pity for her. . . . And he pitied himself too, for his solitude" (p. 149). When he arrives, he doesn't dare glance at Sonya and looks instead at Sonya's proxy, the dog on the blanket spread on her lap. The dog looks at Isaac and "scowls at him . . . and the stick sways in the dog's mouth. Isaac's shoulders recoil and he brings his face back to Sonya and the dog once again looks at him with furious eyes" (p. 150). His look reminds Isaac of Grisha, and suddenly his innocent heart is filled with "wrath and envy" (p. 150). As in other places in the novel, the point of view changes without warning, and the reader is invited to glance at Isaac through Sonya's eyes: "Isaac spoke in a tone like a petit bourgeois on a holiday. And that solemnity drove her out of her mind and made her angry . . . and [she] said, I forgot that you're a Galician, and she spoke Yiddish to him, the way you talk with simple people. . . . Sonya said to herself, For two or three kisses do I owe him anything? And does the fellow think that a girl's kisses enslave her completely? . . . Where would I be if every single fellow I've kissed saw himself like this Galician?" (p. 151). The reversal of the stereotypical roles of men and women maintained in *Only Yesterday* is also obvious. Sonya's new contempt for Isaac, a "class" contempt and a "hormonal" contempt ("A Hebrew teacher . . . round as a herring barrel . . . wore blue socks like the ones you're wearing" [p. 153]), mixed with social haughtiness ("Galician," "simple people"), is intensified because Isaac starts treating her as his fiancée ("if every single fellow I've kissed saw himself like this Galician" [p. 151]). When he comes to her room, she holds out her fingers to him with a needle between them. The erotic stabbing of the needle in Sonya's fingers almost prefigures the dog's bite that is to come.

After the reader sees Sonya through Isaac's worshipful and stunned eyes and Isaac through Sonya's cold eyes, the next chapter, "Brief Commentary on the Preceding Chapter," adds lines to Sonya's character from the point of view of the narrator himself. Sonya Zweiering is depicted in *Only Yesterday* as a superficial, stylish, snobbish girl. The description of Jerusalem through her eyes (book 1, chapter 15) is a comic gem.

Yet, with all the contrast between the innocent Isaac and the experienced Sonya, there is a basic similarity between them that may be obvious in many secondary characters in the novel as well: their orphanhood. The people of the Second Aliya in *Only Yesterday* are mostly young people with no relatives in the Land of Israel, children exiled from their father's table, lovers who cannot start a family and raise children, isolated individuals whose social life attempts to substitute for family life, and they want to be "a mother and a sister" or a father, or a child to each other (e.g., book 2, chapter 21).

When Sonya leaves Isaac, he experiences a religious regression, and a childish regression as well. The religious regression is expressed in the fact that Isaac interprets his torments as divine punishment and torments himself for his sins. The childish regression is evident in his hope that after Sonya finishes darning all her socks, she'll come back to him as to a child who has been punished unjustly and will "appease" him—for he sees Sonya as a continuation of his mother. So Isaac attempts to be "sweet" in her eyes.

The combination of the two regressions leads Isaac to the idea that he should marry Sonya and thus repair the "sin of Rabinovitch" and atone for his other sins, and also win himself a permanent place under her warm apron. But between intention and act, Sonya disappears, and Isaac does not know where to find her in little Jaffa. "Now his anger was calmed and an affection he had never known throbbed in his heart, the affection that starts with yearnings and ends with madness" (p. 153). This is the road that runs between the oppression of Eros and the torments of sin of a person educated in the religious world, the road taken by most of the heroes of Hebrew literature in the "Generation of the Revival." Isaac, who seemed at first to be an exception to the rule, now accepts the rule and joins the heroes of the *Scroll of Fire, Fligelman, Mahanaim, In Winter,* and *Bereavement and Failure*—heroes who also experienced the path that leads from yearnings to madness. The "affection that starts with yearnings and ends with madness" is the very same affection the dog Balak will experience. He, too, will savor the infatuating emotional and physical attraction to someone who humiliated him and threw him out. Balak vis-à-vis Isaac is like Isaac vis-à-vis Sonya: in vain will he try to cut himself off, to forget, to find a substitute, or even to repent. And like Isaac, Balak will be unable to understand the hidden causal connections, the "hidden cause" that undermines the "open wish," and the sources of the vicissitudes in his life. "For no special reason, Sonya changed her ways with Isaac" (p. 143), and for no special reason, the man with the dripping tool, the man who drips affection and unforgettable pleasure on the dog—will suddenly change his way and kick the dog, thus putting him on the way to madness.

In any case, right now, in Jaffa, there is only "a stray dog that shouts arf arf" from a distance. In a short flickering, as if incidentally, the hidden and persistent presence of fate lurking nearby is revealed for a moment, almost like the horrible barking of the fatal dog in Conan Doyle's "The Hound of the Baskervilles," where the dog is also first depicted as a messenger of fate and a staff of rage of hidden forces.

The rejected Isaac approaches Orgelbrand, that "ideal double" who also yearns for Sonya. Like the two ex-wives of the wonderful musician Vittorio Godswill, these two start "going steady."

In the chapter "Pioneers," perhaps for the first time in the novel, the ironic distance between the ornate Zionist rhetoric and the wretched reality in the Land of Israel disappears. Isaac's visit to Eyn Ganim turns into the apotheosis of a handful of workers who succeed in showing a quasi-religious devotion, a full and innocent devotion, "without any calculation." Unlike most of the Zionists in the novel, there is no distinction between their words and their deeds. Isaac judges himself and condemns himself for not being one of the settlers of Eyn Ganim. The words he selects to admit his failure are straight from the Jewish religious world: "he ascribed the failure to himself for not enduring the ordeals" (p. 173).[22] Of course, it is no accident that, right after this religious musing, Isaac is again gnawed by guilt over the sin he is being punished for by Heaven: the sin of Rabinovitch. And again: "Isaac bowed his head and muttered something, like someone who admits his guilt. And what guilt is it, it is the guilt of all of us who came to work the Land and didn't work it" (p. 174). In the first person plural here, the narrator involves himself, his hero, and his hero's comrades, Rabinovitch and Yarkoni and Mittelman and Grisha and Gorishkin and perhaps, by implication, also the author of *Only Yesterday*—all those who ascended to the Land to "build and be rebuilt there," but who forgot to build and tried hard to be rebuilt, or agreed to write the great novel on the building of the Land or to improve the garb of the Land or to renew its colors a little.

And what stops Isaac from staying in Eyn Ganim, now that his affair with Sonya is over, now that Pnina, the girlfriend of Sonya and Yael Hayyot, comes and almost offers herself to him and even admits that she is "a village girl and deserves to settle on the soil" (p. 175)? Pnina asks of Isaac, "that fellow who isn't flooded with theories, why does he live in the city" (p. 175). Ostensibly, Isaac could have responded to Pnina's veiled offer to start a family in Eyn Ganim and begin "working and guarding." If he had, the novel would have ended a third of the way through, Reb Fayesh and Balak and Reb Grunam would have gone on struggling in the dust of Jerusalem, "and we shall tell the deeds of our brothers and sisters, the children of the living God, the nation of the Lord, who work the earth of Israel for a monument and fame and glory" (p. 142). So, what is the "delay"? Why doesn't Isaac take Pnina the village girl and settle in Eyn Ganim? Because of orphanhood and silence and guilt—"The open wish is undermined by the hidden cause" (p. 128).

The visit to Eyn Ganim and the sojourn among the Zionists "worthy of the name," stirs Isaac's memory of his grandfather's grandfather, Reb Yudel Hasid, who once spent a Sabbath with one of the Lamed Vovniks the world stands on. "And when Isaac contemplated those things, he smiled and said, And I . . . descendant of Rabbi Yudel Hasid spent a weekday not with a hidden saint, but with a host of hidden saints on whom the world stands" (p. 176). With those words, by dint of the naïve synthesis, Isaac stitches together for a moment the tragic split between observant Judaism and Zionism, between Hasidism and Pioneering, between the quarry he was hewn from and the aspiration of his soul. Nevertheless, the fact is that when Isaac comes to Eyn Ganim—the point where the two parallel lines of his world miraculously meet—he doesn't stop or sink into it but continues on his way back to the chaotic world of pseudo-Zionist Jaffa and from there to the world of death of the pseudoreligious Meah Shearim.

And that is really what soon happens to Isaac when he finally meets the ideal father figure, one he can cling to more than he clung to Rabinovitch or Sweet Foot, Rabbi Menahemke, called Standing Menahem. Isaac does not learn from Menahem's actions and does not take his road, even though Menahem is walking proof of the possibility of the synthesis of faith and Pioneering Zionism, and the living embodiment of the annulment of the rip between the world of Commandments and keeping the commandment of building the Land. Rabbi Menahemke feels no difficulty or contradiction in keeping all the Commandments of the religion and all the commandments of practical Zionism (book 1, chapter 17; book 4, chapter 10). Like Brenner—and like Agnon himself—Menahem hates all high-flown phraseology, such as the term "religion of work" (which people mistakenly ascribe to Aharon David Gordon, even though Gordon never used it in his writings). Menahem becomes furious over the notion of a "religion of work" with a wonderful blend of Brennerish rage and Agnonian irony. Some see the character of Rabbi Menahemke as an ideal expression of the spiritual "match" Agnon aspired to make between the three "fathers" he adopted when he came to the Land of Israel as a young man: the religious Zionist rabbi Abraham Isaac Ha-Cohen Kook; the ideologue and leader of the labor movement, Berl Katznelson; and the "conscience of the Second Aliya," the writer Yosef-Hayyim Brenner. According to this view, Menahem in *Only Yesterday* bears the heavy burden of an ideal synthesis between these three spiritual leaders.[23] Others say that the character of the standing Menahem is based on the personality of Isaiah Shapiro (1891–1945), one of the spiritual leaders of the Ha-Po'el Ha-Mizrachi (religious labor) movement, a descendant of the Magid of Kozhenitz and "the Seer of Lublin." Shapiro refused to accept the role of a Hasidic Rebbe and lived as a worker on the land in Kfar Pines, and his spirit prevailed over the Bnei Akiva movement before parts of it wandered off toward the nationalist Right.[24]

Along with Sweet Foot and Samson Bloykof the artist and Arzef the taxidermist, Menahem belongs to the small group of strong, dominant characters in *Only Yesterday* who maintain an internal integrity, each in his own way, profoundly indifferent toward society and its conventions. Every one of these four exists outside all defined groups. From a different angle, every one of them loathes propriety and petit bourgeois *glikn* (happiness). Needless to say, the "orphan" Isaac sees every one of them, in turn, as an authoritative and admirable father figure. In Leichtfuss and Bloykof, at any rate, he finds a father substitute. Menahem decrees: "A person has to work, for if he doesn't work, what will he eat? I myself have no need for ideas, not about the Land and not about work. It's enough for a man that he was blessed to dwell in the Land of Israel. And may we not have to be ashamed of the Land" (p. 179). With these few words, Menahem returns things to their original, refined simplicity. Much of *Only Yesterday* is devoted to a cruel mockery of hollow pathos, but here the novel attains a rare expression of genuine pathos the author stands behind. There are very few places in Agnon's work where the author almost comes out directly with a clear personal credo, far from the ambivalence and wittiness with which he usually prefers to disguise his positions. The character of Menahem expresses in an undisguised and undiluted fashion the degree of closeness Agnon felt for the best people of "Torah and Work."

"In those days, Isaac heard about a shoemaker in Jaffa who left his trade and his wife and his little children and ascended to Jerusalem and settled in the prayer house of the Bratslav Hasids . . . because his soul longed to repair himself. . . . There are people who, wherever they are, they live their lives as they want to. Isaac wasn't one of them" (p. 185). Thus, because of a rumor he hears, Isaac is willing to leave Jaffa for Jerusalem and Zionism for the Bratslav Hasids and sin for repentance. But like all the explanations and reasons in *Only Yesterday,* here, too, hidden causes are operating under the open wish. Then comes a paragraph that plays naïve: "And if he had found work in the field or the vineyard, he would have settled on the soil, and we would sing the Song of the Earth. But in spite of himself and not for his own good, Isaac became what he became, that is, seeking work with his brush and his bucket, and we tag along behind him. . . . Either for good or for bad, we won't abandon him in the middle of the road" (p. 185). Once again, the narrator takes the first person plural form and disguises himself as a hidden traveler who goes wherever Isaac goes, even if he doesn't know whether it's "for good or for bad" and surely doesn't profess to shape his hero's fate or to control the plot. But right afterward, the narrator can say that "in spite of himself and not for his own good" did Isaac become a painter, or "[seek] work with his brush" (like begging or "seeking alms").

At this point, the careful reader asks what in fact prevents Isaac from joining Eyn Ganim or adopting Menahem's life-style. And what is the hidden force that makes him respond to the tale of the cobbler (again shoes!) of Jaffa and change his place and his life-style because of an anonymous rumor? Indeed, is it "only by chance" that Isaac doesn't settle on the soil? And only by chance that readers have not been presented with an agricultural novel, because a narrator who preferred to sing the "Song of the Earth" was led down another road by his hero, just as the hero himself would prefer to work in the field and the vineyard but was led down another road by his fate?[25] What is this "in spite of himself"? In religious language, the language of the hero and the narrator, what is the nature of "the delay"? Perhaps that is the secret content of *Only Yesterday*.

Sonya will certainly not prevent Isaac from ascending to Jerusalem. On the contrary, when they see one another, she teases him about his masculinity, which she has wounded, and says: "Anyone who has a drop of blood in him and not colored water goes and sees" (p. 187).

|

The farewell scene between Sonya and Isaac as he leaves for Jerusalem is one of the most marvelous examples of an idle, banal conversation that covers the most intimate subtext. The conversation between Isaac and Sonya, who accompanies him to the railroad station, apparently concerns ice cream and coffee. But in fact, Sonya is confessing to Isaac—although in code—the sexual disappointment he has caused her. (Here, too, she is reminiscent of Yael Hayyot, who in "Hill of Sand" finds a way to hint to Hemdat what Shammai has and he doesn't.) Sonya pities the grieving Isaac. She is suddenly sorry for the torments she has caused this suitor, who is excellent and modest: She "passe[s] all her acquaintances before her mind's eye. Sometimes they were this way and sometimes they were that way, and Isaac always leveled with her and never sinned against her" (p. 188). So "she [takes] his hand and ask[s] his forgiveness" (p. 188). So far, so good. But suddenly Sonya complains about the ice cream she and Isaac ate in the coffeehouse on their way to the railroad station: the ice cream was "lukewarm." So she would like some "strong, sharp coffee." Isaac's taste is different; he's happy with "lukewarm" and not with "strong and sharp." Just to appease Sonya, he consents in a weak voice: "I want" (that is, "they force him until he says 'I want'"). Sonya says: "Your voice is weak, as if you lost the strength of will. I wonder if you have even a hint of will. In all your life, Isaac, you never asked me for anything" (p. 188). These words convey a reproach and an invitation at the same time.

Isaac takes courage and replies that never in his life has he ever asked for anything because with her he didn't lack anything. Then they look at one another, and Isaac dares to take advantage of the "invitation" and to express a wish that she write to him in Jerusalem. Here he closes his eyes and explains to her: "I am reading your letters." Once again, Sonya reproaches him, not exactly for that specific closing of his eyes: "With your eyes closed you read." Isaac makes an unconscious effort to radiate his childish virginity, the tested feature that charmed Sonya at the beginning of their relationship: "In all my life I've never seen a letter from a girl." Sonya tries to rouse him from the slumber of his love: "Letters that weren't written you read" (p. 189). But Isaac refuses to open his eyes (p. 189). (This sleeping beloved is similar to another sleeping beloved, Hemdat, who says of himself: "I'm a sleeping prince whose true love puts him back to sleep" ["Hill of Sand," p. 106].) Thus, once again, Isaac tries unwittingly to give Sonya the role of a lady knight on a white horse, a knight whose kiss will awaken the sleeping beauty from his slumber. (Hirshl in *A Simple Story* wants Bluma to play the same knightly role for him and bears a grudge against her for not fulfilling his expectations.)

In any case, Sonya's patience has run out, and she has already exhausted the game with Isaac. Two or three times she asks him, "When does your train leave?" And each time, she forgets his answer and repeats her question. Until the train leaves, she continues expressing indirectly the sexual disappointment the sleeping beauty bequeathed her. She expresses something she may not be aware of, and Isaac certainly cannot decipher what she says to him. But, as in the scene of peeling oranges and other scenes, the reader can peep at what is not revealed through the trivial conversation between the speakers. Thus, Sonya says: "I wanted to drink a strong and sharp beverage with you, and he brought us coffee with milk. If you want to taste real coffee, go to the Arabs, as Rabinovitch and I used to do" (p. 189).

It is not the "Arabs" who are the main point of this sentence, nor is the coffee its subject, but "as Rabinovitch and I used to do," and "strong and sharp," as opposed to diluted with milk. Even though Isaac doesn't understand what the words say, nevertheless he does sense something, and his face falls so much that Sonya says to him: "Get up and let's go, with head held high and body erect" (p. 189). And as if deliberately to seal their parting with a sign of the role reversal that has characterized their relationship, she closes the circle by paying the bill at the coffeehouse and buying the boy a chocolate bar for the road. As for the boy, he "shorten[s] his steps to lengthen the way" (p. 189), and as the train lingers, he imagines that the train won't come at all and the trip will be canceled: "He started imagining that he returned with Sonya to the city and rented himself a room . . . like Rabinovitch's room, and there . . . Isaac hadn't finished his thoughts when the rumble of the train was heard rattling in" (p. 189).

Even though Isaac seems free to board the train or not, everything appears to be expected and permission isn't given and Isaac goes submissively to the place where his fate awaits him. He will have that same submissiveness at the entrance to Jerusalem, too: "A carter came and took his belongings. Isaac trudged along behind him" (p. 192). And, despite the famous submissiveness in his personality, Isaac has a peculiar power to soften Sonya at the last minute of their parting. As if Isaac cast a spell over her, she momentarily adapts to the softness emanating from him, drops her thorniness and her disgust for the "tepid" fellow in front of her, forgets her gossiping and arrogance, takes his hand, and asks his forgiveness. For one moment, she responds to his mute wish, "be a mother to me and a sister," and she truly treats him as her little son—until "a halo beamed over his closed eyes" (p. 189). That halo seems to envelop Sonya, too, in the last moments of parting. And in this description, as in the description of their first night of love (book 1, chapter 11) and as in other scenes in the novel, it is the passive-feminine man and not the dominant-masculine woman who stamps his seal on what happens, and who "paints" the picture in the soft tint of his personality—another miracle in the minor chain of miracles caused by "Reb Isaac Hasid," who can melt hard hearts and renew dusty souls.

|

The first description of Jerusalem in *Only Yesterday* is gloomy, mysterious, and severe, a striking contrast to the secularism and sands that characterize Jaffa in the novel: "Before him, the Wall of Jerusalem suddenly appeared, woven into a red fire, plaited with gold, surrounded by gray clouds blended with blue clouds" (p. 237). Jaffa is depicted thus: "This is the sand of Jaffa that digs underneath you to swallow you up. As soon as you stand on it, it runs out and turns into holes on top of holes" (p. 40).

The description of Isaac's entrance into Jerusalem, to the melody of the carter's prayer, is ominous: "and a still small voice was heard like the voice of wailing in the mountains. Suddenly a sad stillness enveloped Isaac's heart, as if they came to bring him tidings and he didn't know if those tidings were for good or for bad" (p. 195).

Isaac stops first in the hotel of Shoel Hershel Tefillinsky, and then he rents a room in Nahalat Shiv'a and looks for work painting, a search that takes him to two artists of the Bezalel Art School, an arrogant one and a kind one.

Samson Bloykof, whose name means "blue head," is from Galicia, like Isaac. Perhaps that is why Isaac dares to ask him for help finding work. This Bloykof, who has heart disease and lung disease and knows that his days are numbered, has already given up the business of making a living, and paints with an artistic fervor that is like religious devotion and that includes a religious component. He "paints what Heaven shows him" (p. 218). And the purpose of his painting is also religious, even though he is not an observant person: "Heaven . . . gives him strength to see and to paint, and the Omnipotent Creator of the World must have a special intention" to exalt through the paintings of Samson Bloykof "the splendor of Jerusalem even in her destruction" (p. 218). Bloykof is also eager to leave behind a trace for future generations. The character of Bloykof is one of the most fascinating and amusing in the novel; he is a clever man of penetrating wit, with a profound religious excitement, an eccentric and egocentric man as full of himself as a baby, yet a warm, generous, and loving man. It is as if Agnon had poured several outstanding personal and confessional elements of that artist who "paints out of hunger and out of extreme yearnings" (p. 218). Bloykof's mordant humor is not far from Agnon's own: "If his heart afflicts him because of his illness, he silences it and tells it, Are you better than the lungs? And if his lungs afflict him, he silences them and tells them, Are you better than the heart? And he goes back to his craft. . . . And if hunger attacks him, he strikes his stomach and says, Are you more distinguished than I am? Even if I die of hunger, I don't say a word" (p. 219). Like the writer who created him, Bloykof thinks that "sometimes even if he [the artist] doesn't know what he is painting, at any rate, he knows more than his interpreters" (p. 220). This closeness between Bloykof and the author does not contradict the assumption that Bloykof is modeled on the personality of the artist Samuel Hirshberg (1865–1908), one of the leaders of Bezalel, who painted the famous "Exile."[26]

Like Yohanan Leichtfuss, and in a completely different way, like Rabbi Menahemke, Bloykof appears to be someone who controls his passions, his acts, and, to some extent, even his fate. Like them, he ignores social conventions, lives outside all groups, and sometimes emits a cold contempt and is haughty toward everyone. Bloykof seems to treat his sick and exhausted body as Sweet Foot treated women, dogs, and employers: with amused mastery. Bloykof is one of the few characters in the novel to whom the author grants a "stylistic concession": he is released from the unity of style that applies to all descriptions and to most of the protagonists, and he speaks in his own language. (An outstanding example of this can be found in book 2, chapter 4.) The use of the first person plural on page 219 is almost unique: "When Isaac knocked on the door, Bloykof flinched and shook and he cursed and insulted him in his heart as we tend to do with anyone who comes to divert us from our work. But his anger quickly turned to pity and he greeted him nicely." The "we" in this passage is neither the narrator and the reader, nor the narrator and Isaac, nor the Second Aliya, but rather—distinctly—"we artists." In the next paragraph, another very rare use of the first person plural appears: "We people of Galicia" (p. 219). These two examples also indicate how close the creator felt toward his protagonist Bloykof.

The affection between Isaac and Bloykof is not only the product of the "Galician connection." Like the affection between Isaac and Rabinovitch, and between Isaac and Leichtfuss, the affection between Isaac and Bloykof is also a father-son relation and may also have a trace of latent platonic homosexuality, as Isaac lovingly and gladly accepts the passive role: "Samson Bloykof and Isaac Kumer sit down, . . . and it seems to him that all his life he yearned for nothing but this hour, and it seems to Bloykof that everything he says was kept in his heart for this man. And isn't it a little puzzling, for Kumer is a simple house painter and has nothing to do with art, but Bloykof is confident that if he talks to him, he is surely worth it" (p. 268).

With all the contrast between the dying eccentric artist and the childish house painter, Bloykof seems to sense Isaac's capacity for excitement. Samson Bloykof, like Yohanan Leichtfuss before him, connects to that capacity in Isaac that, as we have said, is a necessary but not sufficient sign of a creative artist. Boaz Arpali has noted that there are capacities in Isaac that are "parallel to the realizing Pioneer on the one hand and to the creative artist on the other." Bloykof himself treats his artistic creation like a religious-Hasidic act, committed with love, awe, devotion, humility, and enthusiasm (book 2, chapter 8). Here, too, they are kindred spirits.

As for women, at first glance, Bloykof, loved passionately by his wife, Tosya, would seem to be the antithesis of Leichtfuss, the bohemian honey sucker, surrounded by women and using them casually and authoritatively for his pleasure. But on a deeper level, Leichtfuss and Bloykof are on the same side of the erotic barricade in *Only Yesterday*, while Isaac is on the other side. The love lives of Sweet Foot and Bloykof are exclamation marks—each in his own way is a lord and master. Isaac's love life is a question mark—like Hemdat, Isaac is "love's beggar walking around with love in a torn old bag" ("Hill of Sand," p. 106).

In any case, Bloykof is almost the last thread that ties Isaac to the world outside ultra-Orthodox Jerusalem and outside religious observance: "If not for Bloykof the painter, Isaac would become a complete Jerusalemite. Milk and honey Isaac did not find in Jerusalem, but he did attain a state of equanimity" (p. 230, and again—almost word for word—in chapter 7, where the issue is spelled out in detail). The state of equanimity is total reconciliation with "all that the Merciful One does, He does for good"; the state of equanimity is the state of Reb Yudel, the complete spiritual balance with nothing at all after it that grants its possessors supreme tranquility and perhaps even some awesome joy—at the price of shriveling all desires and extinguishing emotional life.

When Bloykof dies, and his widow, Tosya—whom Isaac may consider briefly—marries someone else, Isaac is once again orphaned, as he was orphaned when he left his house, and when the old couple on the ship disappeared, and when Rabinovitch left, and when Sonya got fed up with him. "The state of equanimity" is what softens that blow and that loss, depicted here as irreparable (book 2, chapter 10).

Like a decree, it hovers over Isaac Kumer's head: whenever a house is opened to him, whenever he manages to feel at home, the house ends up disappearing and he returns to being orphaned like a stray dog.

|

The preacher Reb Grunam May-Salvation-Arise is modeled on the Jerusalem preacher Rabbi Ben Zion Yadler (1872–1962) and is assigned, as it were, to establish the connection between the dog and Eros in *Only Yesterday*.[27] In his first appearance and sermon in the novel, he castigates

> the sinners whose instinct tempts them to commit sins, and when their instinct sees that they are drawn to sin, it raises the price of sins to them, to wear them down, and at last it draws the sin to one place and the sinners to another place, until their eyes bulge and they don't enjoy anything. Like those who tease dogs, show a dog a chunk of meat and when the dog jumps up to catch it, they remove the meat from him until he finally goes mad with desire. (p. 229)

Not only is there a harsh vision hinting at the future here, but there is also a horrible perspective on the past, on what had already happened to Isaac. Not only the connection between the sex instinct and the dog is emphasized here, but also the almost schizophrenic notion that "sinners" are separate from "their instinct," man is separate from his impulses and appetites. The relation between man and his sex instinct is presented here as a relation between a helpless victim without free choice, and an abusive and ruthless sadistic force. In the game between the sex instinct and its possessors, between Eros and man, everything is expected and permission is not given. And perhaps sin lies at the gate yearning for you, and you can't control it.

Moreover, the dog, who seems to be compared to Eros in several places in the novel, is presented here in Reb Grunam's sermon as the helpless victim of an omnipotent force, and not the "demonic" dog that the critic Kurzweil and others have seen. Even before Balak takes center stage, dogs in *Only Yesterday*—starting with Sweet Foot's dog, Tsutsik, to the guard dog on Sonya's bed, and from the dog that "looks like a stick," in the words of the Arab guard, to the miserable dog in Reb Grunam's parable—do not bear only one allegorical meaning on their back, but rather a variegated symbolic burden: some parallel Isaac himself, some "represent" the female sex, some embody erotic instincts, and some are the helpless victims of a hidden force that is partly moralistic and partly sadistic. Despite various hints the narrator scatters here and there, the dogs of *Only Yesterday* are not allegorical dogs and are not like Mendele Moykher Sforim's "My Mare."

In "the residue of *Only Yesterday*" is a suppressed ninth chapter that Agnon rejected for the novel, which is titled "The Author's Apologies and More to Isaac." In the second paragraph of that suppressed chapter, the narrator addresses the reader in the second person:

> I know you've got a grudge against me for mixing up one
> tale with another and man with livestock. In your opinion,
> innocent reader, I should have separated Isaac and the dog
> and made two stories, one story about the man and one story
> about the dog. And you also scold me for making the dog talk
> in a human language and making him think things that no
> livestock, animal, or fowl needs to do. . . . And you've already
> received your punishment that an arrogant critic has come and
> proved . . . that horses are not wont to talk like humans.

This suppressed chapter may indicate Agnon's hesitations about interweaving the two stories, which may have originated as two separate works, and Sarah Hagar has noted the genealogical metamorphoses in the structure of *Only Yesterday*.[28] (Incidentally, it is interesting to compare Balak's entrance into the structure of *Only Yesterday* with the metamorphoses of a chapter in A. B. Yehoshua's *Late Divorce*, titled "The Last Night," which was suppressed and later revealed. The protagonist of that chapter is also a dog who expresses thoughts in a human tongue.)

|

The stream of Isaac's thoughts again reveals the fact that the "root of his soul" is a Hasidic, religious root, and even his Zionism is merely a Hasidic, religious impulse displaced for a while into a new channel. In Jerusalem, Isaac no longer needs the naïve synthesis between contradictory beliefs and opinions because he has reached "a state of equanimity." Even when he hums to himself at work the songs of Hemdat-Agnon and a pious fellow suspects that he is a Zionist and attacks Zionism, Isaac isn't drawn into an argument and doesn't defend Zionism as he had in his arguments with the old man on the ship. But a state of equanimity doesn't release him from feeling guilty about his

father's house or from feelings of sin about "the iniquity of Rabinovitch" and the incident of Sonya (book 2, chapter 6). The guilt produces an internal "conflict" between himself and the shadow of the old
man on the ship, and between himself and the memory of Reb Yudel
Hasid (book 2, chapter 6).

Unlike his hero, the narrator does not reach a state of equanimity: ultra-Orthodox Jerusalem is depicted in *Only Yesterday* with a
sarcasm as satiric and disgusted as was the fake, Zionistic Jaffa for its
activists and empty people. In both, mouth and heart are not synchro-
nized: in the coastal plain, the Zionist deed and building the Land
turned into empty words, while in Jerusalem, reverence turned into a
desolate, petrified zealous ritual. The narrator depicts that desolation
in colors that are just as hostile as those in which the fighting Maskilim
and the rebellious Zionists depicted the degenerate shtetl.

|

The character of Arzef appears close to the "watershed" of the novel:
Isaac has been removed from the experience of the Second Aliya, has giv-
en up his Pioneering aspirations, has been orphaned by Rabinovitch and
Bloykof and Sonya. Sonya still writes to Isaac from time to time, but her
immature nature, incapable of any sustained contact, becomes obvious
(book 2, chapter 7). Isaac does not really enter Orthodox life, because "a
stranger will not come in" and because a penitent like him is not allowed
into the ultra-Orthodox inner circle. Even when the torments of Eros
aren't "screaming," they are gnawing at him perhaps just as much as they
gnawed at Brenner's Ezekiel Hefetz, who is almost Isaac's "neighbor."

On the Sabbath, Isaac joins a few young craftsmen like himself who stroll around Jerusalem, and they "[go] to visit Arzef" (p. 241),
a yeshiva student who became a heretic and "lives alone like the First
Adam in the Garden of Eden, with no wife and no sons and no cares
and no troubles" (p. 242) in the village of Eyn Rogel, where he practices taxidermy. (Incidentally, the zoologist Israel Aharoni apparently
maintained that the name Arzef is simply an acronym of "Aharoni
head of Zoology of Palestine." The connection between the character
of Arzef in *Only Yesterday* and the historical figure of the zoologist
Israel Aharoni [1882–1946] is fairly flimsy.)

Leichtfuss in his way and Bloykof in his are both erotic
"heroes," but Arzef is superior to both of them because he has
absolutely no need for Eros and is the only one in the novel who "is

exempt from that punishment." Leichtfuss in his way and Bloykof in his are both free of social conventions, but Arzef is superior to both of them because he has no need for any living soul and "lives alone like the First Adam in the Garden of Eden"—before the creation of the woman, the snake, and the apple, and before there was another.

Arzef's mystical tranquility may come from his position at the junction of life and death, or between death and immortality. By taking the souls of the animals he stuffs, he grants them immortal life. The animals themselves are eager to participate in that magical exchange of achieving immortal life through death, "and even when he takes their soul, they don't demand his blood" (p. 242). What Arzef does might look like what the artist does: killing and resurrecting. Stuffing the living—thus guaranteeing them a name and a relic and a memorial. And Arzef is also like the artist in that "it's enough for Arzef to look at his handiwork and know that never in his life has he ruined any creature in the world" (p. 242). No wonder Arzef is depicted as the most extreme and consistent—almost insanely extreme and consistent—expression of the essence represented in the novel by Leichtfuss and Bloykof. And no wonder Isaac is also drawn to him, almost in a "feminine way," as he is always drawn to artists in particular and to hard men who take wild freedoms for themselves in general. Rabbi Menahemke has the power to rise high above all Zionist phraseology and to cut himself off from every group; Sweet Foot stands above women and above concerns about his livelihood; Bloykof is master of his body and his art.

But greater than all of them is Arzef, who is placed above life itself: he is the ultimate distillation of the asocial ideal of the artist in *Only Yesterday*, an ideal that sometimes contradicts the Zionist ideal and even casts it in an absurd light, just as it casts erotic distress and the passion for honor and wealth in a ridiculous light: "Some of Arzef's comrades had made wealth and honor for themselves. Their wealth and honor are as important to Arzef as empty casuistry" (p. 242). That passage should be compared with a similar passage at the beginning of the novel: "Some of Isaac's friends had already taken wives and opened shops for themselves, and they're distinguished in the eyes of folks. . . . And others of Isaac's friends are at the university studying all manner of wisdom that sustains those who possess it" (p. 3). It is not difficult to discern that those twin passages suggest a seemingly ironic parallel between Isaac and Arzef—both are considered unusual eccentrics who are "out of step with the time." In point of fact, what stands out is the contrast between the quintessential petit bourgeois conformist with a Hasidic soul, on the one hand, and the "noble savages," the uninhibited, romantic characters to whom Isaac's heart goes out "from the depths," but, as he says, "who is equal to you." It is no accident that, right after a visit to Arzef, Isaac returns in his thoughts and in the stories he tells his companions, the craftsmen, to his great prototype, his ancestor Reb Yudel Hasid. "One thing I do know," Isaac's father would say when asked about what had happened to his ancestor, "in the past it was good and now it is no good" (p. 243).

|

Bloykof dies, and his wife, Tosya, marries somebody else, and Isaac is once again orphaned. Book 2, chapter 10 is called "Orphanhood," a title that may encompass the entire work. Isaac has now been living in Jerusalem for a year and is still tormenting himself for "his transgressions"—a transgression against the Zionism he did not realize, a transgression against the family he doesn't support, a transgression against Sonya and Rabinovitch, and probably also a transgression against the torments of sex, which are linked here explicitly for the first time to the dog who fills the lunatic demands of Reb Grunam May-Salvation-Arise (book 2, chapter 10). As Isaac's soul returns to its Hasidic, religious sources, the burden of sin continues to depress him, and the torments of passion pursue him relentlessly (book 2, chapter 10). The old struggle between religion and life, a central subject in Hebrew literature for decades, is revealed as one of the main issues of *Only Yesterday*—even though, at first, it seemed that the novel and its hero would avoid that curse by means of the naïve synthesis.

Isaac seems inadvertently to drown in the pious world of Meah Shearim, not because he has experienced a theological conversion in his views or because he has suddenly been granted divine illumination. On the contrary, those very private hopes Isaac once attached to a Zionist-Pioneering "realization" he now attaches to integrating into the ultra-Orthodox environment: finding himself a surrogate family, attaining some slight upward mobility, and, perhaps, as Boaz Arpali hints, even finding an erotic opportunity that has evaded him in the Zionist territory of the coastal plain.

|

In the chapter titled "Two Friends Will Meet but Mountains Never,"[29] there is another one of those encounters that seem accidental at first but are later revealed to be expressions of the hand of fate: Reb Moyshe Amram and his wife, the old couple Isaac met on the ship, encounter him in Jerusalem, take pity on him, and become close to him, as if thus settling the debate begun on the ship and continued in Isaac's heart: are "all the Children of Israel comrades, especially in the Land of Israel," and therefore there is no need for relatives (as Isaac argued), or do comrades come and go while orphanhood remains forever, and therefore woe unto him who has no family (as the old man argued)? The story has sometimes tended to one side and sometimes to the other, and now it starts approaching a paradoxical decision in the argument: Isaac will find himself a home that is not a home far from the circle of comrades in Jaffa and the settlements. But a substitute is a substitute: orphanhood and guilt and catastrophe and there is no license. The first time Isaac's eyes rest on the Amrams' granddaughter, Shifra, "his heart [begins] pounding" but "the eyes of his heart" see Sonya (p. 281). Right after this, as if incidentally and casually, writing on the dog Balak's skin is first mentioned, only to emphasize the quality of Isaac's paints and his abilities as a fine painter (book 2, chapter 13). A stray dog who has already crossed Isaac's path here and there is about to take center stage.

|

The "act" itself should be examined in detail.

One day, after Isaac had finished painting a memorial tablet in the neighborhood of Rehovot, a Bukharan quarter in Jerusalem, and was about to wipe his brush, "he chanced on a stray dog, with . . . hair that looked maybe white or maybe brown or maybe yellow" (p. 286). In the next description, the connection between dogs and erotica and women is so explicit that painting on the dog's skin is designed to be an almost undisguised sexual act: Isaac thrust his brush at the dog, "the dog stuck out his tongue and gazed at him. You can't say he wanted to lick the brush . . . but he didn't want the owner of the brush to put his brush away with no result" (p. 286). Then comes a detailed, semi-veiled description of the love play in which Isaac, for a change, plays the customary male role and Balak the stereotypical female role, until Isaac's brush finally drips onto Balak's skin (book 2, chapter 14).

Before we address the content of the writing, which many critics have already noted, we must note the stages of the act, especially the verbs. "Isaac's arm stretched out and his hand started trembling. He reached out his brush to the dog, and the dog reached himself out to

Isaac" (p. 286). Then: "The dog liked his contact with a human creature who has a kind of dripping vessel, . . . was still waiting for his mois-
ture to drip on him, . . . and barked a weak, obsequious bark. Isaac's
hand began to tingle. . . [and] he rubbed it on his clothes to get rid of
the tingling, but it kept on tingling." And again: "The dog stretched
himself toward him and looked at his brush as if with curiosity. In truth,
there was no curiosity here, but there was desire" ("desire" means
lust).[30] "He raised himself a bit, and raised himself a bit again until between him and the brush there was just a margin of nothing. The brush
started dripping" (p. 287; see Jacob Katz's comments on this issue).

Note that here, more than anywhere else in *Only Yesterday,*
and perhaps more than anywhere else in Agnon's works, is a detailed
and almost open description of copulation.

Just as Sonya treated Isaac and as Leichtfuss treats his lovers
and as Isaac thinks Arab men treat their women—so Isaac treats Balak.
Right after the act, "he kicked the dog. . . . The dog opened his mouth
wide and peered at him in amazement. He treated him with affection
and in the end he kicks him. . . . That one's eyes smile and his feet are
angry. Don't his feet know that he's just having fun? In the meantime,
the dog's spirits drooped" (p. 287). Even without emphasizing the sexual flavor of the word "fun," it is easy to see that right after the act, the
dog stopped representing the female principle. In a flash, he takes on
the character and fate of Isaac, whom Sonya "treated with affection"
and suddenly "kicked" so hard "his spirits drooped."

And once again, we may challenge the tendency of several
readers and critics to state that Balak is Isaac or Balak is Isaac's passion
or Balak is Isaac's orphanhood or Balak is Isaac's "demon" or Balak is
a parable of the Second Aliya or of sin or punishment or woman or
atonement or the past, and so on and so forth. Just because there is a
trace of reason in each of these many contradictory decodings, it is better not to attribute a general and exclusive validity to any one of them.
The decoder who has perhaps gone farthest is Shlomo Tsemakh, who
disagrees with Eli Schweid that all the "modernism" in Agnon, including the episode of Balak in *Only Yesterday,* is just an accident that happened to "a Hebrew author who always wrote pretty things as they are,
and suddenly swerved from his good road and went astray" (and see
Meshulam Tochner's reply to these arguments). Eli Schweid's comments are subtle and direct: "To grasp the meaning of the 'stray dog'
in the work, we must give up all moral fables and discuss 'its personal-

ity' and its fate as one of the protagonists of the plot." But Schweid does talk about a "parallel" between the dog and Isaac and sees Balak as a "poetic borrowing," an expanded metaphor for Isaac, and he sees Isaac himself as an expanded metaphor or symbol for the entire Second Aliya. Schweid does emphasize that, while Isaac Kumer is not a sociological, representative figure who characterizes the Second Aliya, he is the most "consistent" figure. According to Schweid, Balak is like Isaac, and Isaac is like the Second Aliya, and all three take a "pathetic position" vis-à-vis alienated reality.

After Isaac stretches out his brush and empties his lust onto Balak's hide, he seems to extinguish his consciousness and to operate from the depths. The dripping brush is Isaac's brush, but the force that dictates the words written on the dog's skin is not the force of Isaac but an ancient force from the depths: "By the time Isaac stood up, he had written in calligraphy on the dog the letters d-o-g" (p. 286). Then: "the brush didn't dry out until the words Crazy Dog were written on the dog's skin" (p. 287). The two words are written from the unconscious depths, thoughtlessly and without choice. Twice, the text emphasizes "until the words were written."

Isaac does not know why "Crazy Dog," and Balak certainly doesn't know, and the narrator tells us he doesn't know either: "We don't know if, from the start, he meant to write what he wrote. . . . But why should we get into that doubt" (p. 286). Incidentally, here the "we" is the professional "we" that some writers use when they talk about their own writing: "as we said in our previous study," and so forth.

Who would write the word "dog" on a dog's skin? Who would bother to write "wall" on a wall or "hand" on a hand? A child having fun. Or even a person whose certainty is shaken and whose soul is no longer sure of things that are obvious; a person suffering from an emotional shock or from some cognitive debility. For example, some amnesiacs write the name on every object so they don't forget it. The same thing sometimes happens to people who suffer shellshock. Perhaps this is a confirmation "from the depths" of the severity of Isaac's wound. Moreover, throughout this scene, Isaac does not behave as usual, as a fine and modest, shy fellow with "nine measures of sadness" always poured on his face. On the contrary, he is arrogant and emanates some amused haughtiness, like Sweet Foot's, while his "tingling hand" in this scene is related closely to Samson Bloykof's hand, which also "tingles" and paints "as if by itself."

And the dog? After Isaac kicked him, "he picked up his feet and started running." He will run with the writing on his back until he becomes the menace of Jerusalem and will terrify all who see him, except for one single man in Jerusalem who is not afraid of the crazy dog because he himself wrote "Crazy Dog" on his skin, and he knows that the dog isn't crazy and that this book cannot be judged by its cover. Thus, in the end, Isaac becomes one of the "titans" he has always adored, those fearless ones who stand alone outside the human herd. When it comes to the fear of the dog—which spreads like mass hysteria in Jerusalem—Isaac stands alone, outside the panicky herd around him.

Until the horror of mocking fate is revealed. Until Isaac—who isn't afraid of the crazy dog because he is the only one who knows that the crazy dog is not a crazy dog—falls victim to the crazy dog, who has gone crazy because of what Isaac did to him, and who wreaks his vengeance on Isaac.

|

Balak's beginning is a perfect satirical "Maskil" one—the dog runs to Meah Shearim and sets off such a grotesque turmoil and a dark menace there that "all of Meah Shearim [is] shocked" (p. 288). Like a four-legged Maskil artist, a Yosef Perl or an Isaac Erter, he exposes the nakedness of hypocritical and petrified ultra-Orthodox Jewry in general, and the nakedness of the most zealous, Reb Fayesh and Reb Grunam, in particular. The man will see eyes and the dog will see knees; and so Balak is able to discern what the listeners to the sermons of the crazy Ayatolla Reb Grunam do not: even though the preacher screams and wails, "his knees don't move when he groans" (p. 288). Here and there, the narrator takes pains to reinforce that "Maskil" foundation in the Balak episode and even verges on an anti-Semitic caricature: "in that generation the freethinkers were not yet important, and Satan desired to dwell among the pious" (p. 333). But the reader had better not stop at that ideological level but go behind the narrator and the dog to more interesting areas.

From Meah Shearim, Balak goes to the places of the Gentiles, but "all those days his thought [is] bound to Meah Shearim" (p. 295), and he struggles and hesitates but is unable to understand the curse that lies on him when he is among Jews and is removed from him when he is among Gentiles. "Why is it that the Children of Israel see his flaw and the Gentiles don't see his flaw? Or perhaps the flaw in him is a flaw in the eyes of the Children of Israel, but for the others it isn't a flaw" (p. 296). It is easy and even tempting to find here only satire à la Yosef Perl and Mendele, a simple allegory whose sting is aimed at the degeneration and madness of zealous Orthodox Jewry, whose angle of vision is sideways and down, at the dog's eye level, and whose un-equivocal conclusion, as it were, is "the face of the generation in the face of a dog" (Sotah 9:15;) or "orphaned generation" (Sotah 7:12). It is easy to see Isaac and Balak as one, and there is a tendency to see Balak as the other side of Isaac, or as his "alter ego."

As we have said, it may be better to refrain from those tempta-tions of monovalent ideological and allegorical identification and to make do with a less rounded perspective: Isaac, like Balak, bears "on his back" the decree of his fate, and at times it seems that everyone but him can see "what is written on him from above." Isaac's efforts, like Balak's efforts to flee from fate, are like the prayer to God: "From You to You I shall flee." Isaac will die without understanding why he is dying, and so will Balak: "At that moment, all his suffering was naught compared with the search for truth. . . . He was amazed and stunned, Everyone who sees me knows the truth about me, and I, who possess the truth itself, I don't know what it is" (p. 303). Whoever reads the writing on Balak's back knows more than Balak can know; whoever reads *Only Yesterday* understands a little more than Isaac himself can understand. And yet, the menace and brutality of fate remain in darkness.

|

Long before Balak goes mad, the description of him (book 4, chapter 3) fits the signs of a mad dog as enumerated in the Talmud: "Our Rabbis taught five things were mentioned in connection with a mad dog. Its mouth is open, its saliva dripping, its ears flap, its tail is hang-ing between its thighs, it walks on the edge of the road. Some say: Also it barks without its voice being heard" (Yoma, 83, page A). Balak com-pares himself to Satan, to Sammael who is called dog and is in charge of Hell (p. 313), but Balak himself—like the critics of *Only Yesterday*—interprets himself in various and contradictory ways.

When Isaac came to the Land of Israel, he stopped observing the Commandments, apparently without any torments and almost in-advertently. But when he ascended to Jerusalem, he became observant again, also inadvertently and without any struggles—"once Isaac put off shaving his beard" (p. 306)—as if his legs carried him and he didn't direct his own steps.

Reb Fayesh, the son-in-law of Reb Amram and the father of Shifra, "the most zealous of the zealots" (p. 307), stirs a repressed hostility in Isaac. "Crazy Dog should have been written on you and your skin" (p. 309), thinks Isaac. Here is the same hostility Reb Fayesh will stir in Balak, who becomes Isaac's "agent" and Isaac's foe at the same time.

Reb Fayesh is Balak's first victim after the dog's return to Meah Shearim. Thus the "Maskil" satire—in which Balak served as a "latent discoverer" or "a righteous observer" exposing the hypocrisy of the fanatic ultra-Orthodox—ceases to be a Maskil satire and becomes a dark, Gothic nightmare, when the dog terrifies Reb Fayesh, who is permanently petrified.

Some critics have found signs of Kafka's influence in the Balak episode. Shlomo Tsemakh, for example, went so far as to declare that the entire episode of Balak is merely an imitation of Kafka, and that "with the distress of a builder who doesn't know how to put the roof onto his building [Agnon flees] into the dark." Hillel Barzel also noted the Kafkaesque basis of the Balak episode. And Meshulam Tochner's response to Shlomo Tsemakh's harsh claims that Agnon was telling Kafka's tales is especially interesting. Agnon himself claimed that, at the time he was writing *Only Yesterday,* he didn't know Kafka's writings at all, and that Kafka was not "rooted in his soul."

Whether or not there is a whiff of Kafka in the Balak episode, it may be better not to dismiss out of hand Shlomo Tsemakh's suspicion about "structural distress" in the second part of the novel. And this structural distress may be merely an external manifestation of the deeper distress that weighed heavily on the possible conclusion of *Shira,* obscured the end of *A Guest for the Night,* and created an end within an end in *The Bridal Canopy.* Dan Miron thinks that in Agnon's novels, "the general artistic pattern . . . is more a perfect soldering than one single casting." Miron apparently means "a perfect soldering" of the story of Isaac with the tale of Balak. Miron argues that, despite Agnon's great achievements as a writer of novels, the novelistic genre was not "natural" to him because of "a comprehensive cultural and historical problematic." He also emphasizes Agnon's difficulty in concluding his novels. This point of view might be supported without adhering to Miron's more exaggerated assumption that Agnon saw the novelistic genre as essentially "a foreign genre," and that it was precisely when he became an observant Jew that he was assailed by some impulse "to domesticate" or "to convert" that genre, as someone who takes sparks out of the external form. Without any connection to the religious observance of Agnon the man, it is doubtful that the position of the creator of *Only Yesterday* could be considered an orthodox religious position—at least in the accepted sense of the term. Perhaps it is more correct to speak of a theological distress rather than a religious position.

|

The evil that Balak does to Reb Fayesh opens the door of Reb Fayesh's house and family to Isaac and indirectly grants him a father surrogate and a mother surrogate and a Sonya surrogate. Or perhaps Shifra is not a "Sonya surrogate" but Isaac's true mate, or is it that "forty days before a man's birth, a voice comes out and declares the daughter of so-and-so for so-and-so"? The novel does not answer this question in its conclusion or at all, in general, as it does not answer the question of natural law and its meaning. All of *Only Yesterday* is steeped in signs and signals of the existence of a detailed and precise natural order—not a leaf falls to the ground without being directed. But is that order divine predestination, or sociopsychological determinism? Or perhaps the natural law is subject to "the horror of fate." The work does not reply to these questions, and the reader may be invited to reply in his own way, or to be silent.

In any case, Isaac responds to the appearance of Shifra in a religious and predestined way: "From heaven were you summoned here" (p. 354), he tells her in their secret, quasi-accidental encounter (pp. 354–55), which is a distant echo of the "vision of the well" he fantasized while lying on the ship traveling to the Land of Israel (prologue, section 12). The encounter of Isaac and Shifra begins with "A girl came holding a jar" (p. 353) and continues with Isaac rolling away and not rolling away the stone that isn't a stone from the mouth of the well that isn't a well. A repressed and restrained Chekhovian charm fills this scene. The emotional tension between Shifra and Isaac is far from the feelings of sin and guilt, from the male-female role reversal, and from the sensual opposition between the experienced Sonya and the virgin Isaac. Here Isaac does not expect Shifra "to come" and take the place of his angelic white mother. With his shy delicacy, he courts Shifra, who is even more timid than he—until she suddenly flees from him or from herself, and Isaac "start[s] running after her. And he [doesn't] know that she [has] already gone far away, and that creature he [sees] walking [isn't] a human being, but a stray dog. Isaac [doesn't] see that it [is] a dog, but the dog [sees] Isaac" (p. 356).

Book 2 of *Only Yesterday* concludes with the character of Reb Alter, who balances the satirical venom the narrator has cast on the zealots and hypocrites of Meah Shearim. In the same way, at the end of book 1, the character of Menahem balances the satirical venom the narrator cast on the hypocritical prattlers of Zionist Jaffa.

|

On his trip back to Jaffa, Isaac hears the carter Reb Avreml-Zundel tell his tale of lost identity, which isn't far from the fate of Menashe Haim in "And the Crooked Became Straight." There—as in *Only Yesterday*, *A Simple Story*, and other works—at least two systems of explanation are operating: the psychosocial and predestination or fatalism. Indirectly and allusively, what happened to the carter Reb Avreml-Zundel is like what happened to Isaac himself (pp. 378–79). The entire trip is shrouded in a dreamy atmosphere, like a divination, a shimmering revelation. The horses fly off, and the road to Jaffa is not simply a road to Jaffa. When the carter asks Isaac, "What do you do?" and Isaac "[wakes] with a start" and replies, "I don't do anything"—these words emerge from their simplicity, especially when they are immediately confronted with the shade of Reb Yudel Hasid, who "never in his life did he do a thing that wasn't for the sake of heaven" (p. 380).

|

Isaac arrives in Jaffa and comes to Sonya at dusk and doesn't yet know what he will say to her. "It was twilight . . . [and] a sweet darkness from outside mated with that darkness in the room. And in the room was a sweetness of dusk" (p. 384). "Between the sweetness of dusk and the mating of the two darknesses, Sonya sees Isaac with his beard and his Jerusalem clothes and she said, You're festive, Isaac, your face is like the face of a bridegroom. Isaac's face blushed" (p. 385). Isaac, who doesn't know if he came to end the whole affair with Sonya so he can marry Shifra, or whether he came to marry Sonya to end his affair with Shifra and Jerusalem, seems to be asking for Sonya's hand. She bursts out laughing and talks to him in Yiddish, contemptuously—as when she dismissed him, for then, too, she spoke Yiddish with him, "the way you talk with simple people" (p. 151). Sonya explains to Isaac that "if I cast off the yoke of father and mother, I won't put on the yoke of a husband" (p. 386), even though many men want to marry her. Instead of marriage, she invites Isaac for an ice cream. And once again, the ice cream (p. 387) turns into a metynomic expression for Sonya's sexuality.

Thus, Isaac comes to Sonya's room ready for the decision of fate, and here is an invitation to ice cream. He wanted to atone "at one fell swoop" for the sin he committed against Sonya by "tempting" her, as it were, and for the sin he committed against Rabinovitch for "stealing" his girl, as it were, and for the sin he committed against religious prohibitions, and perhaps also for the sin he committed against his father's house. Asking for Sonya's hand is supposed to repair all those transgressions, as a gallant gesture; even though his heart may already be given to Shifra, the obligation of gallantry is imposed on him to take belated responsibility for his deeds. All this stirs in Sonya nothing but a great laugh that may border on slight hysteria. As for Isaac, he may be repressing his failure as a man and concealing it from himself under the guise of "divine punishment." Perhaps it is easier for him to live with a sense of sin than to live with a sense of insult as a man.

Just as the Jerusalem zealotry in the characters of Reb Grunam and Reb Fayesh stirs the narrator's sarcastic mockery, so the hollow loquacity of the Zionist activists of Jaffa stirs his stinging contempt (pp. 388–89). Hemdat, the image of the young Agnon, greets Sonya and Isaac and Yarkoni hospitably, "for Hemdat said, If a person drops in on me it surely has to be, for if not, would divine Providence have taken the trouble to bring us to the same place" (p. 389)—and thus Hemdat jokingly and casually expresses the strict law of encounters that rules autocratically in *Only Yesterday,* a law that recognizes neither chance nor accidental meetings. Thus Hemdat also expresses an echo of "everything the Merciful One does He does for good," the innocent and perfect religious position of Reb Yudel Hasid. When they are joined at Hemdat's by the moldy Dr. Schimmelmann, who is improving the Torah and raising the Prophets of Israel to the level of journalists (compare the description of him on p. 103), a stinging and fascinating confrontation begins between Hemdat-Agnon and Schimmelmann, which may be one of the most poisonous peaks of Agnonian irony (pp. 390–92). Even Yael Hayyot and her lover Shammai from "Hill of Sand," as well as the scholar of seaweed Jacob Rekhnitz and little Tamara from the story "An Oath of Faith," join this splendid gathering in the coffeehouse and later in their creator's garret.

Now that he has asked for Sonya's hand and thus "atoned for his sins," and he is free to marry Shifra with a clear conscience, Isaac Kumer does not feel relief. On the contrary, the sense of guilt still seems to be slicing, even more than before, "for if he had settled his account with Sonya, with Rabinovitch he hadn't settled. A hundred times he said to himself, Rabinovitch has already taken his mind off her, and he doesn't care about anything. But Isaac wasn't satisfied. He started trembling and he started sweating like someone in the grip of malaria. But this wasn't malaria, but the sweat of shame covered him and remorse racked his body" (p. 392). These symptoms are not much different from those experienced by the dog Balak when he goes mad (book 4, chapter 17).

Isaac's erotic dilemma is not resolved by asking for Sonya's hand and by her refusal, because it is a dilemma with no solution: his heart is given to Shifra and his passion draws him to Sonya (almost like Hirshl in *A Simple Story,* whose heart is with his beloved Bluma and whose passion is with his wife, Mina, or like Manfred Herbst, whose heart is with his wife, Henriette, and whose passion is with the nurse Shira).

Isaac "makes a pilgrimage" to Sweet Foot's hut, and finds him so absorbed in the annals of the dogs he had who left and came back that it is hard not to see the similarity between his dogs and his lovers, who return to him whenever he throws them out.[31] One of his dogs, as Leichtfuss tells Isaac, returned to his first master, and "now that he is living with you, he misses me, afterward, when he stays with me, he'll miss you" (p. 395). This can be seen as an echo of Isaac's distress between Jaffa and Jerusalem and between Sonya and Shifra. Later on, in one of the more amusing and bizarre encounters in the novel, Hemdat-Agnon also comes to Sweet Foot's hut, that young poet who "doesn't have anything to do. . . . As long as he was Outside the Land and his heart was in the Land of Israel, he composed poems; now that he lives in the Land of Israel, what shall he do? Would he compose poems about the longings he once had?" (p. 397). Like Bloykof, Hemdat is not afraid of the mystical bond between creation and death (p. 397).

"Hemdat and Isaac are the same age, and should have been conscripted into the army. They slipped away and ascended to the Land of Israel on one and the same day in two different ships" (p. 397). Whether they came on two ships (in those days, two ships didn't come to the Land of Israel from Europe in a week), to his pleasure and amusement, the narrator reveals the biographical closeness between the narrating author and his hero Isaac. He also exposes the half-repressed prosaic reason (far from Zionist romanticism) for at least two of those three Galicians (Isaac, Hemdat, and perhaps Agnon, too) immigrating to the Land of Israel: to escape the danger of conscription. (The prosaic, unromantic draft board is also a reason for Hirshl's madness in *A Simple Story*.)

In the same encounter, Hemdat greets Isaac heartily "even though he [isn't] comfortable with the craft Isaac practice[s], for there is something misleading in it, since painters are wont to embellish ugly things" (p. 397). Thus Hemdat reinforces the symbolic distinction between painting and building: "Like all our brethren of the Second Aliya, the bearers of Our Salvation, Isaac Kumer left his country and his homeland and his city and ascended to the Land of Israel to build it from its destruction and to be rebuilt by it," says the opening sentence of the novel. But Isaac does not carry out his intention and does not build the Land from its destruction but rather paints it, perhaps to beautify its ugliness. Indeed, none of the people gathered in Leichtfuss's hut in this bizarre scene is building the Land; each in his own way may be trying to be rebuilt by it.

Later, at the inn of Jacob Malkhov—who may represent Rabbi Abraham Isaac Ha-Cohen Kook, whom Agnon admired—Yosef-Hayyim Brenner enters the novel, under his real name: "A short man with a blond beard and beautiful blue eyes. . . . His movements are casual and his clothes are tattered, and he is timid in the presence of folks" (p. 402). Malkhov and Brenner, like the standing Rabbi Menahem, both receive a "stylistic concession" from the narrator: they are exempt from the author's hand that stylizes the speech of most of the protagonists and express themselves here in an almost mimetic language. Thus a fascinating scene of a cultural and intellectual conflict develops, which Isaac attends as a passive and admiring witness. Brenner treats Hemdat-Agnon in a warm, paternal way, as if he were a capricious girl, while he treats Malkhov like a brother (pp. 402–7).

Malkhov begins by telling Brenner and the others a tale of Professor Boris Schatz, the founder and director of the Bezalel Art School, who gave a "joyous Hanukah party." Malkhov's tale mocks the Zionist usurpation of the story of the Hasmoneans, a tale of religious zealots and a religious uprising. Zionism turns the story, to its own advantage, into one of a Garibaldian national uprising. This counterfeit Zionist tale led the members of Bezalel to dance around a stat-ue of Mattithiyahu the iconoclast Hasmonean, and if that statue came to life, it would rise up against the celebrants and stab them all with the sword in his hand, "for this Mattithiyahu was a zealot for his religion, for his religion and not for his land" (p. 406). Brenner bursts into coarse laughter, "vulgar" laughter, or "wild" laughter, in his words, at this tale. In this scene, it is the anti-Zionist Malkhov who gets the last word. But the narrator's affection is given both to Malkhov and to Brenner, just as Malkhov and Brenner are fond of each other despite their quarrel. The whole group "comes out gracefully" from the narra-tor's pen.

Brenner's "internal monologue" ("Brenner doesn't share the rejoicing," and so forth [pp. 409–11]) almost constitutes a "Brenner-esque enclave" within Agnon's novel. Perhaps this monologue con-tains a circuitous and significant reply to Malkhov's crushing arguments against secular Zionism. Brenner's reply does not dissipate the doubts but, on the contrary, intensifies and deepens them, and yet it jolts all those who "haven't yet awoken from the hypnosis of the past"—bold words that may be stronger today than when they were said.

Hemdat-Agnon's heart, and perhaps Isaac's, too, goes out to Malkhov and to Brenner, and perhaps most to Yanekele and Yankele's father, until Brenner "respond[s] with a melody and [says], Kinderlakh m'darf geyn aheym" (p. 412; Children, we've got to go home). And everybody laughs, because who has a home? "They [part] from one another and [go] their way, this one to his room, and that one to the corner of his bed in the cheap hotels of Neve Shalom" (p. 412).

In one of those cheap hotels, Isaac spends a strange night: the flood of his thoughts between dream and longing leads him from Sweet Foot—and here he really sees Leichtfuss and himself as a pair of lovers—to Jacob Malkhov, and from him to Arzef and to the dogs barking in the dark of night, to Shifra and Sonya and to Reb Fayesh and to the dog embroidered on Sonya's blanket (pp. 412–13). This flood of associa-tions, which might be defined as a "stream of unconsciousness," reveals among other things Isaac's erotic revulsion for Shifra, and on the other hand his obsessive attraction to Sonya (p. 413). Perhaps Gershon Shaked was wrong when he stated that Isaac "chose" Shifra over Sonya, and that "this choice causes a schizophrenic process." Almost nowhere and never in the novel does Isaac Kumer use the right of choice. Perhaps the heart of the novel is the lack of "a right of choice." Isaac surely did not "choose" Shifra. If Sonya had agreed to his marriage proposal when he came back to Jaffa to be released from his bonds, he might not have returned to Jerusalem and married Shifra.

Once again, Jaffa is spread out before Isaac's eyes in the human expanse between Hemdat and Orgelbrand and between Brenner and Malkhov, as the opposite of Jerusalem—both in the social and cultural intensity of Jaffa, and in its vistas: "And here the sea of Jaffa cheers the heart and the green citrus groves gladden the eyes and the red pomegranate trees are suffused with a loveliness of beauty like a sweet promise. . . . And Jaffa also has this advantage over Jerusalem, that everywhere you go there, you find comrades" (pp. 417–18). These comrades all gather together on Friday evening, in the chapter "Happy People" and in the following chapter, "Continuation," and then "In Hemdat's Garret" (pp. 419–39). Here, in the chapters on Jaffa in the third part of the novel, the melancholy, the stifling, and the menace in the Jerusalem chapters seem to change into youthful joy that is more artistic and bohemian than Pioneering and idealistic.

Historical figures appear here under their real names (Malkhov, Brenner, Mordechai ben Hillel HaCohen, Michael Heilperin, Aharon David Gordon, Arthur Ruppin, Levi Yitzhak the hotelier), while others appear under fictional and slightly camouflaged names (the young Hemdat-Agnon, Falk Shpaltleder, Gorishkin, Yarkoni);[32] and there are also fictional characters (Sonya, Shammai and Pnina, Yael Hayyot, the two inseparable ex-wives of Vitorio Godswill). Orphanhood is contrasted with exultant youthful freedom: these "happy people," released from the yoke of tradition, liberated from the presence of demanding parents, free from the compulsions of a job and a career, from the yoke of marriage and child rearing, are described here not as a handful of heroic Pioneers devoted to the sanctity of the Zionist commandments, but rather as a group of young men and women (mostly men) who live in a constant summer camp of sweet ragamuffin licentiousness. Jaffa suddenly appears to be a liberated Arcadia of youth and joy, almost a prototype of a hippie commune of the sixties, despite the bitter arguments between these youths—or perhaps even the arguments merely add spice to the overflowing adolescent energy.

Jaffa seems to hold Isaac and keep him from going back to Jerusalem, even though the novel continues moving back and forth between the temperamental Jaffa and the gloomy home of the paralyzed Reb Fayesh, where Shifra and her mother, Rebecca, come to despair because of Isaac's disappearance (book 3, chapters 13 and 14).

Rabinovitch's return from Outside the Land once again stirs in Isaac the dread of the sin that poisons his life: "Even though his affairs with Sonya were over, his affairs with himself weren't over. And if Rabinovitch had never been out of his mind's eye for a day, those days he grew severalfold. And as he grew so did that sin. . . . And if he put Shifra before his mind's eye to prove that he has nothing to do with Sonya, He Who reproaches him evokes Sonya in his mind's eye" (p. 465). Isaac, who lives as a guard for free in the hut of Sweet Foot, gone on his wanderings, encounters Arzef in the sands when Arzef comes from Jerusalem on a matter of taxidermy. Not only does Isaac want to cling to Leichtfuss and Arzef (as once he did to Rabinovitch and Bloykof), but he also longs to be like them, to live outside social compulsions and erotic humility—in short, "outside the system." But Isaac isn't made of egocentric or narcissistic material; he has no aggressiveness or cruelty or any characteristic of a Nietzschean "Superman" (as it was grasped in the imaginations of small-town Jewish boys in those days). Thus, over and over again, his legs carry him to the one he is destined for, to his "ideal double," Jonathan Orgelbrand, the "established" bachelor with a regular income and a respectable position, whose dreams about Sonya are like Isaac's visions about her (pp. 466–68).

When Isaac meets the new Rabinovitch, Rabinovitch the rich merchant (pp. 469–71), he learns that his former friend is now married and doesn't reproach him at all for the "transgression of Sonya" and in fact doesn't feel anything for Sonya except contempt mixed with slight hostility (p. 470, and even more on p. 474).

Rabinovitch found his wife Hilda "through a dog" (a tale that is almost a small parody on Chekhov's "The Woman with the Puppy"). When Isaac hears this story from Rabinovitch (p. 476), the narrator plays the innocent and states piously: "In everything the Holy-One-Blessed-Be-He carries out His mission, sometimes in the open and sometimes in secret. What is done in the open, we see, what is done in secret, we don't see" (p. 476). This religious thought may contain more dread of darkness than do several deterministic or fatalistic musings of the author in other places in the novel, for if the horror is lying in wait for Isaac, it is produced by "the agent of the Holy-One-Blessed-Be-He." In the same way, the dog who matched Rabinovitch and his

Hilda acted as an agent of the Holy-One-Blessed-Be-He, for the natural order is a satanic order. One who sins is not punished, and one who is punished has almost not sinned, and punishment is not proportionate to what the human mind tolerates as a banal transgression, and transgression is also decreed on the victim from the start and without any choice or "permission given." It is not "the earth [that] is given into the hand of the wicked," but Heaven.

Isaac returns to Sweet Foot's hut and finds that its owner has come back, taken over his bed, fallen asleep in it, and does not need the key to the hut that was in Isaac's keeping. Isaac reluctantly moves for one night to a hotel and reluctantly gets up the next day and returns to Jerusalem. At the railroad station: "The porters saw him and started wrangling with each other to serve him. Isaac saw one man standing alone with his hands folded behind his back, he called him. That porter was a porter of the Burial Society. . . . He untied his ropes and followed Isaac" (p. 482). Thus ends book 3 of *Only Yesterday.* Guilt and orphanhood and fate; Isaac is going to be bound. Here is the hangman, and here is the rope.

|

Book 4, "Epilogue," opens with the dog Balak and unfolds a wicked satire about a kind of "scandal in Clochemerle" that swells whenever the episode of the dog fills the newspapers of Jerusalem and is then transformed into an allegorical, didactic metamorphosis for the newspapers of Jaffa, and back to the yards of the rabbis of Jerusalem, until it also resonates overseas and Balak puts his stamp on Hasidism and politics and art and everything else in the world (pp. 485–94). This episode, which may not be one of the best of *Only Yesterday,* does connect well—albeit at a low and ridiculous level—with the world prevailing in all parts of the novel, in which a dense causal network that does not allow any room for accident is spread from one end of the world to the other. A dog doesn't bark in Jerusalem without starting a chain of reasons and causing a development of ramified results whose scope is the whole world—and who can predict how it will end?

There has been a great deal of criticism of the chapter on Balak's nature and pedigree (pp. 495–98), as well as discussion of canine mythology and the Midrash on the canine Genesis, from the ancient camel to the biting of the firmament, Balak's licentiousness and loss of religious faith (pp. 499–506)—on its four levels of meaning—

literal, allusion, exegesis, and secret. And here and there that discussion may have indulged in exaggerated hairsplitting. The short fragment in which the remnants of Balak's fear of heaven are destroyed (p. 502) deserves special mention, not necessarily because of the parallel (which doesn't exist here) between the dog and Isaac, but because of the (supposed) closeness between the torments of faith and heresy of the dog and the torments of faith and heresy that may have been experienced by the creator of Isaac and Balak. Nevertheless, despite the efforts of several interpreters, the reader may not be obliged to attribute a psychological, ideological, historical, or religious moral to every one of Balak's barks and gasps. It is enough to note that the main theme of Balak in the novel is the orphanhood and abandonment of a dog who is and is not like a proper Jewish dog, is and is not like every other obsequious stray dog looking for a house and love and attention, is and is not out of his mind; but with all his beatings, he did not and could not leave the path fate decreed for him for no sin he had committed.

"Even before Isaac reached Jerusalem, Jaffa was uprooted from his heart. . . . And when he reached Jerusalem, his soul woke up and his heart began to beat" (p. 519). What is depicted in the first parts of *Only Yesterday* as a bridge of the naïve synthesis that spanned all the cleavages that have split the Jewish people in the last two hundred years—above all, a bridge spanning the awful opposition between religion and life—is now revealed to be a paper bridge that is torn to shreds: there is no room or coexistence for Jaffa and Jerusalem in Isaac's heart. One comes and the other goes. Thus he confronts a Hobson's choice far beyond his strength, and hence he cannot choose. Isaac "chances on," "winds up," "is swept away" from here to there and back again. In the narrator's words: "His feet moved by themselves, and he was dragged along with his feet" (p. 19).

Once again Isaac winds up in Jerusalem, and once again his feet carry him to the house of Reb Fayesh, Shifra's house. The Jerusalem of *Only Yesterday* is a sublime and filthy city, mysterious and ugly, characterized by barrenness and dryness even before they are reified in a drought at the end of the novel. The narrator uses a stray dog in the role of eyes, ears, and nose, absorbing and conveying the filth and decadence of Jerusalem. Only the visionary eyes of a child, like Bloykof or Isaac, sometimes see the splendor behind the ugliness. (Dov Sadan has written several pertinent lines about the "double image of Jerusalem" in *Only Yesterday*.)

Returning to the inn, Isaac discovers among his bundles "a small Tallit" his father had given him for the road, but that he hadn't used so far. Therefore, he sits down and composes a letter to his father in pious terminology, as if he hadn't sat just a few days before with Brenner and Sonya and Pnina, as if he had never gone with Sonya to Café Hermon. In his letter, Isaac tells his father "a bit about his affairs with Shifra" (p. 526), reporting on the match even before it is concluded (pp. 525–26).

After he rents himself a room and goes back to work painting, Isaac visits Shifra and her mother, Rebecca. (The old couple he met on the ship, Shifra's grandparents, have meanwhile moved to Safed.) And this time, Isaac dares to do what he has not done before; he tells the two women about his family, about his dead mother, and they also tell him their family stories (pp. 544–49). Thus, that match is shaped in a more traditional, small-town way than rolling a stone off the mouth of the well, as in his fantasy. It has charm and grace and mercy and even the calculation of practicality, but it does not have one spark of the erotic fire that Sonya kindled in Isaac. The more Isaac wraps himself in the ultra-Orthodox bosom of Jerusalem, the more the image of the Zionist Pioneer he had in Jaffa and the settlement leaves him. He reverts to what he was in his small town: a lowly son of a lowly family, the son of shopkeepers who declined in fortune, with no hope of bourgeois social climbing and no characteristics of a scholar, merely a simple laborer who can expect nothing more in the "marriage market" than a bride of poor social quality, or a bride with some defect in herself or her family that lowers her value—like Shifra the daughter of Reb Fayesh, who got caught in a bad deal and became paralyzed. In "The Beginning of Isaac," he had the flame of the Zionist dream and longings to work the soil, and now he has nothing but the sadness of an orphan seeking a home.

As a modest and submissive fellow, a small-town boy who has come of age and has neither father nor mother, Isaac goes to his towns-folk in Jerusalem and hopes they will help him with his match, for after all a fellow doesn't make a match for himself (pp. 560–63). Reb Alter, the ritual slaughterer, along with the blind Reb Haim Rafael, show the warm, good-hearted aspect of religious Judaism. Each in his own way agrees to be a father surrogate for Isaac. It is the people of his home-town who help Isaac make a match with Shifra's family—just as they would certainly have helped him with his match if he and they had not left their hometown. Thus, the circle is closed that opened with the splendid and modest fellow's rebellion and his decision "to break the traditional rules," and he now reaches submission and a return to obedience to the Jewish bosom he tried to escape by joining the Zionist revolution. Boaz Arpali thinks that Isaac is "a hero who flees from all conscious choice and any genuine ethical decision." Perhaps. But the internal question at the base of the work seems to be whether a person can make a conscious choice, an ethical decision, or whether from the start, everything is in the hands of irresistible forces.

In the nightmares that visit him (p. 573), Isaac is swept back to the sea, to the forgotten shoes, the bare head, until he sees himself in his dream in a house whose first story is ruined and whose second story is a prayer house, and he climbs a ladder and puts his head into the prayer house and the door closes on him, his head inside and his body outside. This is Isaac's existential situation after he has cut himself off from his other world and his other persona, the physical and passionate one, and from his other faith and the other commandments and his other love.

Isaac spends more time with the old men of his hometown who live in Jerusalem—because they are old and because they are from his hometown: "Isaac was a simple fellow who didn't engage in profound inquiry. And like the simple Children of Israel, who, if they sometimes stray from the path, in the end they return" (p. 574). In another dream, he sees himself standing "in a warm place without shade" and almost dying of thirst; he sees a channel of water, but he can't get to it. Pnina, whom he met in Jaffa and in Eyn Ganim, appears in that dream, and her voice is the voice of Shifra, and she is plowing the soil and tells Isaac that this is Um G'uni, that is Degania (where Isaac had never been). In his dream, he picks up a hoe and starts hoeing the soil, and here's Makherovitch with a photographer coming to take his picture at work, and the dog barks and wakes him up (p. 575). If in the first dream his head is in the prayer house and his body is outside and all of him is neither swallowed up nor vomited, in the second dream (almost as in the dream about the magus and the caravan in Bialik's "Gleanings"), Degania is a source of flowing water, and the hoe is the heart's desire, and Pnina and Shifra are combined in a "proper" female Pioneer image, but the lie comes (Makherovitch and the photographer) and makes everything ugly.

On the eve of his wedding, Isaac goes to "show his face" to Reb Alter and his wife, Hinda-Puah, who promises to come to his wedding, reducing all of Isaac's essence to one awful sentence: "A child solitary as a stone in the field and I would refrain from dancing at his wedding" (p. 581). After receiving Reb Alter's blessing, he goes to blind Reb Haim Raphael to invite him to the wedding and to receive his blessing. The old man recalls an incident at the wedding of Isaac's grandfather, when Haim Raphael the blind child groped his way there and was offended and wept bitterly, and now he makes a wish for Isaac and himself: "I hope I may repair at your wedding what I ruined at your grandfather's wedding" (p. 586). This memory joins a long list of ominous signs, beginning with the porter of the Burial Society who clung to Isaac as he went from Jaffa to Jerusalem.

Shifra and Isaac's paltry wedding, shrouded in hostility and suspicion on the part of the zealous ultra-Orthodox and overshadowed by the calamity of Reb Fayesh, the bride's father, is almost reminiscent of the grotesque offense of the wedding of Dinah and the doctor in "The Doctor's Divorce."[33] Before the wedding, Isaac received a telegram of congratulation from Rabinovitch and didn't read it but put it in his pocket. A few hours before the ceremony, while waiting his turn for the barber, Isaac reads the story "Tishrei," a first version of "Hill of Sand," in *The Young Laborer.*[34] Meanwhile, he suddenly forgets Sonya's last name, like a person who wants to blot out of his memory on his wedding day the earlier rings that haunt him.

And right in the middle of the horrifying and hostile marriage ceremony, a miracle happens to Isaac like the miracle that happened to Reb Yudel his ancestor: a great rabbi who ascended to Israel from Hungary takes pity on the family of Reb Moyshe Amram, whom he knew in his youth, and goes to the wedding, and with him flow all the people of Meah Shearim, "and they [bring] bread and wine and meat and fish and other delicacies" (p. 588). Note the narrator's bitter, caustic vision here: within the ultra-Orthodox world, it is neither a measure of compassion nor a measure of justice that is the determining factor, but rather the rabbinical hierarchy, which can turn a horror into a holiday.

Right after the wedding come the Ten Plagues to smite Jerusalem: diseases and epidemics and drought. The ultra-Orthodox communities recite prayers, institute fasts, organize proclamations and assemblies and excommunications and prostrations on the graves of Saints and the wedding of an orphan boy and girl, but nothing helps. In the torments and parching, speculation flourishes, along with prayers and ardent, zealous preaching, steeped in superstition and

hatred of man, by Rabbi Grunam May-Salvation-Arise, "as expert in
the transgressions of the generation as were the destructive angels, . . .
as if Satan had deposited his notebook with him" (p. 192). With all his
mockery of Zionist Jaffa with its prattlers and its emptiness, the narrator's fury at the ultra-Orthodox Judaism of Jerusalem is clearly greater
than his contempt for the hypocrisy of Jaffa.

Words of theodicy, of justification of God, in the mouth of
the narrator sound increasingly so hollow and forced that the bitter
irony pierces the submission, and pierces perhaps more than any
overt heresy: "And if you ever saw a star jumping out of its place and
getting out of line, know that it is His will, Blessed-Be-He, for even
things that look out of line are lined up" (p. 598). And after this paragraph comes chapter 14 of book 4, "Balak Gets Out of Line." This is
the "system" or the ultra-Orthodox "line" described in the previous
chapter in colors that are almost the gloomiest and most disgusting in
all Hebrew literature.

|

Balak goes mad and turns, like Isaac before him, to go back to Meah
Shearim, explaining: "I want a meaningful life" (p. 605). When he
comes to the neighborhood, he is described strictly according to the
five signs the Talmud finds in a mad dog.[35] Balak comes upon the
crowd listening to the sermon of Reb Grunam May-Salvation-Arise.
The drought is at its height, giving the rabbi the ideal opportunity to
castigate his audience and to torment them with scorpions or, more
precisely, to torment them with dogs:

> And now, gentlemen, what shall we say and what shall we
> claim, for we see the face of the generation as the face of a
> dog. And not just an ordinary dog, but a mad dog, and they
> are even worse than a mad dog, for they think that they are
> great sages. . . . While the mad dog, gentlemen, is better than
> them, for he declares that he is mad, as we found in that dog
> that tormented Jerusalem who had Crazy Dog written on his
> skin to warn folks to stay away from him. This is what I say,
> the face of the generation is like the face of a dog. And not
> just an ordinary dog, but a crazy dog. (p. 621)

Strangely, several scholars and critics have accepted these mad
preacher's words as if they stated Agnon's own position and have

almost turned them into their own position. Thus, the dog Balak is perceived by several readers as if it was S. Y. Agnon who wrote on his skin his opinion of the generation. The narrator himself refutes this error and turns it into a joke when the concrete dog—whom Reb Grunam and the other sages, writers, journalists, and politicians have turned for their own benefit into a metaphorical, allegorical, sociological, and historiosophical dog—"sallies forth" again suddenly from Reb Grunam's rhetorical flood, and in one of the most grotesque feuilleton-like fragments of the novel, he becomes a flesh-and-blood dog—a tormented dog, victimized for nothing, a wretched soul seeking solace or revenge: "That proverb, the face of the generation is the face of a dog, had donned skin and bones and put on flesh" (p. 621).

"At that moment, Isaac stood and didn't see anything for his soul clung to his wife like a bridegroom in the wedding week. His thoughts wandered off to Sonya and Rabinovitch and he was amazed. . . . Isaac was suddenly jostled aside . . . and didn't know why he was jostled or why they were jostling him" (p. 623). And thus, between his soul "that clung to his wife" and the reminder of the sin against Sonya and Rabinovitch, Isaac's life is about to end as it has always been conducted: "jostled aside" and not knowing "why he was jostled or why they were jostling him." While the neighborhood crowd, gripped by hysteria, shouts at him to join the mob fleeing the mad dog, Isaac refuses to panic until everyone thinks "he is mad" (p. 624) and allows him to read what is written on the dog's skin. Now, at long last, Isaac is free to show arrogance à la Leichtfuss or Arzef, for he himself has written the dreaded words on the dog's skin. But the truth stops being truth and the joke gets teeth.

For the one and only time since he ascended to the Land, Isaac understands and isn't swept up in the stream or dragged behind his milieu. For the only time, he seems suddenly endowed with those hidden powers of soul he has yearned for and envied so much all his life. For that one time, his fate closes in on him (pp. 624–31). The joke makes the joker mad. A dim echo of the myth of "Appointment in Samarra" comes through in this scene, which closes Isaac's circles. One is the "erotic circle": when Isaac wets the skin of the dog Balak with his brush, the act is described—in a semitransparent disguise—as a coitus in which Isaac plays the male-giving role, and Balak the role of the seducing woman, receiving what drips from Isaac's brush. Now comes Balak's bite, which produces the last role reversal in the novel: the bite is also shaped, in disguise, as a sexual act—even though this time the act is depicted as a rape and not as a game of courtship and seduction, as in the scene of the painting. This time, Balak is the one who takes the role of aggressive male: "A sweet bubble began bubbling between his teeth. All his heartaches were drowned and a kind of long-ing gushed in him like a spring, up to his teeth. His teeth stood erect and his whole body was taut. Before Isaac could start walking, the dog leaped on him and sank his teeth in him" (p. 630). Note "a kind of longing gushed in him like a spring," and the words "bubble," "taut," "erect" that give this scene an erotic tone and connect it to its "nega-tive" in the scene of Isaac painting on Balak's skin. Moreover, Balak's rape of Isaac's body is conceived as an emission of semen, as when someone tries to comfort the bitten Isaac with the words: "since he bit you through your clothes, his saliva didn't reach your flesh" (p. 630). And three weeks later: "His wounds began to swell up and turn red, and finally they opened by themselves and a stinking pus began bub-bling out of them" (p. 635). The phrase "stinking pus" is, like "a putrid drop," connected with spilling semen.[36]

|

Does Isaac Kumer at last receive his punishment? Is *Only Yesterday* a novel of sin and punishment? The boldest words of heresy in the entire novel seem to come at the end from the two pious and observant women who never sinned, thinking of the qualities of the Master of the Whole Universe. Rebecca, Shifra's mother, grasps the arm of Hinda-Puah, Reb Alter's wife, Isaac's "mother," as it were, "and [says] to her, Tell me, good woman, why did he do that to my daughter? [Says] Hinda-Puah to Rebecca, Who do you mean? [Says] Rebecca, Who do I mean? I mean the Holy-One-Blessed-Be-He. [Says] Hinda-Puah, Why did he do that to our Itsikl?" (pp. 637–38). Ephraim the plasterer quickly scolds the two women and recites the acceptance of judgment: "Everything the Merciful One does He does for good" (p. 638). But he himself seems to say those words halfheartedly, and "thus they wrestled with the issue that everyone who has ever come into the world has wres-tled with from the day the world was created until now" (p. 638).

The narrator also adds his voice to the fray, not on the side of the plasterer Ephraim who lives in his faith, but on the side of the good women whose perfect faith is cracked: "And now, good friends, as we observe the adventures of Isaac, we are shaken and stunned. This Isaac who is no worse than any other person, why is he punished so harshly?

. . . Moreover the end of Isaac Kumer is not inherent in his beginning" (p. 639). Really? Isn't the dark connection between Isaac's beginning and his end the essence of the novel *Only Yesterday!*

Perhaps in his heart, S. Y. Agnon wanted that dark connection to be less dark. In his literary estate is a short passage, perhaps an advance on the promised "Parcel of Land."[37] This fragment is a belated sequel to *Only Yesterday,* in which we are told that Shifra, Isaac's widow, managed to get pregnant before his death and gave birth to a daughter named Judith, after Isaac's mother. This daughter lives in a *kevutsa* and falls in love with Gideon, the son of Sonya and Yarkoni, who lives in the same *kevutsa.* While Judith Kumer and Gideon Yarkoni build the Land and work its soil, Sonya recalls in her bed at night "that Galician, that Isaac Kumer," and concludes that "there are souls who win after the soul departs the body, that the sons and daughters get what they did not get in their physical life." Does Isaac's soul find solace in "the physical life" of his daughter with Sonya's son? Gershon Shaked notes correctly that Agnon concealed that epilogue because the promise of the Zionist utopia in *Only Yesterday* had to remain a promise, and a "happy ending" would grate as a denial of both the artistic and the intellectual logic of the work.

The chord that concludes *Only Yesterday,* like its presentation, is not a chord of acceptance of the judgment, but of protesting to Heaven and of wounded faith.

In any case, the reader should always keep in mind that the novel is set during the Second Aliya, between 1908 and 1911, but was written during the Nazi period (1931–1945).

Isaac's punishment is horrifying and visible. It is hinted at in the very beginning of the novel, and when it comes it may stun the reader but is not surprising. But what is the sin? At every juncture of his life, except perhaps for his decision to ascend to the Land of Israel, Isaac was passive; he did not choose the path to walk on but was hurled here and there. And even his ascent to the Land, an act originating in the silent force of his will in his struggle with his father, is also based on a "genetic" impulse more than on a considered rational decision. Forces stronger than Isaac shape his acts at every one of his crossroads. It is not he who is responsible for meeting an ultra-Orthodox old couple on the ship and getting into an argument with them about whether "all the Children of Israel are comrades." It is not his fault that he helped the assistant chef paint in exchange for his food and became a painter. It was not by his will that he became friends with Rabinovitch and was dragged after him and met Sonya. Not out of choice did he return to Jaffa, and not by his free decision did he start earning his living as a painter. It wasn't he who chose Sonya, and it wasn't he who broke up with her. As in a dream, he ascended to Jerusalem and by luck he met Bloykof and happened to come upon the old couple from the ship and met their daughter and their granddaughter. And once again, as in a dream, he held out his brush and played a joke on a hot day on a wretched stray dog. Without deciding it, "he made a match" with Shifra, and to get out of his obligation, he went down to Jaffa to ask for Sonya's hand. Only because the owner of the hut came back was Isaac pushed to return to Jerusalem, and when he returned, he married Shifra. Casually, he left his house a few days after the wedding, "as a bridegroom leaves his wedding canopy," and quite logically refused to join those fleeing the crazy dog because he knew the dog wasn't crazy since he himself had written Crazy Dog on him for fun. And how could he know that what was written as a joke would come true with an awful seriousness that could not be treated with laughter or frivolity?

In the suppressed chapter of *Only Yesterday,* the narrator says: "But human sense and the sense of acts are two different senses, and have nothing whatever to do with one another."

Even after we finish *Only Yesterday,* the question remains: Isaac's punishment is horrifying and visible—but what is his sin? Various critics, such as Abraham Band and Baruch Kurzweil, offer different answers. Both Band and Kurzweil know what Isaac's sin is and what he is punished for. They certainly know that better than Isaac and—who knows— perhaps they know it a little better than Agnon himself.

Is Isaac condemned to death because he didn't refrain from taking the last pennies from his father and brother and sisters and didn't bother to support them even when "an extra penny fell into his hand"? That is the family transgression. Or perhaps he is condemned to death because he violated the prohibitions of the faith "Thou shalt not covet" and "Thou shalt not commit adultery," or for the sin between a man and his fellow man, for his friend deposited his girlfriend in his hands and he embezzled the deposit? Or perhaps he sinned against Zionism by not fulfilling the intention of his immigration, not working the soil of the Land, and not building it, but only painting it? He did not become a new man, but only painted himself for a while with a new paint. Can we say that Isaac's sin is a sin of cutting off attachments (family, religious, social, and Zionist)? Can we suppose that Isaac wanders around in the Land like a stray dog until he finds his punishment, which he had unconsciously and incessantly been seeking from the start?

To answer one or some of those questions positively, we must assume the existence of a private providence and free will. Without free will, there is no choice, and without choice, there is no sin.

Is Isaac Kumer's will free, and is his choice free? What will a person do in a world where "the open wish is undermined by the hidden cause," always and without exception. Is this whole work ruled by an indifferent determinism, or a precise predestination that governs every last detail, or a cruel, blind, wanton fate? And which of those three?

There does not seem to be an unequivocal answer to that question in *Only Yesterday*. Dov Sadan, pondering Agnon's theological position in *The Bridal Canopy*, says: "Here you don't know and you wouldn't know, even if the author published a declaration about it." Leah Goldberg, however, has not hesitated to express some disappointment with the conclusion of the novel, which she thinks is too rounded. David Canaani points to the existence of the "realm of terrors" in a world without Providence. Eli Schweid writes: "This is a tragedy . . . nothing is left in it or around it except the anguish that extinguishes itself and sinks with the roar of a mad laugh into empty space." Isaiah Rabinovitch finds in the end of *Only Yesterday* no less than "a spirit of mercy . . . pastoral amnesty." He is amazed that, at the end, "all the ironic, expressionistic ugliness" in the novel "is changed," and believes that he who hears it will enjoy. Dov Sadan, however, firmly insists on Agnon's refusal to hold onto "divine appeasement," and, on this issue, Adi Tsemakh, who went farthest, pointing out the shocking anti-God, nihilistic irony, even theophobia in the novel, may have come closest to the truth. (The term "theophobia" is not in Adi Tsemakh's work but is in the same vein as his position.)

How much did Agnon agonize over how to end Isaac's life and *Only Yesterday*? Dan Miron writes: "The great difficulties Agnon came upon appear in both his Eretz-Israeli novels" (i.e., *Only Yesterday* and *Shira*). "Agnon had trouble writing these novels because he had trouble determining his relation to that reality." And Miron adds: "Agnon and his readers were bothered here by several unanswerable questions—

ethical and theological questions," as well as ideological and historical questions, "and above all, Agnon was oppressed by the question of the religious meaning of Isaac's death." Miron doesn't seem to wonder if "unanswerable" ethical and theological questions really do disturb the novel or perhaps help it. Some of the greatest novels in world literature originate in torments of unanswerable historical, ideological, theological, and ethical questions, while several "neat solutions" to such questions have engendered a plethora of mediocre and didactic novels.

Many fine critics have found ample space in *Only Yesterday* for generalizations about the Second Aliya, or the whole return to Zion, which had fallen away, as it were, from religion and family and tradition and had at last also fallen away from its own Pioneering ideals.

True or false, what is found in *Only Yesterday* about the connection between a person's acts and his fate is awful; it is as difficult for the reader as it seems to have been for the writer. Agnon himself writes to Baruch Kurzweil in reply to a question about *Only Yesterday:* "I don't see myself as someone who has been shown the mysteries of life, but a little something of the terrifying entity is revealed to me from time to time."

Consolation will come with the end of the drought and the rainfall, when Heaven receives the human sacrifice, as in a pagan appeasement ceremony, as in *Oedipus Rex.* But in *Oedipus*, there is a horrible sin, and the punishment is not of an "innocent lamb." In *Only Yesterday*, the furious or jesting gods are appeased only on condition that they are served an offering of clean blood: the sacrifice of Isaac, without a ram and without grace. The harmonic, idyllic tone in the final chapter of the novel, twin of the harmonic, idyllic tone in its opening chapter, is not theodicy or acceptance of the Judgment. After the sacrifice and after the burial of Isaac, the windows of Heaven are opened and the blessing descends upon the Land. The narrator once again sings in the first person plural, as the proxy for all the inhabitants of the Land. The novel concludes with an apotheosis of pastoral bliss, as "the earth was smiling with its plants and its flowers," and "from the soaked earth rose the voice of the sheep, and they were answered by the birds of the skies. And a great rejoicing was in the world" (p. 641). Once again the balanced harmonic structural parallelism appears, a sign of "the religious style" that sees the world as a good and fine and balanced place (p. 641). Within the idyll is the sentence "Like a blessed dwelling was the whole Land and its inhabitants were blessed by the Lord"

(p. 142), a reflection of Isaac's hopes and dreams in the opening paragraph of the novel: "A blessed dwelling place was his image of the whole Land of Israel and its inhabitants were blessed by the Lord" (p. 3).

Isaac's image of the Land was realized at last, but without him, and at the cost of his life. And perhaps the only purpose of the novel's last paragraph is to maintain an old custom of not finishing a book with something bad. In this, too, *Only Yesterday* is close to the Book of Ecclesiastes.

1991–1992

C H A P T E R   1

The Heart, the Dead Space, and the Way Back

1. The title of a well-known story by M. Z. Feyerberg, "Whither."

2. S. Y. Agnon, *A Guest for the Night,* trans. Misha Louvish (London: Victor Gollancz, 1968), pp. 4, 34.

3. Ibid., p. 206.

4. Baruch Kurzweil (1907–1972), Israeli literary critic, author, and educator.

5. S. Y. Agnon, "Tehilah," trans. Walter Lever, in *Israeli Stories,* ed. Joel Blocker (New York: Schocken, 1965), p. 30.

6. Agnon himself was called Tshatshkes at the time, and "Agnon" was the pseudonym of a new and unknown writer.

7. S. Y. Agnon, "Edo and Enam," trans. Walter Lever, in *Two Tales by S. Y. Agnon* (New York: Schocken, 1966), p. 207.

8. Adiel Amzeh, "Forever," trans. Joel Blocker, in *Israeli Stories,* ed. Joel Blocker (New York: Schocken, 1965), p. 249.

C H A P T E R   2

The Mockery of Fate and the Madness of the Righteous Woman

1. S. Y. Agnon, *A Guest for the Night,* trans. Misha Louvish (London: Victor Gollancz, 1968), p. 181: "If it is a question of repentance, it is the Holy One, blessed be He—if I may say so—who ought to repent [!]."

2. Adi Tsemakh is an exception. He rejects the harmonistic view and suggests a midrashic interpretation of Tehilah, in which the righteous woman committed the sin of adultery (by bringing up the image of Shraga), for which she receives divine punishment.

3. Page numbers in the remainder of this chapter refer to S. Y. Agnon, "Tehilah," trans. Walter Lever, in *Israeli Stories,* ed. Joel Blocker (New York: Schocken, 1965), pp. 23–64.

4. Cf. Agnon's story of his journey with a tourist in Jerusalem, in *From Myself to Myself.* My friend Haim Be'er found that the tourist was the Austrian painter Oskar Kokoschka.

5. I am grateful to my friend Nitza Ben-Dov for pointing out this and several other issues.

6. There are few places in Agnon's works where the word "perhaps" is doubled as here. Cf. "Perhaps if Mr. Rigel had behaved with Babtchi as at first, her heart might perhaps have changed in his favor," *A Guest for the Night* [my translation—B.H.].

7. See Gershon Shaked, "Parallelisms and Encounters," in *Art of the Story of S. Y. Agnon* (Mirhavia and Tel Aviv: Sifriat Poalim, 1973), pp. 47–64 [Hebrew]. In this essay, Shaked does not discuss "Tehilah," but what he says can also apply to that story. If Baruch Kurzweil saw a "polar" opposition between the harmonious "Tehilah" and the demonic *Book of Tales*, Shaked demonstrates that "as Agnon's stories become more 'modern' in their form, this aspect shrinks in them: The plot is determined by a chain of encounters . . . coincidences, as it were" (p. 48). In terms of this distinction, "Tehilah" is among Agnon's modern works and not among his naïve folk tales. But perhaps the time has come for a fundamental reexamination of the distinction made by several scholars between the "traditional" Agnon and the "modern" Agnon, between the "harmonic" Agnon and the "demonic" Agnon, as they have recently protested correctly against the customary distinction between Bialik's "poems of individual grief" and his "poems of collective grief." It is my hope that this book will contribute to wiping out this distinction in Agnon's work.

8. See the remarks of Rabbi Hanina in the Tractate Ta'anit, 8, p. A; and Rashi, Tosephet, "Pakhad Yitzhak"; and, in detail, the entry HLD in *Arukh Ha-Shalem*; and see, for example, the poem of Moshe Laski, "The Faithful of the Land, or the Weasel and the Well" (Warsaw, 1840), and Eliahu Mordechai Werbel in his poem "The Weasel and the Well, or Loyal Witnesses" (1852), and Abraham Goldfaden in his play *Shulamith*, in Y. D. Eizenshteyn, *Otsar Midrashim* (New York, 1915), pp. 161–62. And closer to our own concern, Agnon's "Week of Faith"; and perhaps the legend of the weasel and the well also reverberates in "The Prime of Life," *A Simple Story, Only Yesterday*, and others.

9. Micah Yosef Ben-Gurion Berdichevski, "The Kaddish or Two Distant Persons," in *Writings of Yosef bin-Gurion* (Tel Aviv: Dvir, 1920), pp. 160–72 [Hebrew]. The story was first included in the collection *From the Close Past* (Warsaw: Sefer, 1909).

10. S. Y. Agnon, "In the Prime of Life," in *Al Kapot HaManul, S. Y. Agnon's Stories*, vol. 3 (Jerusalem and Tel Aviv: Schocken, 1960), p. 8.

11. Ada Shosheim has pointed out that Tehilah was a *pointe* story, whose end leads the reader to reexamine its beginning.

12. S. Y. Agnon, *A Simple Story*, trans. Hillel Halkin (New York: Schocken, 1985), p. 127.

CHAPTER 3
Stolen Waters and Bread Eaten in Secret

1. (Trans.) The externs were nonresident Jewish students in Russia preparing for matriculation exams, who were barred from attending classes and who populate Hebrew fiction.

2. The term "polyphony" is used in a different sense than in Bakhtin, "The Polyphonous Novel and Literary Criticism," *Problems in the Poetics of Doestoyevski*.

3. As I learned from Raphael Weiser, *A Simple Story* is set in about 1903 to 1907, since the Russo-Japanese war is mentioned as a current event, while,

according to various issues mentioned in *Only Yesterday*, Isaac Kumer immigrates to the Land of Israel in 1908, the same year that Agnon himself immigrated there. Hirshl may be three or four years older than Isaac. Hirshl and Mina are betrothed in early December 1904, according to Raphael Weiser, and married in the summer of 1905. In about January 1906, Mina is at the beginning of her first pregnancy. Hirshl is put in Dr. Langsam's hospital in the summer of 1906 and returns home at about Rosh Hashanah 1907 (see p. 197), according to the dispute over the citrons from Corfu (p. 202), Dreyfus (p. 209), and the issue of the Russian refugees (pp. 133–34).

4. *A Simple Story*, trans. Hillel Halkin (New York: Schocken, 1985), pp. 1–2.

5. Cf. "[Isaac's] clothes will come and indicate that he's the son of a good house," *Only Yesterday*, pp. 10–11.

6. Let us not deduce from this, Heaven forbid, that there is any similarity between lunacy on the one hand and Zionism and immigration to Israel on the other, even though Chaim Weizmann once said that "to be a Zionist you don't have to be crazy—but it helps a lot."

7. Agnon, *Only Yesterday*, pp. 89–90. And compare the description of Tirza Mazel, née Mintz, of her mother, Leah, at the beginning of "In the Prime of Her Life" (Jerusalem and Tel Aviv: Schocken, 1960), a story that first appeared in 1923.

8. Agnon, *Only Yesterday*, p. 90 (my emphasis—A.O.).

9. Agnon, *Only Yesterday*, p. 149.

10. Also cf. Ps. 109:22: "For I am poor and needy, and my heart is wounded within me."

11. A detailed discussion of the words "his heart bore a grudge" appears later in this book.

12. "Hill of Sand." And see Shamir, "The Torn Bag," and G. Shaked, "The Sleeping Prince," pp. 151–76.

13. And perhaps Tsirl and Toyber should not be lumped together in this matter, for there is at least a shadow of a hint in the story that Toyber himself succeeded in finding in the hunchback he married, the sister of Getsel Stein, something of what Hirshl found in Mina. Who knows, maybe there was more than one underground cell in the city in those days. . . .

14. I am grateful to my old friend Rabbi Joel Ben-Nun for putting me onto this point, which enriches our understanding of *A Simple Story*.

CHAPTER 4
Guilt and Orphanhood and Fate

1. Eliezar Schweid discusses the question of whether Isaac Kumer is characteristic or representative of the Pioneers of the Second Aliya: "If Isaac Kumer represents the Second Aliya, he symbolizes it in the rare and correct sense of a symbol: He is not the most common, but the most consequential."

2. *Babylonian Talmud*, Nidah, 30, p. 2.

3. S. Y. Agnon, "With Our Young and Our Old," in *Al Kapot HaManul, S. Y. Agnon's Stories*, vol. 3 (Jerusalem and Tel Aviv: Schocken, 1960).

4. Gustav Kroyanker has noted the gradual emptying of traditional Jewish life in the small town and discusses the status there of socialism and Zionism, a status that "lacked any uniqueness . . . an issue for societies of young bourgeois to dwell on."

5. Sukkah, p. 51, p. 2, from Jacob Neusner, *The Mishnah: A New Translation* (New Haven: Yale University Press, 1988), p. 288.

6. For example, Bialik's use of "the wing of the *Shekhina*" in the poem, "Alone."

7. Like S. Y. Agnon's "Hemdat," in *From Myself to Myself* (Jerusalem and Tel Aviv: Schocken, 1976).

8. Sotah, 1:7, Neusner, *The Mishnah*, p. 449.

9. S. Y. Agnon, *Shira*, trans. Zeva Shapiro (New York: Schocken, 1989).

10. Agnon, *Shira*, pp. 85–88, esp. p. 85.

11. Yehoshua Knaz, *Heart Murmur* (Tel Aviv: Am Oved, 1986), p. 391.

12. Agnon, *Shira*, pp. 68, 239.

13. For the question of causation in *Only Yesterday*, see Arnold Band's profound discussion, *Nostalgia and Nightmare* (Berkeley and Los Angeles: University of California Press, 1968), pp. 425–28.

14. Cf. Ezek. 23:20. "Sinew" is also a euphemism for the male sex organ.

15. Arnold Band provides an expansive discussion of the novel's place and its relation to other works of Agnon in *Nostalgia and Nightmare*, pp. 414–47.

16. E. M. Forster, *Aspects of the Novel* (San Diego: Harcourt Brace Jovanovich, 1955), pp. 65–82.

17. Cf. the character of the coachman, Stach, in Agnon, *A Simple Story*, pp. 122, 164, 266–68.

18. Cf. Sanhedrin 105, p. A: "A parable of two dogs in a pack and were yellow to each other" [i.e., hated each other].

19. S. Y. Agnon, "The Doctor's Divorce," trans. Robert Alter, in *A Book That Was Lost and Other Stories*, ed. Alan Mintz and Anne Golomb Hoffman (New York: Schocken, 1995), p. 302.

20. (Trans.) In Hebrew, there is an implied linguistic link between painting (*Tsav'a*) and hypocrisy (*Tsvi'ut*).

21. S. Y. Agnon, "Hill of Sand," trans. Hillel Halkin, in *A Book That Was Lost and Other Stories*, pp. 87–122.

22. And compare this with his recurrent thoughts that he has not stood the Zionist test, e.g., book 4, chapter 4.

23. My friend Haim Be'er thinks that this character is based on the personality of Rabbi Mordechai Gimpel Yoffe, "the rabbi from Yehud" (1820–1892; immigrated to the Land of Israel in 1888).

24. I am grateful to my friend Professor Amos Altshuler, who directed my attention to this hypothetical identification.

25. Agnon, "Epilogue."

26. Gideon Efrat found the painter Samuel Hirshberg, master of "Exile," a source of inspiration for the character of Samson Bloykof, with the help of Raphael Weiser, according to a note found in Dov Sadan's handwriting on the margins of a pamphlet in Yiddish by Yosef Sandel on Hirshberg.

27. My friend Haim Be'er pointed out the model for Reb Grunam.

28. The story "Tubal Cain" was not found, but Tubal-Cain, as we recall, is one of the ancestors of the dog Balak. This is what Agnon wrote to Baruch Kurzweil, who asked him what the connection was between Balak and Isaac: "I'll tell you the truth, I often asked myself what Balak's connection with Isaac is. And whenever I wanted to drop the matter of Balak from the story, I saw a much greater need for it than before. I don't see Balak as symbolic, especially

not as a unified symbolism, but I know that the incident of Balak adds to the story what Isaac and all our friends cannot. . . . You know I don't like allegories, and I never intended Balak as an allegory, but I wanted to put in the mouth of an animal what I couldn't do with a man." And see Sotah, 3, p. B, "She is tied to him as a dog."

29. "Two friends will meet but mountains never"—a popular saying in medieval literature.

30. Cf. "Do not desire—you have desire" *(Psikta Rabati,* 20) and "Desire is the root of all iniquity" *(Melamed Hatalmidim,* Yethro); and in the narrow meaning of sexual lust, "It is the blood of desire (Nidah, 20, p. B) and "lest she saw blood out of the lust of desire" (Rashi, Nidah, 66, p. A).

31. Some say that the character of Jonathan Leichtfuss, Sweet Foot, is similar to the personality of Baruch Kauschenski-Agadati (1895–1976)—artist, dancer, choreographer, a founder of the Aldleyada festival Tel Aviv, and one of the fathers of both silent and sound cinema in Israel.

32. Gorishkin is apparently close to the figure of Yakov Ya'ari-Poleskin (1886–1944), and Yarkoni may be reminiscent of Shlomo Tsemakh (1886–1974). In the figure of Dr. Schimmelmann, there may be a few lines reminiscent of the personality of Dr. Ben-Zion Mosinson (1878–1942; immigrated to Israel in 1907), and some say that Falk Shpaltleder is similar to Yakov Vitkin-Zerubavel (1887–1967).

33. Agnon, "The Doctor's Divorce," p. 301.

34. This allows us to know in which months Isaac Kumer got married and died: The first version of "Hill of Sand" and its name "Tishrei" were printed serially in *Ha-Po'el Ha-Tsa'ir* during 1911 and 1912. The issue the barber gave Isaac is almost certainly no. 3–4, which appeared on December 1, 1911. As for the harsh drought of autumn 1911, it ended with a sudden downpour on December 11, 1911, which also enables us to "determine" on what day Isaac was buried at the end of *Only Yesterday.*

35. Yoma, 80, p. B.

36. For "stinking pus," see Tractate Makhshirin, 6, 8 (Neusner, *The Mishnah,* p. 1107); for "a putrid drop," see Abot, 3, 1; Neusner, *The Mishnah,* p. 678.

37. No. 1:381, Agnon Archive.